MAKING LAWS THAT W

This book examines why laws fail and provides strategies for making laws that work.

Why do some laws fail? And how can we make laws that actually work? This helpful guide, written by a leading jurist, provides answers to these questions and gives practical strategies for law-making. It looks at a range of laws which have failed; the 'damp squibs' that achieve little or nothing in practice; laws that overshoot their policy goals; laws that produce nasty surprises; and laws that backfire, undermining the very goals they were intended to advance.

It goes on to examine some of the reasons why such failures occur, drawing on insights from psychology and economics, including the work of Kahneman and others on how humans develop narratives about the ways in which the world works and make predictions about the future.

It provides strategies to reduce the risk of failure of legislative projects, including adopting a more structured and systematic approach to analysing the likely effects of the legislation; ensuring we identify the limits of our knowledge and the uncertainties of our predictions; and framing laws in a way that enables us to adjust the way they operate as new information becomes available or circumstances change.

Key themes include the importance of the institutions that administer the legislation, of default outcomes, and of the 'stickiness' of those defaults.

The book concludes with helpful checklists of questions to ask and issues to consider, which will be of benefit to anyone involved in designing legislation.

For Linda,

with love !

David

Making Laws That Work

How Laws Fail and How We Can Do Better

David Goddard

·HART·

OXFORD · LONDON · NEW YORK · NEW DELHI · SYDNEY

HART PUBLISHING

Bloomsbury Publishing Plc

Kemp House, Chawley Park, Cumnor Hill, Oxford, OX2 9PH, UK

1385 Broadway, New York, NY 10018, USA

29 Earlsfort Terrace, Dublin 2, Ireland

HART PUBLISHING, the Hart/Stag logo, BLOOMSBURY and the Diana logo are
trademarks of Bloomsbury Publishing Plc

First published in Great Britain 2022

A catalogue record for this book is available from the British Library.

A catalogue record for this book is available from the Library of Congress.

Library of Congress Control Number: 2022934277

ISBN:	PB:	978-1-50995-536-7
	ePDF:	978-1-50995-539-8
	ePub:	978-1-50995-538-1

Typeset by Compuscript Ltd, Shannon
Printed and bound in Great Britain by CPI Group (UK) Ltd, Croydon CR0 4YY

To find out more about our authors and books visit www.hartpublishing.co.uk.
Here you will find extracts, author information, details of forthcoming events
and the option to sign up for our newsletters.

FOREWORD

There are good reasons why lawmakers should be humble about their role in shaping society. For too many people the law is too expensive and too complex to be useful to them. Policy in general has become abstract as the policy institutions have lost sight of the customers and become prisoners of inertia and virtue signalling. Politics remains as messy as ever, mixing vision inspiration and poor short-term decisions.

David Goddard wants to close the gap between intellectual frameworks and reality, between the constitutional process and the people. Our legislative process often makes mistakes which cause unnecessary damage to people and economic uncertainty. The self-correction mechanisms of common law and policy review work eventually, but they take time.

David Goddard demonstrates a unique grasp of how design thinking, technology and ubiquitous data can enhance the legislative process reducing mistakes and correcting mistakes more quickly.

We share the same conviction that spending time understanding behaviour as well as concepts is essential. Engaging with the people actually affected by a law and understanding their perspective works better than politicians and bureaucrats sitting around in meeting rooms with abstract theories of goodness.

I like most the self-awareness of this book. Public and legal institutions are not good at understanding their own power, their biases and their impact on people. David Goddard is an insider who has looked hard at his own world and cared enough to question its ways and work through a coherent scheme for improvement. This intellectual integrity is at the core of his persuasive argument.

Sir Bill English
Former Prime Minister of New Zealand

ACKNOWLEDGEMENTS

I did much of the research for this book, and wrote a first draft, in the 2018–19 academic year which I spent at the NYU Law School as a Senior Global Fellow from Practice and Government. I am very grateful to the Hauser Global Law School at NYU for providing a stimulating and supportive environment in which to work on this project, and in particular to Linda Silberman and Jeremy Waldron for their warm welcome and encouragement.

I owe a huge debt of gratitude to friends and colleagues who read early drafts of this book, and provided insightful comments along the way, including Jonathan Ayto, Paul Beaumont, Ross Carter, Bill English, Andrew Goddard, Ian Govey, Mark Hickford, Ken Keith, Helen McQueen, Andy Nicholls, Cassie Nicholson, Julie Nind, Geoffrey Palmer, Richard Revesz, Joseph Weiler, and five anonymous reviewers.

Above all, I am grateful to Liesle Theron, my brilliant, loving and generous wife, for her encouragement and support. From the time I first conceived the project, Liesle has been a critical sounding board for many of the ideas it explores. She encouraged me to take time out of legal practice to work on the project; was instrumental in the choice of NYU as my academic home for the year; and bore the brunt of uprooting the family to spend the year overseas. Without her, this book would not exist. I dedicate it to her, with love and gratitude.

CONTENTS

PART I
SETTING THE SCENE

PART II
LESSONS FOR LEGAL DESIGNERS

PART III
THE CHECKLISTS

APPENDICES

LIST OF ILLUSTRATIONS

Figure	Illustration	Copyright details
1.1	Building with blocked up windows	Creative commons licence CC BY-SA 3.0: Photograph by Whilesteps, own work by Gary Burt (2008), available at: commons.wikimedia.org/wiki/File:Window_Tax.jpg
1.2	Rembrandt, 'The Anatomy Lesson of Dr Tulp'	Photograph of work out of copyright – credit Mauritshuis, The Hague. Use in publications is permitted by the gallery, available at: www.mauritshuis.nl/en/explore/the-collection/artworks/the-anatomy-lesson-of-dr-nicolaes-tulp-146/detailgegevens/
2.1	King Canute	Painting by Alphonse-Marie-Adolphe de Neuville, reproduced in John H Haaren and AB Poland, *Famous Men of the Middle Ages* (University Publishing Company, 1904) 153, available at: commons.wikimedia.org/wiki/File:Canute_rebukes_his_courtiers.png Image of painting out of copyright – artist died 1885
2.2	Indian cobra	Creative commons licence CC BY 3.0: Photograph by Kamalnv, own work (2008), available at: commons.wikimedia.org/wiki/File:Indiancobra.jpg
2.3	Mexico City with smog	Creative commons licence CC BY-SA 3.0: Image by Fidel Gonzalez, own work (2010), available at: commons.wikimedia.org/wiki/File:AerialViewPhotochemicalSmogMexico City_2.jpg

Introduction

Who is this Book For?

This book is for anyone involved in the business of making legislation – written laws: decision-makers; officials and other advisers; law drafters; people seeking to influence the law-making process. The aim of the book is to improve the quality and effectiveness of legislation. I begin by looking at the different ways in which laws fail, and some of the reasons why they fail. From this I draw some lessons that will reduce the risk of your legislative projects failing in the same ways.

The issues I identify in this book may seem challenging. But it is better to be realistic about the challenges we face in legislating than it is to engage in serial over-optimism, followed by serial failure. Some of the suggestions I make for how to respond to these challenges may seem obvious. But my experience is that these are the things we get wrong time after time in both wealthy developed countries and less wealthy countries.

Key Themes

Much of what I have to say is about quality of information, and clarity of goals. We can't even begin to have a conversation about the effectiveness of legislation until we know what that legislation is intended to achieve. It is question begging, and hopelessly circular, to describe the policy goal of proposed legislation as 'changing the law from X to Y'. Rather, we need to focus on how the law is intended to change what people do – how people behave. A coherent proposal to change the law requires as its starting point:[1]

- A clear and accurate statement of the current position – what is the law now? What are the facts – how does that law operate (or fail to operate) in practice?
- Identification of the problem – what is it about the current situation that is unsatisfactory?
- A description of what the world would look like – of how the people concerned would behave – if the problem were solved. What does success look like?

With answers to these questions – answers which, depending on your role, you may either be responsible for developing or which you may need to look to others to provide – it is possible to think about the form that the proposed legislation should take to improve its prospects of success. My starting point for tackling that question is to ask how and why laws fail, so we can think in a more systematic way about how to reduce the risk of failure.

As I explain below, reducing the risk of failure requires a careful analysis of whether, and how, legislation can bring about the changes in behaviour that would count as success. Or contribute to bringing about those changes, when coupled with other measures. It also requires a careful analysis of the risk of unexpected and undesired changes in behaviour.

It turns out, unfortunately, that analysis of this kind does not come naturally to us humans. Our intuition swiftly generates narratives about how our society currently works, and predictions about how it will work in the future, that are simple, clear, confident – and frequently wrong. A great deal of research in recent decades has shown that people (experts included) are very good at coming up with plausible and confident explanations for how the world currently works – and why – based on inadequate information. We are not good at identifying what we do not know, or assessing the implications of that lack of knowledge. We do a very bad job of predicting future developments in the complex societies in which we live. The confidence with which we make our predictions far outpaces their accuracy. The more complex the situation, and the longer term the predictions, the worse we perform. The exercise is inherently difficult – and we routinely fail to appreciate that difficulty, and factor it into our analysis.

If legislating requires us to understand the current dynamics of the society we live in and predict its future dynamics, and if we struggle to do just that, is the enterprise of legislating doomed? Not necessarily. It is not easy to design legislation that is effective – but if we have a realistic picture of the challenges we face, we can do a much better job of addressing them. In this book I identify two strategies we can adopt to respond to the intrinsic challenge of legislating effectively.

The first is to adopt a structured approach to identifying the problem that the proposed legislation is intended to address, and thinking about the ways in which that legislation will affect the behaviour of its various audiences: citizens, businesses, officials, public agencies and other institutions involved in applying the law. We can break broad questions about how the law in a given field might be changed down into a number of more manageable sub-issues, and address each of those in turn. We can gather information about each of those sub-issues more systematically. We can draw on a range of perspectives to ensure we do not become captured by superficially plausible but inaccurate narratives, or by any one over-simplified model. We can improve our predictions about the effect of the proposed legislation on the behaviour of each of the various groups to whom it is addressed, despite the inherent difficulty of that task. A more structured and systematic approach to designing laws can significantly improve the quality of our analysis.

The second strategy, closely related to the first, is to ensure we identify the limits of our knowledge and the uncertainty of our predictions, and factor these into the design of our laws. We should legislate in a way that enables us to identify when outcomes differ from our predictions in ways that matter; and to respond to unexpected developments in a timely and appropriate manner. That requires us to track what is happening over time – how the legislation operates in practice. It will often require building into the legislation mechanisms for adjusting the way it operates, as and when we obtain new information, or circumstances change in ways that were not anticipated when the law was made. I call this *adaptive legislation*. The 'set and forget' approach to legislation pretty much guarantees frequent failures.

Throughout this book I emphasise the importance of the institutions that implement the law – applying it, interpreting it, enforcing it. It is impossible to design laws well without paying close attention to these institutions, and how they work in practice. Laws are like the code running in the background on your computer or your phone; the institutions that implement the law are the hardware and user interface through which we interact with that code. What matters in law, as in technology, is the outcomes that users experience. Bad code pretty much guarantees bad outcomes. But even the best-written code will fail to deliver good outcomes if the code and the hardware don't work well together – if the code makes demands on the hardware that it cannot handle, for example, so the system runs unacceptably slowly or crashes. Or if the code is optimised for a desktop computer with a large screen – and you are trying to run it on an ageing smartphone, so you can barely read the text and none of the drop-down menus works. Good law is law that is optimised for the environment in which it will operate. Achieving that may require changes to the law, changes to institutional arrangements, or both.

I also emphasise a closely related point: the importance of default outcomes, and the 'stickiness' of those defaults – how hard it is to move away from the default. The easier it is for a person to access the benefit that a law is intended to provide for them, the more likely it is that the benefit will be received in practice. The easier it is to comply with a legal requirement, the greater the prospect of compliance. This sounds pretty obvious: but I frequently encounter legislation that requires people to jump through unnecessary and time-consuming hoops. Well-designed laws and institutions make it as easy as possible to get to the outcome that the law is intended to achieve. The design of laws needs to pay close attention to default settings, and to the process for departing from those default settings.

Some may argue that the suggestions I make in this book are unrealistic – that I am asking more of legislators and their advisers than is workable in practice. But responsible legislators and officials should hold themselves to the same standards that they apply to other measures that have a far-reaching impact on the public. A responsible government wouldn't introduce a new public health initiative (say, a new vaccination regime), or a new drinking water treatment technology, or new design standards for bridges, unless there was a reliable basis for expecting the new approach to work, and a reasonable level of confidence that it would not produce serious adverse effects. A responsible government would insist on proper monitoring mechanisms, so we know if and when serious problems emerge and we can respond in a timely way. It seems odd to suggest that the exercise of legislative power – which affects all citizens, and invokes the coercive power of the state – requires less justification, or a less disciplined approach.

If those of us who are involved in the business of legislating hold ourselves to the same standards that we expect of other professionals whose work affects public wellbeing, then we don't have the luxury of continuing to legislate based on inadequate information and analysis, and disproportionate confidence. We need to do better.

The Book's Structure

Part I of the book sets the scene, and looks at how and why laws fail. Part II explores some of the lessons we can learn from the ways in which laws have failed in the past, and identifies some options for reducing the risk that your legislative projects will fail in the same ways. Part III suggests a possible structure for bringing these insights to bear on your projects. It contains checklists of questions to ask, and issues to consider, when you set out to design legislation. The process of working through the checklists in part III should help to identify the key risks that are relevant to your project, and how you might manage those risks.

The Perspectives from which I have Written this Book

I should say a word – if only by way of disclosure – about the perspectives from which I have written this book. For the last few years I have been an appellate judge in New Zealand. Much of my time is spent reading and applying legislation. Some of that legislation is of very high quality. But much is not. All too often, the legal design process has overlooked key features of the world in which the legislation is intended to operate. Or the world has changed, and the legislation has not aged well. The result is avoidable complexity and uncertainty, and much wasted time and cost. If a fraction of the resources that are spent on arguments before our courts about the operation of legislation were invested in better legal design, our laws could be dramatically improved.

Before I became a judge, I worked as an academic (briefly); a practising lawyer and appellate advocate; a civil servant providing policy advice, assisting ministers to shepherd legislation through the parliamentary process, and representing New Zealand in bilateral and multilateral negotiations; a policy consultant in New Zealand and the Asia-Pacific region; and a drafter (of primary and secondary legislation, and international instruments). I have been involved in law-making at very different scales and in very different environments: from advising on and drafting legislation for Niue (population around 2,000), Samoa (population around 200,000) and New Zealand (population around five million) to chairing multilateral treaty negotiations in The Hague involving more than 80 states. From this experience I am acutely conscious of the challenges of legal design – it isn't as easy as it looks from outside. But I have seen the same problems crop up time and again, and I am pretty confident we can do better.

I have also tried to write the book from the perspective on legislation that is most important, but often overlooked: the end user of the legislation, the person to whom it is meant to apply. Lawyers tend to forget that most people to whom legislation is addressed will never read it, or pay for legal advice about it. The vast majority of people's interactions with legislation do not involve referring directly to the legislation. (Imagine going out into the street and asking passers-by when they last read their country's tax legislation? Road traffic legislation? Legislation governing their rights as a tenant? Legislation governing what they can build on a property that they own?) How do individuals and businesses find out what legislation is relevant to them, and what that legislation enables them to do, or requires them to do? (Spoiler alert: often, they don't.) What determines whether the law works (or fails) from their perspective? The 'user interfaces' of our laws – the institutional arrangements through which the laws are implemented, and touch the lives of affected citizens – are at least as important as the content of the legislation itself. Legal designers need to pay much more attention to those user interfaces.

Where to Next?

In this book I seek to map the broad contours of the discipline of legal design. Inevitably, I can only scratch the surface of this large and important topic. The book is long on questions, and short on answers. It is the start of a conversation, no more.

My hope is that the book will encourage a more realistic and more effective approach to the design of new laws. If some readers use this book as a prompt to ask simple but challenging questions about the legislative projects they are working on, the book will have achieved one of its core goals. I look forward to hearing from readers – especially those who have used the checklists – who can tell me what works in their environment, and what can be improved to be more useful for them and for others. I am sure there are important issues I have overlooked, and useful design options I have not mentioned. Tell me, so the next edition of this book will be better.

My broader goal is to champion the idea of legal design as a distinct discipline – the study of how the design of laws contributes to their success or failure, and how we can do better in this important field. There is enormous scope for further research and writing on legal design, drawing on a wide range of disciplines including law, economics, psychology and public policy. Every topic I touch on in this book would benefit from further study by academics and policy practitioners. We need to know more about how laws fail, and why: my incomplete and anecdotal account of failed laws should be superseded by more comprehensive and systematic reviews of this terrain. We need to study how people become aware of the benefits that laws offer them, and the ways in which we can design laws to facilitate access to those benefits. We need to look at ways to design laws and legal institutions to reduce barriers to access to justice: the issue of how to transform rights on paper into real-world rights is a pressing issue for anyone concerned with the rule of law and social inclusion. How can laws be designed to make it easier for people who have obligations under those laws to be informed about, and comply with, those obligations? How can laws be designed to make better use of technology to reduce complexity as experienced by the audiences for those laws? Is (part of) the answer making greater use of technologies such as artificial intelligence (AI) to resolve simpler cases, with human decision-makers as a back-up for hard cases? What are the most pressing cross-border issues that legal designers encounter, and what is the toolbox available to legal designers for responding to those issues? The list goes on and on: there are many hundreds of law review articles and theses waiting to be written in this domain.

Another goal of this book is to stimulate teaching of legal design in law schools. The teaching of law remains focused for the most part on how legislation and case law are used in courtrooms to determine disputes. Clinical legal education also tends to focus on advocacy and dispute resolution, in courts and other forums. Some law schools offer courses that look at how law is used in the context of commercial transactions. Some offer courses on legislation, which look at topics such as the process by which laws are made, the structure of legislation, and the interpretation of legislation. There are a few courses aimed at legislative drafters. But few if any law schools offer courses on the design of legislation – on how laws succeed or fail in achieving their policy goals, and on how to design laws to reduce the risk of failure and increase the prospect of success.[2] To me at least, this is a surprising gap. The field of legal design is both interesting and practically important. It could be taught jointly across law schools and public policy schools. It would appeal to students doing first degrees, and – perhaps especially – to students doing further study while working in government or in organisations that seek to influence governments.

A well-functioning legal system is an essential foundation for a flourishing society in which we can lead safe, meaningful and rewarding lives. Most of the time we take this critical social infrastructure for granted. But its quality is at best uneven. For many, there is a large gap between the promise of the law on paper and the reality of the law in practice. Too many laws are damp squibs whose benefits fail to materialise in the real world. Too many laws produce nasty surprises, or backfire and make the problem worse. There is a great deal of room for improvement. We can, and must, do better to make law work for all members of the societies in which we live. I am convinced that better legal design can help to achieve this fundamentally important goal. Legal design founded on asking better questions, insisting on better information, and paying intelligent attention to the gaps in our knowledge and the inevitability of change. Legal design that focuses on what people actually do, and how they experience the law, not just on words on paper. Law that speaks to people in ways they can understand. Law that works for people. If we bear that goal squarely in mind in our work as legal designers, we will have taken the first and most important step towards making our laws work better.

---

[1] An early inspiration for this book was Sir Kenneth Keith's paper 'Philosophies of Law Reform' (1991) 7 *Otago Law Review* 363. He poses four questions in relation to any law reform: What is the question? What are the facts? Who should handle the particular reform and how? By reference to what principles? Although I come at the issues in a slightly different way, and focus on the narrower perspective of legislative design once a policy direction has been set, Sir Kenneth's emphasis on keeping the policy goal squarely in view, and understanding the facts, underpins this work.

[2] The Institute of Advanced Legal Studies at the University of London offers an LLM in Drafting Legislation, Regulation, and Policy. Sir Geoffrey Palmer, a law professor and former Prime Minister, has for some years taught a course on Legislative Design, Drafting and Law-Making at Victoria University of Wellington, New Zealand. For a review of tertiary courses in Europe and the United Kingdom with a focus on legislation and 'legisprudence' (the field of legal studies dedicated to researching and teaching about the theory and practice of legislation), see Marta Tavares de Almeida and Chris Moll, 'Legislative Training' in Ulrich Karpen and Helen Xanthaki (eds), *Legislation in Europe* (Oxford, Hart Publishing, 2017). See also Ulrich Karpen and Helen Xanthaki, 'Legislation in European Countries' in Ulrich Karpen and Helen Xanthaki (eds), *Legislation in Europe: A Country by Country Guide* (Oxford, Hart Publishing, 2020), esp [1.6]. The journal *The Theory and Practice of Legislation* is a useful source of material in the field of legal design.

PART I

Setting the Scene

1

When Legislation Fails

Laws fail in many ways. The consequences of those failures can be both serious and long-lasting. One striking example from more than three hundred years ago, the peculiar results of which are still visible today, is the window tax enacted by the English Parliament in 1696. This progressive tax, calculated by reference to the number of windows in a dwelling, initially produced substantial and much-needed revenue to fund replacement of the Kingdom's debased coinage. But over time, and despite a number of reforms, the revenue from the new tax fell away. Owners of existing houses blocked up windows. New houses were built with few windows. In many British cities today you can still see bricked in spaces where windows used to be – the enduring evidence of early tax mitigation schemes.[1]

Figure 1.1 The enduring legacy of the window tax

So the window tax became ever less effective as a revenue-raising measure. More problematically still, it led to reduced ventilation and light in many houses, especially those of the poor, and in the city tenements where workers congregated as the Industrial Revolution got under way. As early as the 1730s pamphlets were circulating that decried the adverse health effects of this 'tax on light and air'. This revenue-raising measure exacerbated the spread of disease and caused, or hastened, many deaths. In 1850 Charles Dickens attacked the tax in his magazine *Household Words*, saying:

> The adage 'free as air' has become obsolete by Act of Parliament. Neither air nor light have been free since the imposition of the window-tax. We are obliged to pay for what nature lavishly supplies to all, at so much per window per year; and the poor who cannot afford the expense are stinted in two of the most urgent necessities of life. The effects produced by a deprivation of them are not immediate, and are therefore unheeded. When a poor man or woman in a dark, close, smoky house is laid up with scrofula, consumption, water in the head, wasting, or a complication of epidemic diseases, nobody thinks of attributing the illness to the right cause; – which may be a want of light and air. If he or she were struck down by a flash of lightning, there would be an immediate outcry against the authorities, whoever they may be, for not providing proper lightning conductors; but because the poison – generated by the absence of light and air – is not seen at work, the victim dies unheeded, and the window tax, which shuts out the remedies, is continued without a murmur.[2]

Nor was this a peculiarly British eccentricity. France introduced a window tax in 1798, and similar taxes were subsequently adopted in other parts of Europe, including the Netherlands. In those countries too we can still see evidence of the enduring appeal of tax minimisation schemes in bricked up windows, and other tax-driven architectural quirks. And there too it is likely that many thousands of people, mostly poor, suffered ill health and accelerated deaths as a direct result of this revenue-raising measure.

The window tax survived in various forms in England until 1851. In France, the window tax was not finally abolished until 1926. Poorly designed laws are not always short-lived: once they are on the books, it can be hard to get rid of them.

It would be reassuring to think that we have learned something in the last few hundred years, and that lawmakers today would readily avoid making similar mistakes. Unfortunately, the evidence suggests that isn't the case. In this book I will look at laws that fail to achieve anything much; laws that overshoot their intended goals; laws – like the window taxes – that have unexpected and undesired consequences; even laws that undermine their own core objectives and make things worse in the very respect that they were intended to improve. Laws from large wealthy countries (such as the United States and the United Kingdom), small wealthy countries (like my home country New Zealand), and some less wealthy countries (small Pacific States, and some larger Asian States). The examples I have chosen are illustrative, not comprehensive: an inventory of failed laws over the ages would be a very long and depressing work. What these examples tell us, though, is that these issues are pervasive. No country is immune. Lawmakers and policy advisers the world over can learn something from studying these failures.

A famous painting by Rembrandt in The Hague's Mauritshuis, one of my favourite galleries, is titled 'The Anatomy Lesson of Dr Tulp'. It shows, in rather grisly detail, a dissection of a cadaver for educational purposes back in 1632.[3]

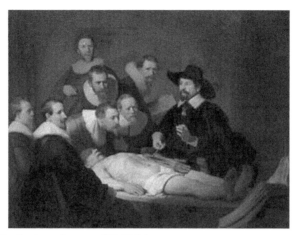

Figure 1.2 'The Anatomy Lesson of Dr Tulp'

Dissections continue to play an important role in medical education. And autopsies remain an important method for ascertaining causes of death. This book is intended to serve a similar purpose: we will dissect some failed laws to better understand what went wrong, and how lawmakers can avoid repeating those errors today.

One more preliminary comment, this time concerned with what the book is *not* about. This book is not – or at least, not mainly – about how to assess whether a policy goal is good or bad. It is not about how to undertake a cost–benefit analysis of a policy proposal – there are excellent books on that topic already.[4] Nor is it about the art of legislative drafting – again, there are excellent books in that field already.[5] Rather, it is about the narrower question of how written laws succeed, or fail, in advancing their proponents' policy goals. If there is a proposal to use legislation to advance a policy goal, will the legislation actually achieve that goal: will it work? Can it be made to work better? Can the legislation be reframed to advance the policy goal more effectively, or at lower cost, or with a lower risk of unexpected and undesired consequences?

Those questions are obviously relevant to the overall evaluation of a policy proposal. And they are essential inputs into any cost–benefit analysis. If legislation is unlikely to actually deliver the desired results, or will be very costly to implement, or risks producing other undesirable consequences, then the appropriateness of legislating to pursue that policy needs to be rethought. Other options that do not involve legislating need to be considered. The viability of the policy goal may need to be revisited. But these are broader issues, which are beyond the scope of this book.

---

[1] The enduring evidence of dynamic responses to the English window tax. Photograph by Whilesteps, own work by Gary Burt (2008), CC BY-SA 3.0, available at: commons.wikimedia.org/wiki/File:Window_Tax.jpg.

[2] Charles Dickens, *Household Words*, vol 1 (London, Bradbury and Evans, 1850) 461. Facsimile available at: www.djo.org.uk/household-words/volume-i/page-461.html.

[3] Image courtesy of Mauritshuis, The Hague. See: www.mauritshuis.nl/en/explore/the-collection/artworks/the-anatomy-lesson-of-dr-nicolaes-tulp-146/detailgegevens/.

[4] See especially, Cass R Sunstein, *The Cost–Benefit Revolution* (Cambridge, MA, MIT Press, 2018).

[5] See, eg, Helen Xanthaki, *Drafting Legislation: Art and Technology of Rules for Regulation* (Oxford, Hart Publishing, 2014); Helen Xanthaki, *Thornton's Legislative Drafting* (West Sussex, Bloomsbury Professional, 2013).

2

The Ways in which Legislation Fails

King Cnut (or 'Canute', as it is sometimes written) is a victim of 'fake news'. Cnut the Great was king of Denmark, England and Norway in the early eleventh century. He is often portrayed as a foolish and arrogant king, who attempted to command the tide not to come in – with a predictable lack of success. But early sources tell the story differently: they suggest that this was a carefully staged performance designed to illustrate the powerlessness of mortal kings, by demonstrating to Cnut's fawning courtiers that he could not command the incoming tide.

Figure 2.1 King Cnut demonstrates the limits of law-making[1]

If this really happened, and if those early sources are right, then Cnut had grasped the most fundamental feature of law-making. It isn't a form of magic. A legislator cannot, simply by passing a law, make the world different – in great ways or small. Rather, the most a law can do is change how people – citizens, businesses, officials, judges and others – behave. If the lawmaker has correctly understood how the relevant people currently behave, and how passing the law will change that behaviour, then (and only then) does it become possible for the law to advance the desired outcome.

So for example it would be easy to pass a law that reads 'hunger is hereby abolished'. Easy, but pointless. Similarly, however tempting it may be to pass a law that provides that 'the Covid-19 virus shall cease to circulate in this country', that would be an empty gesture. If reducing the spread of Covid-19 is the goal, and it is to be pursued through legislation, it is necessary to understand what people do now that contributes to the spread of the virus, and design legislation that is effective to modify that behaviour – for example, by requiring people to use masks, or restricting their movement during a 'lockdown', or requiring them to provide proof of vaccination before engaging in certain activities. And it is necessary to ensure that people know about the requirements that apply to them, and that there are effective mechanisms in place to encourage, monitor and (if necessary) enforce compliance.

This sounds obvious. But it is overlooked all too often. There's a social problem? Easy: we'll pass a law prohibiting the things we don't like, or mandating the things we wish were happening. This '*Harry Potter*' approach to law-making – wave a magic (legislative) wand and the problem will be solved – is attractive to some politicians. And sometimes it is enough – especially for a politician operating on a short electoral time frame – to be seen to be 'doing something' about a problem, regardless of how effective that 'something' subsequently turns out to be. However for legislators who genuinely want to achieve social change, and for advisers responsible for promoting high-quality effective legislation, it is essential to bear in mind that the only way that a law can be effective – the only way it can succeed – is if it changes the behaviour of the people to whom that law is addressed. Legislation is, at its core, a technology for changing behaviour in the society to which that legislation will apply.[2]

What, then, does it mean to say a law has failed? At one level, we can say that a law fails if it does not achieve the ultimate social goals of the lawmaker. So for example a law designed to improve educational outcomes in primary schools will have failed if pupils' achievement stays the same, or gets worse. (I assume here that the proponents of a new law are intending to bring about some sort of change in the society to which the law applies. This seems a reasonable assumption: law-making is an inherently purposive activity.[3] It would be odd for a proponent of a new law to say, if asked, that they did not expect it would change anything at all.)

But this book is not about the ultimate social goals of legislation, which are often value-laden and politically contested. The opponents of the law may consider that the law will make their society worse off, and that it would be a good thing if the law did not work in practice. That is the proper domain of political debate. But it is not the subject of this book. Rather, when I speak of a law failing, I am concerned with the *effectiveness* of the law: whether it does in fact produce the changes in behaviour that it was intended to bring about. The only way a law can 'work' is by changing the behaviour of the people to whom it is addressed. A law does not work – it fails – if it does not bring about the desired changes in how the relevant people behave.[4]

Seen in this light, a law plainly fails where the behaviour of the relevant people doesn't change at all. I discuss these 'damp squibs' in more detail below.[5]

Importantly, a law also fails where it changes how people behave in ways that are significantly different from what was expected and desired at the time the law was made.[6] We do not want to be surprised by the consequences of the laws we make: that is never a good outcome, even if those consequences are (fortunately!) reasonably benign. Law-making is not meant to be a lottery, or a 'lucky dip'. And all too often the unexpected and undesired consequences of a law change are not benign: if they had been expected, the law would not have been made in the same terms. The law's proponents would have recognised that changes to the law were needed, or that it should not be made at all. This is a more complex form of failure, which I describe below in three broad (and sometimes overlapping) categories: overshoots, nasty surprises and backfires.

The Damp Squib

Some legislation simply fails to produce the desired result. The legislation is enacted, but the world doesn't change – or doesn't change much. That is, the legislation is a 'damp squib'.[7] There are many factors that can contribute to this form of failure.

One depressingly common problem is that the people whose behaviour the legislation is intended to influence are not aware of it, or don't understand it. This cause of failure underscores the importance of accessibility of the law, and accessibility of information about what the law requires people to do. Access to law is widely accepted as a fundamental aspect of the rule of law.[8] At the most basic level, it is an essential prerequisite for law to be effective. If key actors are not aware of the law, or of its implications for them – what it enables them to do, or requires them to do or refrain from doing – then their behaviour will not change and the law will not work.[9]

This doesn't just mean publishing legislation on a website – though that is a useful first step. Nor does it mean drafting the legislation in language that is as clear and understandable as possible, though again that is plainly desirable. If you want to influence the behaviour of a section of the public, information explaining what the law enables them to do, or requires them to do, must actually reach the relevant group in a form that they can understand at the time when that information is relevant to them.[10] This is an integral element of effective law-making.

Another common barrier to the effectiveness of legislation is that the people the legislation is intended to benefit do not have the knowledge, skills and resources (in particular, financial resources) to be able to invoke it effectively.[11] For example, it is all too common for legislators to pass laws intended to protect disadvantaged individuals that can only be enforced by those individuals taking some sort of action through the courts. But these are precisely the individuals who lack the resources to bring court proceedings on their own, or to coordinate with others in the same situation to bring collective proceedings (in countries where that is an available option).[12] So the law is disregarded with impunity by the powerful companies or individuals against whom it was intended to provide protection. Debtor protection laws in many countries provide stark examples of this problem. It is all very well to give disadvantaged borrowers the right to challenge the terms of an oppressive or exploitative loan agreement. But if individual borrowers have to go to court to pursue that challenge, the law will largely be a dead letter. The borrower's lack of resources, and the imbalance of power in the relationship between lender and borrower, mean that rights on paper will not translate into protection in the real world. Some other more effective mechanism is needed for laws of this kind to have any real world impact.

The examples of damp squibs I discuss in later chapters include New Zealand's 2001 reform of the law governing division of property between separating couples to address the issue of disparity in post-separation earning potential as a result of the division of roles within the family. This is often a significant issue where one partner has continued to work and the other has given up a career to focus on caring for the family. The new regime was complex and opaque, and was administered by the courts in a way that made it slow and expensive to apply. The result was that the reform was essentially a dead letter – very few of the economically disadvantaged people (mostly women) who were intended to benefit from this reform were able to invoke it and obtain meaningful and timely relief.

For most people who encounter legal issues in their daily lives (a breach of contract; their landlord failing to comply with tenancy laws; the need to divide assets when a relationship ends) the cost of resolving that issue through formal legal channels is prohibitive. The law on paper provides little or no protection in practice.[13] If the goal of the legislation is real-world outcomes, rather than rhetoric, this outcome represents failure. And in every society I have worked in, failures of this kind are pervasive.

Similar problems arise for many people entitled to some form of government support or assistance. The time and difficulty involved in obtaining that benefit (visiting the right government offices; standing in long lines; filling in complex forms; providing information and documents) make it all too hard: they are discouraged from attempting to apply for the benefit, or abandon the exercise part-way through, or fail to successfully complete all the necessary steps and miss out.[14] Their entitlements on paper do not translate into entitlements in practice.

Laws will also be ineffective where the institutions responsible for administering the law do not do this job well – or at all. They may lack the necessary resources: people, systems, funding. They may actively choose not to enforce the law because they are not sympathetic to its goals. The way they administer the law may be influenced by stakeholders through lobbying, or political influence, or outright corruption.

These issues are especially acute in less wealthy countries with fewer resources to devote to administering the law, and in countries where institutions are weak and corruption is pervasive. Another example of a damp squib that I discuss below is the contract law of Bangladesh. When I did some work there in the 1990s I found the courts were so backlogged, and faced so many other institutional challenges, that contracts were for all practical purposes unenforceable. The law on paper looked fine, but was useless in practice.

But wealthy countries with large and sophisticated institutions are by no means immune from these challenges. It is common to see additional responsibilities conferred on agencies without the provision of additional funding. Legislation often provides for new agencies to be established, or for existing agencies to take on new tasks, without adequate thought being given to implementation issues: the personnel and IT systems and funding and lead times needed to make the proposals work. Or whether implementation is in fact possible in practice.[15] Courts in many countries are expected to hear and decide a growing caseload, without a corresponding increase in the number of judges or court facilities, leading to increasing delays. There is an extensive literature on agency 'capture' by vested interests, and on the many ways in which the incentives of agencies and their personnel can lead to behaviour at odds with the goals of the laws those agencies administer. Political influence over agency activity is common in many wealthy countries, especially where agency heads are political appointees: there are many ways in which this can distort agency decision-making, and undermine the effectiveness of the laws those agencies administer.[16] The law on paper will not change the real world in the desired way unless the institutions to which the law is addressed have the capacity – including the necessary human and financial resources – to administer it effectively, and the will to do so. Some implementation failures do of course result from unpredictable events that occur after the legislation has been enacted. But many – I suspect, most – implementation failures can fairly be attributed to flaws in the initial design of the legislation, as a result of insufficient attention being paid to the institutional arrangements for implementation of the law.

A further cause of ineffective legislation, which overlaps with the first and third causes mentioned above, is where enforcement miscues: where there is a gap between the understanding of the law on the part of its framers on the one hand, and the understanding of that law on the part of the officials, agencies and judges responsible for interpreting and applying that law on the other. That gap means that the behaviour of the relevant institutions either does not change or does not change much, so the desired outcomes are not achieved.

Laws often fail to have much of an impact where they run counter to a society's deep-seated beliefs or customs: simply passing a law is usually not enough, by itself, to bring about significant cultural change. So for example anti-discrimination laws can serve an important expressive function by conveying a society's commitment to equal treatment, which may help to shift attitudes and behaviours.[17] The enactment and enforcement of those laws plays an essential role in the elimination of discriminatory attitudes and practices. But to achieve enduring social change those laws need to be coupled with effective education, leadership from prominent members of the community, and other active measures. Similarly, it is not possible to change social attitudes to smoking or alcohol or drugs merely by passing laws: such laws are at most one component of an effective intervention.

Laws also fail in the all too common scenario where the gains to be made from breaking the law significantly outweigh the expected cost of any sanctions. Fines or other penalties are simply seen as a cost of doing business. For many years New Zealand had laws designed to protect the government-owned railways from competition, by restricting the carriage of goods by road between locations served by rail. The staple diet of traffic courts around the country included sentencing trucking firms for breaches of this law. The truckers' lists of prior convictions would be solemnly placed before the court – and in the early days of computerisation, when I had the dubious pleasure of observing some of these hearings, those lists were often long scrolls of continuous printouts that reached from the prosecutor's hands right down to the floor. But the fines were small, and the revenues from trucking goods were substantial. Trucking firms could charge prices that reflected the cost of paying the fines, and still be cheaper than rail. So the goods continued to go by truck; roadside inspections continued to detect regular breaches; the solemn ritual of prosecuting these offences continued to clog the courts; and rail revenues continued to decline.

This is an insidious factor in the effectiveness of laws, as it often becomes worse over time: sanctions that were appropriate when the law was first passed become less effective as the years pass, as a result of inflation or changes in the economic environment which alter the relative costs and benefits of non-compliance.[18] Many countries have adopted mechanisms for automatically adjusting monetary penalties to reflect inflation at least. But (rather surprisingly) many others have not. And inflation is only part of the picture. This illustrates the need to keep laws under review to ensure that they *remain* effective.

The Overshoot

Some laws deliver what they were intended to achieve, but fail to stop there – they overshoot. And as anyone who has eaten too much ice-cream knows, too much of something you once desired can become a problem. That problem is exacerbated if the result of an overshoot in objectives is also an overshoot in the cost of administering the law.

One recent example is provided by New Zealand's 2013 bail law reforms. The government responded to public concern about a handful of high-profile offences committed by people on bail awaiting trial by tightening the criteria for granting bail.[19] The changes included reversing the burden of proof for a wider range of people facing charges: instead of the prosecutor having to persuade the court that the individual was a flight risk, that individual had the burden of satisfying the court that they met the requirements for bail. The new law also set more demanding requirements for the accommodation that a bailed person could live in while on bail, at a time when housing was becoming ever less affordable, and social housing was under significant pressure.

It was an integral part of this law change that more people would be incarcerated: the policy goal was after all to imprison a small additional number of high-risk individuals pre-trial to ensure that those individuals would not reoffend while on bail awaiting trial.[20] The changes were predicted to result in a modest increase of about 50 additional remand prisoners in the daily New Zealand prison population.[21] But the law overshot, by a wide margin. Although exact figures are not available, it is likely that the actual result was many hundreds of additional prisoners on remand on any given day.[22] Remand rates went from 6.1 per cent of people awaiting trial in 2010 to 8.5 per cent in 2015 – an increase of more than a third. In the same period, the number of prisoners on remand at any one time went from around 1,830 to around 3,000.[23] The reverse onus of proof, coupled with more demanding criteria for accommodation for people on bail, left many people facing charges unable to satisfy a judge that they should be granted bail. The risk-averse approach to bail signalled by the law also appears to have influenced judicial approaches to bail more generally.[24] The consequences of these changes were particularly acute for the most disadvantaged members of society, as they faced the greatest difficulty in finding acceptable accommodation and in providing the necessary evidence to qualify for bail.

In New Zealand each prison inmate on remand costs the government about $100,000 per annum on average.[25] So the expected financial cost of the 2013 changes was around $5 million per annum. If the law change increased the prison population by more than 200, which seems a plausible lower-end estimate, then the actual cost would have been more than $20 million per annum: four times what was predicted. If the 2013 changes were responsible for half of the approximately 1,200 increase in prison numbers between 2010 and 2015, then the cost would be higher still: around $60 million per annum. It is impossible to know for sure – there are gaps in the data, and tracing causation would be difficult even with better data.[26]

The financial costs described above are not the only adverse consequences of this law change, or even the most serious. The human costs also need to be counted. Many individuals suffered serious and lasting harms. Those who were ultimately acquitted, or received non-custodial sentences, should not have spent any time in prison. But they lost their liberty, often for many months. As a result, many of these individuals lost their jobs, and – because they could not pay the rent or make mortgage payments –their homes. Families were deprived of fathers and mothers, and family relationships were put under severe stress. While these individuals were in prison on remand they were exposed to influences that increased the likelihood that they would be involved in offending in the future.[27] All of this in the absence of any trial or conviction: these harsh consequences were suffered by people who had not been found guilty of any offence, who had not been shown to be flight risks, and who were entitled to the benefit of the presumption of innocence while they awaited trial.

In 2018 concern about these trends led to administrative initiatives aimed at assisting people facing charges to meet bail requirements, and to provide the necessary information to the courts to qualify for bail. This initiative substantially reduced the remand population – down from a peak of 4,000 to around 3,000 in October 2018.[28] That reduction suggests that the 'overshoot' from the 2013 reforms may have been as many as 1,000 additional prisoners on remand at any given time, at a cost of $100 million per annum. It also suggests that much of this overshoot could have been avoided by making relatively simple changes to the way in which the bail regime was administered in tandem with the change in the law. That brings us back to the importance of institutions – and to the importance of default outcomes, and the impact of changing default settings. These topics are discussed in more detail below.

It seems pretty clear, despite the lack of robust data, that the 2013 change in bail laws, coupled with a failure to review and adapt existing administrative practices, led to far more people being incarcerated than was intended. Including many who posed no real danger to society, and no real flight risk. They were in prison because they were poor, or lacked the literacy skills and support networks to understand what they needed to do to get bail, to work through those requirements and to establish them to the court's satisfaction. The cost to New Zealanders was substantial – many times what was predicted. By any measure, this was a significant policy failure.[29]

Nasty Surprises

Some laws achieve their intended goals, but produce other unexpected and undesired results. The window taxes described in chapter one are a good example of this class of failed laws. They raised substantial revenue (initially at least, though this fell away over time). They were less intrusive and more easily administered than a tax on income, or the 'hearth tax' (a tax on chimneys) that preceded the English window tax. But they had an enduring adverse effect on the housing stock in the UK and elsewhere, and on the quality of life and health of many citizens.

The window tax example illustrates a common theme in many 'nasty surprise' legislative failures: a failure to think through the longer-term consequences of a law, and how people are likely to respond to it. The law may work well in a static environment, with everything else held constant. But people are creative, and they don't like paying taxes. So over time they change their behaviour – in the case of the window tax, they brick up existing windows, and build new houses with fewer windows. Revenue goes down, and people suffer and die. We live in a dynamic world in which people respond to incentives. Legislation that ignores this feature of the world we inhabit is very likely to fail.

The other common theme in 'nasty surprise' failures is a lack of institutional capacity – or will – to administer the law in accordance with its policy goals. This happens all too often when laws from wealthy countries with strong institutions are transplanted into developing countries that have not yet had the time and resources to build equally strong institutions. In one developing country I visited some years ago, I was told that a recently enacted competition law was based on advice from highly respected overseas lawyers, and represented 'global best practice'. That law gave the newly established competition regulator the power to block mergers and acquisitions that would harm competition. However the agency did not have the expertise or resources to carry out an orthodox economic analysis of the competitive implications of a merger. At the time of my visit, it did not employ a single economist. Its staff were all public servants transferred from other agencies, without any background in the fields of competition law or economics. The agency clearly lacked the ability to perform its core functions. But it had recently used its new powers to block a deal. It prevented the purchase by the highest bidder of a state-owned business that was being privatised. There was no possible competition concern: the highest bidder was an overseas company with no existing presence in the local market. That bidder withdrew – it didn't want to go through the long and uncertain process of challenging the regulator's decision in the courts. So the second-highest bidder was successful with its (substantially lower) bid. The state was paid much less for the business. According to some well-informed people I spoke to, the suspicion was that the regulator's decision had been made to benefit an influential politician whose brother had a major stake in the second-highest bidder. But even if this decision was the result of simple incompetence rather than corruption, it involved the misuse of newly created powers at a significant cost to the public purse, and to the credibility of future state enterprise sales processes.

Nasty surprises caused by lack of institutional capacity are also common in wealthy countries. Laws are often passed without much thought being given to how they will be administered – or even if they can be effectively administered. As discussed in chapter eight below, New Zealand's introduction of performance-based building regulation in the early 1990s led to a multibillion-dollar 'leaky building' crisis. There was a strong case for reform of the existing highly prescriptive regulatory regime, to permit more flexibility and innovation in how buildings were designed and built. But lack of capacity to administer the new regime effectively on the part of local regulators, and on the part of the national agency responsible for oversight of the regime, led to serious and costly failures.

In their fascinating (but rather depressing) book *The Blunders of our Governments* Anthony King and Ivor Crewe identify a number of spectacular failures by UK governments in recent decades, many of which involved the enactment of legislation. They define a blunder as:

> [A]n episode in which a government adopts a specific course of action in order to achieve one or more objectives and, as a result largely or wholly of its own mistakes, either fails completely to achieve those objectives, or does achieve some or all of them but at a totally disproportionate cost, or else does achieve some or all of them but contrives at the same time to cause a significant amount of 'collateral damage' in the form of unintended and undesired consequences.

The first category of blunders – failure to achieve the law's objectives – corresponds with my 'damp squib' category. The others, involving disproportionate costs or other undesired consequences, correspond with my 'nasty surprise' category. The blunders that led to many of the spectacular nasty surprises they describe – including the mis-selling of personal pensions in the late 1980s and early 1990s, the introduction of a new child support regime in the early 1990s, 'individual learning accounts' in the late 1990s, and the introduction of a new system of tax credits in 2002 – involved serious implementation failures that could and should have been foreseen by the politicians and officials responsible for the legislation.[30] It is worth adding that the categories of damp squib and nasty surprise can overlap; this occurs where a law fails to achieve its intended purpose *and* produces an unforeseen and undesirable consequence. The introduction of the new child support regime in the United Kingdom, as described by King and Crewe, is an example of failure on both these dimensions.

Perhaps the most common form of nasty surprise is implementation costs far in excess of what was originally anticipated. If expenditure on implementation of the law is capped (for example, by an allocation of government funding for the programme which cannot be exceeded), then higher than expected implementation costs tend to result in a damp (or, at least, damp-ish) squib – the intended benefits simply cannot be achieved with the available funds. Where expenditure is not subject to effective limits – for example, the cost of imprisoning offenders sentenced by judges whose case-by-case decisions are not constrained by budget allocations for running prisons, or the cost of publicly funded demand-driven health services – cost overruns mean nasty surprises for the public purse.

One especially nasty subset of the 'nasty surprises' school of failures is the law that backfires, exacerbating the very problem it aimed to solve. This is sometimes referred to in the economics literature as the 'cobra effect', after a famous policy failure in British India. Many of these backfires stem from the dynamic consequences of a law that has been conceived in static terms. Failures of this kind are so obviously unsatisfactory, and their causes so informative, that I discuss them as a separate category below.

The Backfire

The 'cobra effect' is named after a policy adopted by the British Raj in Delhi in the late nineteenth century.[31] Troubled by the large population of poisonous cobras in the city, the governor issued a proclamation offering a bounty for cobra skins.

Figure 2.2 Indian cobra

The goal was, of course, to encourage the killing of cobras and reduce the cobra population. However some enterprising Delhi residents quickly realised that the cost of breeding, raising and skinning cobras was substantially less than the bounty payable on their skins, and began to farm cobras in order to earn the bounty. Once the governor realised that the bounty programme was costing much more than expected, and was not producing any noticeable reduction in Delhi's cobra population, the bounty scheme was terminated. The farmed cobras were now worthless – so the breeders released them.[32] The ultimate result? An increase in the cobra population, and a waste of government funds that could have been better spent on other goals.

The same scenario played out in Hanoi in the early twentieth century, under French rule.[33] This time, the problem was rats. Concerned by the growing rat population in the city's newly constructed sewers, the government offered a bounty on rat tails. But it turned out that it was easier to farm rats than it was to catch and kill wild rats: rat farms soon appeared on the edges of the city. More problematically still, it made sense for the bounty hunters to cut the tails off the rats – wild or farmed – and let the rats live in order to produce more rats, which in turn would provide more bounty opportunities in the future. The endgame was, with the benefit of hindsight, inevitable: ever-escalating bounty payments; no apparent headway in terms of the Hanoi rat population (though it seems there were frequent sightings of tail-less rats); cancellation of the bounty; and release of the farmed rats – making the original problem worse.

Nor is this a problem confined to a previous era, or to colonial administrations in distant lands. In 2007, a US military base, Fort Benning, introduced a bounty scheme to attempt to control the abundant (and destructive) local population of wild pigs. For each pig tail, the government paid $40. The scheme was abandoned some three years later, when it became clear it wasn't working: studies suggest that the wild pig population actually increased during the period when the bounty programme was in effect.[34] As the ghost of the French Governor of Hanoi might say with a wry smile, '*plus ça change, plus c'est la même chose!*'

There are many other examples of laws that make the problem they were aimed at worse. In Mexico City, a 1989 ban restricted each car from driving on a specified weekday (based on its number plate) in order to reduce congestion and air pollution. Several studies found that the ban actually made these problems worse. Many households bought an additional car to get around the ban. The increased use of these second cars – many of which were cheaper, older and more polluting than the household's first car – contributed to an increase in congestion and a deterioration in air quality.[35] The behaviour of the targeted group – residents of Mexico City – changed; but it changed in ways that the framers of the law failed to anticipate. Similar schemes restricting the use of cars have been tried in many other places at many other times, for various reasons – typically with just as little success. Many such schemes continue to operate in congested cities worldwide, despite the documented failures in Mexico City and elsewhere.[36]

Figure 2.3 When laws backfire – Mexico City, blanketed by smog[37]

The economic literature provides many more examples of 'backfires' of this kind, especially (and tragically) in the field of environmental regulation.[38] Laws to protect endangered species, some features of which may actually accelerate loss of habitat and population.[39] Creation of pollution standards for new vehicles, while excluding existing vehicles from the scheme (a practice often referred to as 'grandparenting'), with the result that the cost of vehicle replacement increases and old dirty vehicles stay on the roads longer than they otherwise would have.[40] Rent control regimes that reduce the supply of housing for worst-off groups.[41] Disclosure requirements that leave people less informed on key dimensions.[42] And so the list continues.

A Focus on how Legislation Changes Behaviour

The common thread in all four of these scenarios – damp squibs, overshoots, nasty surprises and backfires – is that the behaviour of the relevant people either did not change in the desired manner, or changed in an unexpected and undesired way. By studying some law-making failures that we can identify after the event, and focusing on how those failures came about, we can shed light on the questions we should be asking ourselves when we design laws. A focus on how legislation is likely to change behaviour draws our attention away from the words on the page to the actions of the various people to whom the legislation is addressed – affected citizens and businesses, officials, courts and others. What do they do now? How will the legislation change what they do – in the short run, and in the longer term? How sure are we about that? If we are not very sure, what does that mean for the design of the legislation, or for whether we should legislate at all? These important questions are explored in more detail below.

---

[1] This lesson about the limits of law-making is captured in a painting by Alphonse-Marie-Adolphe de Neuville, reproduced in John H Haaren and AB Poland, *Famous Men of the Middle Ages* (University Publishing Company, 1904) 153, available at: commons.wikimedia.org/wiki/File:Canute_rebukes_his_courtiers.png.

[2] More generally, laws can be seen as a technology for channelling behaviour in a society – which in many contexts means maintaining existing patterns of behaviour. Making new laws – legislating – is a technology for changing that behaviour. The technology may on occasion be used to make declaratory statements about the law or aspirational policy statements that change nothing – see Andrew Burrows, *Thinking About Statutes: Interpretation, Interaction, Improvement* (Cambridge, Cambridge University Press, 2018) 106–07. But this is not the core purpose of legislation. And in the eyes of many commentators, including Professor Burrows, legislation is not an appropriate vehicle for such statements.

[3] Law-making is generally treated as a purposive activity by those who engage in it. And rightly so. The making of a new law requires justification for three related reasons. First, the law-making process makes significant calls on the (scarce, and costly) time and attention of the institutions through which we govern our society: the law-making institutions themselves, and the institutions (bureaucracies, courts etc) that apply those laws. Second, new laws demand the time and attention of members of our society, who need to ascertain whether, and how, those laws may apply to them. Third, most laws invoke the coercive power of the state, either directly (by imposing enforceable obligations) or indirectly (by providing for activities that will be funded through taxation). The demands that laws make on our time and attention, and the burdens they impose, require justification by reference to the ways in which the proponents of the law believe that our society will be different, and better off, if the law is made.

[4] This has also been described as the 'impact' of a law: see, eg, Lawrence M Friedman, *Impact: How Law Affects Behavior* (Cambridge, MA, Harvard University Press, 2016) ch 3.

[5] This concept is often framed in terms of *effectiveness*: is the legislation effective in achieving its direct goals? See Maria Mousmouti, *Designing Effective Legislation* (Cheltenham, Edward Elgar Publishing, 2019) ch 1, esp 9; Helen Xanthaki, *Drafting Legislation: Art and Technology of Rules for Regulation* (Oxford, Hart Publishing, 2014) ch 1. But the terminology is not uniform – see, eg, Friedman (n 4).

[6] There are conflicting views on whether a law can be described as effective if and only if it achieves its direct goals *and does not have significant unanticipated and undesired results*. A law plainly is not effective where it produces the undesired results in place of the desired results. Where the desired results are achieved, but they are accompanied by significant undesired results, some commentators would not see this as going to effectiveness and would frame the concern in terms of efficiency: do the (unexpected) social costs of achieving the desired results outweigh the social benefits from those results? See Mousmouti (n 5). At the end of the day, the label seems less important than recognising that a law that produces significant unanticipated and undesired results can hardly be seen as a success.

[7] A figure of speech referring to something that fails ignominiously to satisfy the expectations aroused by it; an anti-climax, a disappointment. Literally, a small firework or firecracker that – having become damp – may fizz a little, but fails to explode.

[8] Lord Bingham, a former United Kingdom Supreme Court judge, identifies eight principles that underpin the concept of the rule of law. The first of those principles is a requirement that the law be accessible, clear and predictable. See Tom Bingham, *The Rule of Law* (London, Penguin Books, 2011).

[9] The legal philosopher Lon Fuller identifies, in *The Morality of Law*, eight 'distinct routes to disaster' in the law-making process. The second of these is 'a failure to publicize, or at least to make available to the affected party, the rules he is expected to observe'. Closely related are the fourth – a failure to make rules understandable, the fifth – the enactment of contradictory rules, and the seventh – introducing such frequent changes in the rules that the subject cannot orient his action by them: Lon Fuller, *The Morality of Law*, revised edn (New Haven, CT, Yale University Press, 1969) 38–39. For a more recent discussion of legislative failure see, eg Mousmouti (n 5) ch 7.

[10] See, eg Friedman (n 4) ch 2; Hazel Genn, 'Business Responses to the Regulation of Health and Safety in England' (1993) 15 *Law & Policy* 219.

[11] Lon Fuller's sixth 'route to disaster' is where 'rules … require conduct beyond the powers of the affected party': Fuller (n 9) 39.

[12] In addition to the obvious difficulty of the cost of court proceedings, there will often be barriers to bringing such proceedings as a result of lack of knowledge of and familiarity with the relevant institutions, and lack of the necessary 'bandwidth' to initiate and pursue such claims. On the impact of lack of resources on this form of human 'bandwidth' see, eg Sendhil Mullainathan and Eldar Shafir, *Scarcity: Why Having Too Little Means So Much* (London, Allen Lane, 2013).

[13] For a discussion of the gap between rights on paper and rights in practice see, eg, Ross Cranston, *How Law Works: The Machinery and Impact of Civil Justice* (Oxford, Oxford University Press, 2006) ch 7. For studies of the proportion of people who pursue legal claims, and the reasons for not doing so see, eg, Hazel Genn, *Paths to Justice: What People Do and Think About Going to Law* (Oxford, Hart Publishing, 1999); Pascoe Pleasence, Nigel Balmer and Rebecca Sandefur, *Paths to Justice: A Past, Present and Future Roadmap* (London, UCL Centre for Empirical Legal Studies, 2013), available at: www.nuffieldfoundation.org/sites/default/files/files/PTJ%20Roadmap%20NUFFIELD%20Published. pdf.

[14] See, eg, the discussion of the student aid process in the United States in Cass R Sunstein's book *Simpler: The Future of Government* (New York, Simon & Schuster, 2013) 122–23.

[15] Many of the 'blunders' described in Anthony King and Ivor Crewe, *The Blunders of Our Governments* (London, Oneworld Publications, 2013) involved the enactment of legislation that established new agencies, or gave new roles to existing agencies, without adequate (or any) attention being paid to the challenges of implementing the legislation. See especially ch 19.

[16] For a striking example of the many ways in which a politicised leadership can undermine the effectiveness of an agency and of the laws it administers see, eg, Richard Revesz 'Institutional Pathologies in the Regulatory State: What Scott Pruitt Taught Us About Regulatory Policy' (2019) 34 *Journal of Land Use & Environmental Law* 211.

[17] See, eg, Cass R Sunstein, *How Change Happens* (Cambridge, MA, MIT Press, 2019) ch 3.

[18] Similar issues may rise in relation to monetary benefits prescribed in legislation, such as social security payments or pensions, if they are not inflation indexed. As with sanctions, there is considerable variation both within and between countries when it comes to indexation of such benefits.

[19] Public concern that was increased by an 'availability cascade': see Timur Kuran and Cass R Sunstein, 'Availability Cascades and Risk Regulation' (1999) 51 *Stanford Law Review* 683.

[20] However as time spent in prison on remand is counted against any sentence ultimately imposed by the courts, under New Zealand law, the total time served in prison would not change for individuals who were convicted of a serious offence and sentenced to imprisonment. See text at n 29 below.

[21] New Zealand's imprisonment rate is already one of the highest among Western developed countries: Office of the Prime Minister's Chief Science Advisor, *Using Evidence to Build a Better Justice System: The Challenge of Rising Prison Costs* (2018) 5, available at: dpmc.govt.nz/sites/default/files/2021-10/pmcsa-Using-evidence-to-build-a-better-justice-system.pdf. For the original estimate of the likely increase in remand prisoner numbers as a result of the 2013 bail law reform, see Ministry of Justice, 'Regulatory Impact Statement for the Bail Amendment Bill 2012' (2012), available at: www.treasury.govt.nz/sites/default/files/2012-03/ris-justice-bab-may12.pdf.

[22] The 2013 bail law changes were described as a 'major cause' contributing to large overall increases in the New Zealand prison population since 2000 in a recent Department of Corrections report: see Department of Corrections, 'Briefing to the Incoming Minister' (2016), available at: www.corrections.govt.nz/__data/assets/pdf_file/0009/28917/Corrections_BIM_December_2016_Redacted.pdf.
The precise impact on the prison population is difficult to assess for a number of reasons. One difficulty is that if an offender receives a prison sentence, time spent on remand is counted towards the sentence – so for this group, time on remand represents an accelerated period in prison rather than an incremental period in prison. Additional time in prison is served by remand prisoners who are acquitted, or do not receive a custodial sentence, or receive a custodial sentence but their time on remand exceeds the time they are required to serve under that sentence (after allowing for parole). However no data are available on the sentences received by remand prisoners, and how these compare to the time served on remand by those prisoners, so it is not possible to assess the extent of incremental prison time served as a result of the 2013 changes. The absence of such data is a serious flaw in the law-making process in this field – it is not easy to see how informed decisions can be made without it. And the failure to recognise that this lack of data meant that predictions about the law's impact were highly uncertain, and that a wide range of outcomes was possible and needed to be evaluated, was a serious flaw in the 2013 law change process. The implications of uncertainty for law-making are discussed in chapter 11 below.

[23] Department of Corrections, 'Corrections Volumes 2016–2017' (2017), available at: www.corrections.govt.nz/resources/statistics/corrections-volumes-report/corrections_volumes_report_201617. Another contributing factor was extended time frames from initial charge to sentence, as a result of other changes to the trial and sentencing processes.

[24] Office of the Prime Minister's Chief Science Advisor, *Using Evidence to Build a Better Justice System: The Challenge of Rising Prison Costs* (2018) 5, available at: www.pmcsa.org.nz/wp-content/uploads/Using-evidence-to-build-a-better-justice-system.pdf 9.

[25] In 2018/19 the estimated average cost per remand prisoner was $302 per day: Department of Corrections, 'Annual Report 1 July 2018–30 June 2019' (2019) 16, available at: www.corrections.govt.nz/__data/assets/pdf_file/0008/38852/Annual_Report_2018_2019_Web_Version_Final.pdf. The long-run incremental cost of additional remand prisoners is likely to be close to this average cost figure, and may exceed it if the figures provided by the Department of Corrections do not include the annualised cost of capital expenditure on new facilities.

[26] The absence of a baseline, and the failure to collect data that would enable the evaluation of the changes after the event, are further failures in the law change process that are discussed below.

[27] Office of the Prime Minister's Chief Science Advisor, *Using Evidence* (n 24).

[28] Interview with Minister for the Department of Corrections, Kelvin Davis: Laura Walters, 'Davis: Prison System Crisis Averted For Now' *Newsroom* (Auckland, 8 October 2018), available at: www.newsroom.co.nz/prison-system-crisis-averted.

[29] The New Zealand figures pale beside those of India. According to an article in *The Economist*, some two-thirds of the 400,000 inmates in Indian prisons were awaiting trial: 'Dropping the Scales' *The Economist* (London, 19 May 2016), citing a government report from 2014. The article went on to say that '[i]t is also estimated that more than half of prisoners who could seek release on bail do not do so. Either they cannot afford it or they have not been made to understand that this is a right'. This is a spectacular injustice, caused by the gap between the laws on paper and their application by the responsible institutions.

[30] King and Crewe (n 15). See especially ch 5 on personal pensions, ch 6 on the Child Support Act 1991, ch 9 on individual learning accounts, ch 10 on tax credits, and ch 15 on the Identity Cards Act 2006. The authors emphasise failure to pay attention to implementation – to institutional arrangements – as a major contributor to these failures: see especially ch 19 on 'Operational disconnect'.

[31] The term was coined by a German economist: see Horst Siebert, *Der Kobra-Effekt: wie man Irrwege der Wirtschaftspolitik vermeidet* (Munich, Deutsche Verlags-Anstalt, 2001). The phenomenon has been explained in a characteristically entertaining and enlightening way by the 'Freakonomics'

team: Stephen J Dubner, 'The Cobra Effect' (*Freakonomics*, 11 October 2012), available at: www.freako-nomics.com/podcast/the-cobra-effect-a-new-freakonomics-radio-podcast/ (full transcript available at: www.freakonomics.com/2012/10/11/the-cobra-effect-full-transcript/).

[32] An Indian cobra, of the kind farmed to exploit the cobra bounty a little over a hundred years ago. Photograph by Kamalnv, own work (2008), CC BY 3.0, available at: commons.wikimedia.org/wiki/File:Indiancobra.jpg.

[33] Michael G Vann, 'Of Rats, Rice, and Race: The Great Hanoi Rat Massacre, an Episode in French Colonial History' (2003) 4 *French Colonial History* 191.

[34] Stephen S Ditchkoff, Robert W Holtfreter and Brian L Williams, 'Effectiveness of a Bounty Program For Reducing Wild Pig Densities' (2017) 41(3) *Wildlife Society Bulletin* 548, available at: www.doi.org/10.1002/wsb.787.

[35] Gunnar S Eskeland and Tarhan Feyzioglu, 'Rationing Can Backfire: The "Day Without a Car" in Mexico City' (1997) 11(3) *World Bank Economic Review* 383; Lucas W Davis, 'The Effect of Driving Restrictions on Air Quality in Mexico City' (2008) 116 *Journal of Political Economy* 38. In 2008 the Mexico City programme was extended from weekday restrictions to Saturdays. A 15% reduction in vehicle emissions on Saturdays was forecast. A recent study suggests there was no measurable reduction in emissions as a result of this law change: Lucas W Davis, 'Saturday Driving Restrictions Fail to Improve Air Quality in Mexico City' (2017) 7 *Scientific Reports* 41652.

[36] See, eg, Davis, 'Saturday Driving Restrictions' (2017), figure 1, identifying 12 cities with a total population in excess of 145 million that have, or have recently had, such restrictions. The Bogota scheme is discussed by the Freakonomics team: see Dubner (n 31).

[37] Image by Fidel Gonzalez, own work (2010), CC BY-SA 3.0, available at: commons.wikimedia.org/wiki/File:AerialViewPhotochemicalSmogMexicoCity_2.jpg.

[38] Cass R Sunstein, 'Paradoxes of the Regulatory State' (1990) 57 *University of Chicago Law Review* 407; Patrick Walker, 'Self-Defeating Regulation' (2013) 9(1) *International Zeitschrift* 31; Siebert (n 31).

[39] John A List, Michael Margolis and Daniel E Osgood, 'Is the Endangered Species Act Endangering Species?' (2006) National Bureau of Economic Research Working Paper 12777, available at: www.nber.org/papers/w12777.

[40] Robert W Crandall et al, *Regulating the Automobile* (Washington DC, Brookings Institution Press, 1986) 89–90. As Sunstein explains in 'Paradoxes of the Regulatory State' (n 38), this is one example of the common phenomenon of regulating existing risks differently from new sources of risk: an approach that is common, but that carries a risk of ineffectiveness or even backfiring that needs to be identified and taken into account in the regulatory design.

[41] Sunstein, 'Paradoxes of the Regulatory State' (n 38) 422–23. See also Rebecca Diamond, Tim McQuade and Franklin Qian, 'The Effects of Rent Control Expansion on Tenants, Landlords, and Inequality: Evidence from San Francisco' (2019) 109 *American Economic Review* 3365, available at: www.web.stanford.edu/~diamondr/DMQ.pdf.

[42] Sunstein, 'Paradoxes of the Regulatory State' (n 38) 424–25; Cass R Sunstein, *Too Much Information* (Cambridge, MA, MIT Press, 2020).

3

Learning from Past Failures

How can we reduce the risk that our legislative projects will fail in one or more of the ways I have just outlined? Experience in other fields suggests that a number of relatively simple steps can go a long way. The first step is to understand the most common factors that lead to the different types of legislative failure. The second is to pay attention to those factors as we design new legislation, and do the best we can – in a world of limited resources and limited human and institutional bandwidth – to anticipate and address those factors. The third, and perhaps most important, is to design laws against the backdrop of a realistic appreciation of what we do not know and cannot confidently predict.

Learning from Failure

One of the most inspiring books I have read in recent years is Atul Gawande's *The Checklist Manifesto*.[1] Gawande, a leading US surgeon, tells the story of how checklists came to be widely used in the aviation industry. He goes on to explain how checklists have begun to be used in surgery, and the surprisingly big difference that such checklists can make. He also describes how checklists are used in other settings – construction, investment banking, natural disaster response. His book explores the difference that a good checklist can make in a wide range of contexts, and how it is that such a simple tool can be so effective.

As Gawande explains, checklists help users to navigate certain types of complexity. In an environment where human decision-makers risk being overwhelmed by the information available to them and the choices they need to make about how to respond to that information, the structure and discipline of a checklist can make the difference between success and failure. And the starting point for a good checklist is … failure. The best checklists target the key things that can and do go wrong in a particular context, and guide the checklist users to take steps that will reduce the risk of such failures.

Lawmakers – like medics – can learn a great deal from the commitment of the aviation safety community to learning from failure. Accidents are carefully studied by aviation safety agencies not for the purpose of attributing blame, but rather to learn for the future. If we are serious about improving the quality and effectiveness of our laws, we need to do the same. We need to identify successes and failures. Where laws fail, we need to study how that came about: not in order to find scapegoats, but to learn what went wrong and to share that learning with others. If we have a better understanding of what hasn't worked in the past, and why, our odds of making laws that do work will be much improved. As the philosopher Karl Popper wrote, 'Every discovery of a mistake constitutes a real advance in our knowledge'.[2]

The challenges of learning from our law-making failures should not however be underestimated. Most laws are never evaluated in a systematic way. Their merits are debated in the political arena, which is long on point-scoring and attribution of blame, and light on lessons for the future. For a number of reasons, which I come back to below, governments rarely undertake objective evaluations of whether a law has succeeded in achieving its intended goals.[3] In other words, we don't even take the first step of systematically identifying failures, let alone go on to study how those failures came about, and what we can learn from that experience for the future.

Nor, of course, is it possible to simply transplant the sort of checklist that is used by pilots, or surgeons, into the legal design context. Checklists for pilots take two main forms: the 'READ-DO' checklist, and the 'DO-CONFIRM' checklist. With a READ-DO checklist, the pilots carry out the listed tasks as they read through the checklist. With a DO-CONFIRM checklist, the pilots rely on their memory and expertise to carry out the tasks, then pause and run through the checklist to ensure that they haven't missed anything.

READ-DO checklists aren't much use to legal designers. Nor – unlike in surgery, for example – is there much scope for DO-CONFIRM checklists.[4] Legal designers have to grapple with complexity. But the decision-making processes are different in important respects, and the complexity encountered in the law-making context is also different. The law-making process doesn't (normally, or healthily!) involve making choices about what to do next under extreme time pressure, in situations that repeat themselves frequently. There is time to consult. The ultimate decision is made following input from a range of stakeholders and advisers. Often, it is made by a deliberative body – a legislature, an independent government agency or a local authority. The process is iterative – where concerns are identified about a proposed law, new options are generated which then need to be evaluated.

And, very importantly, the complexity that lawmakers encounter is not the product of a large amount of available and well-documented information about the challenges they will encounter, and how to anticipate or respond to those challenges. To the contrary, lawmakers often find themselves dealing with issues that have novel features, with little or no information about identical scenarios on which they can draw. In order to do so, they need to predict how different design options will play out over an extended period, in a society that is itself constantly changing. This is inherently difficult – sometimes, impossible. And as I will explain in more detail shortly, research suggests that this is not something that comes naturally to us, or that most of us do particularly well.

Against that backdrop, perhaps the most surprising observation I have made in my more than 30 years of involvement in law reform is how consistently confident legal designers are about their projects. All too often I see legal designers – especially, but not only, politicians – make intuitive leaps to solutions when it is clear that they do not have the information needed to decide whether that solution has a good prospect of succeeding. They express confident views about how the world currently works, and about the change that their proposed law will produce. But if you ask some simple – almost embarrassingly naïve – questions about the basis for those views, it turns out they are founded on limited (and often anecdotal) information, and irrationally optimistic assumptions about how the law will operate in practice. Critical issues – for example, the ability of people to access the benefits that the law is intended to provide, or the ability of relevant institutions to administer the law – are ignored, or put to one side on the basis that they will be addressed further down the road as an implementation issue. (Deferring practical questions of this kind is especially common where different people are responsible for designing the law and for implementing it.)

This is a recipe for failure. Failure that comes as a surprise to those confident legal designers, if they are aware of it.[5] All too often we are not even aware of such failures, given how rare it is to carry out a systematic evaluation of whether a law has succeeded in achieving its goals. But sometimes failures are sufficiently stark that we cannot ignore them. The 'blunders' in the United Kingdom described by Crewe and King fall into that category. Sometimes, if you have been in law reform long enough, you find yourself working on reviews of a law that you were involved in developing 10 or 20 years earlier. It's an uncomfortable – but salutary – experience to appear before a parliamentary committee to explain that a particular provision did not operate in the way you had expected, and needs to be amended to work better. And all too often in my current role as a judge I find myself trying to make a statute work sensibly in circumstances that plainly were not anticipated by its framers, even though the issue was always likely to arise, and should have been provided for.

Causes of Legal Design Failures

If our legal design failures are the product of process failures – failures to ask important questions, and failures to understand the limits of our knowledge and our ability to make predictions – why do we keep making the same mistakes year after year, project after project? And how can we do better?

The reasons we keep making these mistakes, it turns out, lie deep in human psychology. Two important books published in the last decade provide a rich source of insights into the way we humans make decisions. First in time is the book *Thinking, Fast and Slow* written by the brilliant psychologist and Nobel Prize winner Daniel Kahneman.[6] And, a decade later, its companion *Noise* written by Daniel Kahneman with Olivier Sibony, a professor of strategy at HEC Paris, and Cass Sunstein, a law professor at Harvard (and probably the world's most influential legal scholar today).[7]

Research into the way people actually make decisions suggests that people think in two broad ways, which Kahneman describes as System 1 and System 2. System 1 is the domain of intuition – it is fast, automatic and unconscious. We use System 1 to talk, walk, ride a bicycle, add two plus two, and recognise familiar faces ('that's my friend Helen over there across the road!'). System 2 involves slower, deliberate, effortful, conscious thinking. When we are conscious that we are thinking, we are using System 2.

System 1 is essential for making many decisions in our daily lives, and deals with those issues swiftly and effectively. But we also deploy System 1 to answer questions for which it is not well equipped. And even when we bring System 2 to bear, often we have a ready answer provided almost instantaneously by System 1. System 2 tends to take that intuitive answer as its starting point – and frequently does little more than find some evidence to confirm that ready answer, then stops there. The result of the interplay between these two systems is that we make many judgements using shortcuts – heuristics – that are driven by factors of little or no relevance to the question we are attempting to address. I describe some of these heuristics in more detail in chapter four.

The interplay between systems 1 and 2, and the heuristics that drive our decision-making, will in some contexts result in 'noise' – the chance variability of judgements. Random factors – the weather, your mood, what you had for lunch – affect the consistency of decision-making of a person over time, and consistency between decision-makers. The authors of *Noise* offer an aphorism: 'Where there is judgment, there is noise – and usually more of it than you think'.[8]

In other contexts, those heuristics result in systematic biases in the decisions people make about an issue. For example, systematic over-optimism and over-confidence in the correctness of your own views about how society works.

The insights provided by these books are relevant to legal designers in three distinct ways.

The Stories We Tell Ourselves about the Laws We Design

First, and most importantly for present purposes, these books shed light on why legal designers are so persistently confident about their projects, even where the foundation for that confidence appears rather thin. A great deal of research confirms that humans are very good at identifying apparent patterns in the information available to them, and developing plausible explanations for those patterns. We do this even though the available information is limited and unreliable – and even though we know it is limited and unreliable. Kahneman describes the human mind as a 'machine for jumping to conclusions': 'We are prone to overestimate how much we understand about the world and to underestimate the role of chance in events. Over-confidence is fed by the illusory certainty of hindsight'.[9]

The confidence that people feel in their assessments is essentially unrelated to the correctness of those assessments, or to the adequacy and reliability of the information on which those assessments are based. Rather, the confidence we feel in our judgements is a function of the coherence of the narrative we construct based on the information available to us. We pay insufficient attention to the information we don't have – as Kahneman puts it, 'What You See Is All There Is!' The less information we have, the fewer pieces in the jigsaw puzzle – so the easier it is to construct a coherent narrative that fits all those pieces, and the greater our confidence in that narrative. A number of studies have found that exposing decision-makers to additional relevant information actually *reduces* the confidence with which they reach their conclusions. The clear message is that we should not confuse confidence with correctness – whether in relation to the judgements of others, or our own judgements.

Experts are not immune from these tendencies in human decision-making. There are fields in which experts develop more accurate and reliable intuitions than non-experts, based on prolonged practice in the relevant field. Even so, many studies confirm that the intuitions of experts are distorted by the heuristics (decision-making shortcuts, or rules of thumb) that Kahneman describes. Still more sobering is his discussion of the circumstances in which it is possible to develop meaningful expertise, and why it is that the (confident!) intuitions of professionals in many fields do not stem from reliable expertise. There are numerous fields in which claims to expertise outstrip the actual ability of experts to consistently make high-quality decisions. Expertise of this kind is difficult or impossible to develop in areas where the environment is not sufficiently regular to be predictable, or where feedback is insufficiently frequent, immediate and unequivocal to provide an opportunity to learn through prolonged practice. In such fields the intuitions of 'experts' will still often be confidently held and confidently expressed, and that confidence may be very well remunerated.[10] But those intuitions will be no more reliable than random guesswork.

Many studies confirm that predictions based on the subjective impressions of trained professionals are typically less accurate than statistical predictions produced using a simple algorithm.[11] This disturbing result (for professionals – and for those who seek out and pay for their advice!) has been confirmed in studies in many fields, including forecasts of academic success; violations of parole; success in pilot training; criminal reoffending; diagnosis of a number of medical conditions; predicting length of hospital stays and a wide range of other medical outcomes; and many economic forecasts.

The disconnect between accuracy and confidence is especially acute when it comes to predicting developments in complex social settings – an exercise that designing legislation often requires. The results obtained by researchers make sobering reading for legal designers. One important contribution to this field is a book written by the psychologist Philip Tetlock called *Expert Political Judgment: How Good Is It?*[12] The book summarises a 20-year study conducted by the author. Tetlock interviewed experts in various fields and asked them to assess the probability of various events occurring in the near to medium term. They were asked to make predictions both within and outside their areas of specialisation. Tetlock then evaluated the accuracy of those predictions.

Experts did perform better than non-specialists – just. Their expertise gave them an edge in the short to medium term, though they did poorly in the longer term. As Tetlock observed, 'We reach the point of diminishing marginal predictive returns for knowledge disconcertingly quickly'. Another important finding from this study was that the experts were far more confident than non-experts about their predictions: their belief in their own expertise led them to think that their predictions were far more accurate than they actually were. When you think about it, that's not too surprising: the world prefers bold and confident predictions to more timid and qualified suggestions. In every field in which I have worked, the experts and advisers who are in demand are the ones who radiate confidence in their own expertise and in the accuracy of their own judgements.[13]

My experience of law reform projects in many countries has been consistent with these findings. It is common for politicians and their advisers to have a clear and confident view of the problem that needs to be addressed, and of the solution to that problem, based on minimal anecdotal information and a plausible narrative that they have constructed about the situation. They might be right (though sometimes the narrative is sufficiently surprising that the odds seem low). But their confidence is almost certainly misplaced in the absence of much better information about both the status quo and the likely impact of the proposed reform.

One of the central themes of this book is that we should be realistic about what we do and do not know about complex social phenomena.[14] We should design laws in a way which takes account of the limited information and difficulty of making reliable predictions that are a common feature of law reform exercises. The confidence we feel in a narrative that we have developed about a particular policy issue is not a safe guide to the accuracy and reliability of that narrative.

Another central theme, closely related to the first, is that because intuition is an unreliable guide when it comes to forecasting the future there is no substitute for doing the hard work – painstakingly gathering information from a wide range of sources, and using the available tools to analyse that information. Even then our understanding is likely to be partial, and our predictions uncertain. But if we articulate both what we do know based on the best available information, and the uncertainties that remain, we are well on the way to a more realistic and more successful approach to the formulation of our laws.

The Importance of Team Composition and Dynamics

Second, these books shed light on why so many legal design teams fail to harness all the information and insights available to team members. A well-functioning legal design team that includes people from a range of backgrounds and with different fields of expertise can significantly improve the process of gathering and analysing relevant information. But all too often, teams fail to take advantage of the information and ideas that some team members have to offer. Key people are not in the loop, or their concerns are discounted, or they are not empowered to share those concerns in the first place.

As the authors of *Noise* explain, group decision-making can amplify noise, and reduce the quality of the decisions that are made.[15] A helpful overview of what we currently know about group decision-making is provided by Cass Sunstein and Reid Hastie in their short book *Wiser: Getting Beyond Groupthink to Make Groups Smarter*.[16] They identify four common failures of deliberating groups:

1.   Sometimes individual errors are amplified, not merely propagated, as a result of deliberation.
2.   Groups fall victim to cascade effects, as the early speakers or actors ensure that people do not learn what is known by their successors.
3.   Because of group polarization, members of deliberating groups often end up in a more extreme position in line with their predeliberation tendencies.
4.   In deliberating groups, shared information often dominates or crowds out unshared information, ensuring that groups do not learn everything that their members know.[17]

All too often the strongly expressed views of senior participants in a legal design exercise – expert advisers, senior officials, politicians – crowd out the information that other team members have to offer. I have seen overseas consultants give advice about the design of laws in a developing country on the basis of assumptions about the local environment and institutions that were simply incorrect: tacit assumptions based on their familiar home environment, the relevance of which they had not thought to question. The local officials had critical information about the environment in which the proposed law would need to operate: about how things work on the ground. But group dynamics – exacerbated by cultural factors and, sometimes, language factors – resulted in those concerns not being articulated, or not being pressed. And I have attended many meetings in New Zealand and other wealthy countries where politicians or senior officials expressed views about how a proposal was likely to play out that some people in the room knew were misconceived – but the group dynamics strongly discouraged raising those concerns at the time, and decisions were made that were difficult or impossible to revisit.

It is hard to overstate the importance for successful legal design projects of putting together an appropriate team to work on the project, and adopting working methods that enable the team to take advantage of the information and insights of all team members.

A Better Model of the World for which We are Designing

Third, the insights in these books shed important light on how the people for whom the law is being designed actually behave. They provide a more sophisticated model for understanding the behaviour of individuals and of social groups.

As I emphasised above, the evaluation of proposed legislation turns on describing how people behave now, and how the legislation is expected to change their behaviour. The better our model of how people actually behave, the more likely it is that our evaluations will be reasonably accurate. As a famous statistician once said, 'all models are wrong – but some models are useful'.[18] The whole point of a model is that it simplifies the reality that it is intended to represent. The simplification is what makes the model easier to understand and apply than the complex reality that it describes. Sometimes those simplifications do not matter, or do not matter much. The model gets us close enough. It is (slightly) wrong, but very useful. But at other times the model simplifies away key features of the reality we are seeking to describe, with the result that the model is wrong in ways that matter. It all depends on what we are trying to achieve – our model needs to be fit for purpose. We can use Newtonian mechanics to predict the trajectory of a projectile on earth, and even to land a space ship on the moon. We could use a more sophisticated model that took into account Einsteinian physics – special relativity and general relativity – but doing so would add a lot more complexity to the analysis, and wouldn't improve accuracy in a way that matters. However that Newtonian model is no use for the teams who design and maintain the Global Positioning System (GPS) that underpins so much modern technology (from the navigation tools used by airline pilots, to the Uber app that helps you get to the airport on time). GPS designers need to work with a model that factors in both special and general relativity. You can't build a working GPS using the simpler Newtonian model: its predictions aren't accurate enough for that purpose.[19]

Many of the failed laws that I described above are the result of defects in the framers' models of how the relevant people would behave in response to the law. The cobra bounty is a good example. The framers of that law thought about the incentives the bounty created to catch and kill cobras. But their model of how the population would respond to the bounty assumed that everything else would remain constant. It didn't take account of the longer-term incentives that the bounty would create to breed more cobras. A model that ignores the dynamic effects of incentives created by a new law is likely to be both wrong and useless. This is perhaps the most important insight that classical economics has to offer for legal designers.

Behavioural economics offers further insights in some settings because it focuses on how people make decisions – how they actually behave – and the significant ways in which that behaviour departs from the base assumptions of classical economics. It provides a more sophisticated model of human behaviour and social dynamics. In some contexts we can improve the accuracy of our analysis in ways that matter by using this more sophisticated model to explain how people currently behave, and to make predictions about how that behaviour is likely to change if proposed legislation is enacted.

How Can We Do Better?

The authors of *Noise* provide a number of suggestions, based on their research, for improving decision-making. They describe a number of elements of what they call 'decision hygiene': steps we can take to improve the quality of the judgements that we make. All of these decision hygiene strategies are relevant to legal design, to varying degrees. But the most directly relevant is the strategy they describe as 'structuring complex judgments'. This involves decomposing a judgement into its component parts, managing the process of data collection to ensure the inputs are independent of one another, and delaying the final judgement until all these inputs have been collected. The need for a more structured approach to legal design is one of the central themes of this book. The checklists in part III describe what such a structure might look like.

Philip Tetlock's more recent research, summarised in his book *Superforecasting*, confirms that we can do better in predicting complex social phenomena – if we do the necessary work.[20] We can significantly improve the quality of our near term forecasts by adopting a more structured and systematic approach to making those forecasts; by systematically reviewing their accuracy; and by revising our approach in light of that feedback. Tetlock identifies two key conclusions from his research:

> One, foresight is real. Some people ... have it in spades. They aren't gurus or oracles with the power to peer decades into the future, but they do have a real, measurable skill at judging how high-stakes events are likely to unfold three months, six months, a year, or a year and a half in advance. The other conclusion is what makes these superforecasters so good. It's not really who they are. It is what they do. Foresight isn't a mysterious gift bestowed at birth. It is the product of particular ways of thinking, of gathering information, of updating beliefs. These habits of thought can be learned and cultivated by any intelligent, thoughtful, determined person.[21]

A few years ago when I was first thinking about writing this book, I told a brilliant economist I have had the good fortune to work with that I was planning to write a book on how to improve the ways in which we design laws. He was politely sceptical. 'What are you going to say', he asked, 'apart from "get really smart people to do it"?' The good news for those of us who are not fully accredited members of Mensa is that Tetlock's research suggests we can do better – perhaps even a whole lot better – by taking a more systematic and structured approach to decision-making in the face of complexity and uncertainty, rather than simply relying on intuition or on plausible narratives based on modest amounts of relevant information. Tetlock's superforecasters had IQs in the top 20 per cent of the population – they were more intelligent than most people, but not 'geniuses' with IQs in the top 1 per cent of the population. If you have made it this far into this book, you have the intellectual grunt to be a superforecaster! The key is to *use* that intellect to take a more sophisticated approach to predicting the future – in our case, for the purpose of designing more effective legislation – rather than fall back on intuition and instinct.

In particular, we need to engage in actively open-minded thinking: that is, we need to actively search for information that contradicts our current views, including new evidence and the views of others who disagree with our current views.[22] We need to relish the opportunity to update our views in light of that new material. We need to say, as John Maynard Keynes reputedly said, 'When the facts change, I change my mind. What do you do?'

Tetlock's research confirms that diverse teams that communicate effectively can significantly outperform individual forecasters. They do a better job of identifying key questions, gathering information, adopting different perspectives on a problem, and testing each other's analysis. Other things being equal, the more complementary the backgrounds and skills of the team members, the more effective the team is likely to be.[23]

Tetlock also tackles the puzzling question of why, if we know we can do a better job of understanding the present and predicting the future, that isn't already standard practice. Tetlock attributes this largely to 'the psychology that convinces us we know things we really don't'; the notion that our subjective experiences and perceptions will provide us with the answers we seek. He explains that it was when the medical profession finally rejected this notion and turned to scientific testing that the field began to make huge leaps forward, and argues that '[t]he same revolution needs to happen in forecasting'.[24]

Figure 3.1 So ... how will this law affect the prison population?[25]

Legislative design requires a similar revolution. We need to do a better job of predicting the social consequences of proposed legislation. We can only do this by adopting a more structured approach to designing legislation, and tracking its results.

In *Superforecasting*, Tetlock writes about a British physician, Archie Cochrane, who spent many years campaigning for greater use of randomised trials in medicine and other fields. He complained that the British healthcare system in the 1950s and 1960s had 'far too little interest in proving and promoting what was effective'. The medical establishment was committed to continuing to do things largely as they had always been done, and relying on their own judgement and the support of their peers to validate what they were doing. They didn't need scientific validation. Cochrane, Tetlock says, 'despised this attitude. He called it "the God complex"'. Cochrane encountered the same 'God complex' when his attention turned to the British justice system. Decision-makers – prison wardens, judges, government officials – were content to rely on their experience and their judgement to make decisions about significant aspects of the criminal justice system, and about the likely effects of reforms to that system. They had no appetite for his proposals for controlled experiments, properly designed and monitored. But as Tetlock says, '[w]hat people didn't grasp is that the only alternative to a controlled experiment that delivers real insight is an uncontrolled experiment that produces merely the illusion of insight'.[26] Tetlock continues, in a passage that should prompt anxious reflection by all committed legal designers:

> Cochrane cited the Thatcher government's 'short, sharp, shock' approach to young offenders, which called for brief incarceration in spartan jails governed by strict rules. Did it work? The government had simply implemented it throughout the justice system, making it impossible to answer. If the policy was introduced and crime went down, that might mean the policy worked, or perhaps crime went down for any of a hundred other possible reasons. If crime went up, that might show the policy was useless or even harmful, or it might mean crime would have risen even more but for the beneficial effects of the policy. Naturally, politicians would claim otherwise. Those in power would say it worked; their opponents would say it failed. But nobody would really know. The politicians would be blind men arguing over the colours of the rainbow. If the government had submitted its policy 'to a randomised controlled trial then we might, by now, have known its true worth and be some way ahead in our thinking', Cochrane observed. But it hadn't. It had just assumed that its policy would work as expected. This was the same toxic brew of ignorance and confidence that had kept medicine in the dark ages for millennia.

The Implications of Our Limited Ability to Make Reliable Predictions

Even with the best decision hygiene, the research described by Kahneman, Tetlock and others underscores that we need to be modest – very modest – about our ability to predict the future effects of reforms. Especially when it comes to the long-term effects of far-reaching reforms. Many important features of our societies are so complex, so path dependent and so significantly influenced by unpredictable chance events that attempts to forecast social outcomes in any detail are futile. As the authors of *Noise* explain, 'intractable uncertainty (what cannot possibly be known) and imperfect information (what could be known but isn't) make perfect predictions impossible. These unknowns are not problems of bias or noise in your judgment; they are objective characteristics of the task'.[27]

Asserting that the future is unpredictable is hardly a conceptual breakthrough, as the authors of *Noise* acknowledge. However, as they go on to say, 'the obviousness of this fact is matched only by the regularity with which it is ignored, as the consistent findings about predictive over-confidence demonstrate'.[28]

The limits of our ability to make reliable predictions about social dynamics are explored in some detail in two more books on my essential reading list: Duncan Watts' *Everything is Obvious*: *Once You Know the Answer* and Nassim Nicholas Taleb's *The Black Swan: The Impact of the Highly Improbable*.[29] Trying to predict complex social dynamics 10 years out? As they say in New York, where I wrote much of this book, 'fuhgeddaboudit'!

Fortunately, lawmakers don't generally need to predict 'Black Swan' upheavals that change the whole landscape in fundamental ways. If major shifts of that kind occur, it will usually be both necessary and constitutionally appropriate for the legislator to amend or replace the relevant laws to respond to that shift.

However we cannot avoid the need to make some predictions about the interplay between laws, institutions and the society we live in over extended periods: most laws are intended to operate for many years before they are revisited. We can do this better – perhaps much better – than we currently do. Even so, we should remain realistic about the reliability of such predictions.

In a curious way, the impossibility of making consistently accurate long-term predictions is also good news – or at least, helpful information about our task. It tells us that we can design legislation that will work better if we take seriously the prospect that circumstances will change in ways we haven't foreseen, and that the law may need to adapt to work as intended in those changed circumstances. If you design a car on the assumption that all roads are straight, you probably won't bother with a steering wheel. But if you know that roads change direction in many ways, following no predetermined pattern, then a steering wheel that lets the driver redirect the car as bends come into view becomes an essential feature. A car with a steering wheel is much less likely to go off the road than one that heads in a straight line, come what may – at least so long as there is a driver at the wheel, and they are awake! I discuss below the form that legislation would take if it were informed by a more realistic approach to our ability to predict the future course of events in a complex social setting: what I call *adaptive legislation*. And I look at what it would mean in this context to have a driver at the wheel.

This book aims to encourage a more structured and systematic approach to the design of legislation. An approach that reflects the limits of our knowledge about the present and our ability to predict the future. But before I turn to how we might do this, I will spend a little more time on the lessons that behavioural economics provides for legal designers. Lessons about the ways in which people make decisions, and how that shapes their behaviour. And lessons about our own mental processes when we engage in our work as legal designers, developing and reviewing proposals for new laws.

---

[1] Atul Gawande, *The Checklist Manifesto: How to Get Things Right*, 1st edn (New York, Metropolitan Books, 2009).

[2] Karl Popper, *The Open Society and Its Enemies*, vol 2 (London, Routledge & Kegan Paul, 1945), addendum.

[3] For a helpful discussion of the reasons why laws are rarely evaluated after they have been passed, written by a former Prime Minister and eminent law professor, see Geoffrey Palmer, 'Law-Making in New Zealand: Is There a Better Way?' (2014) 22 *Waikato Law Review* 1, 29–30. For the United Kingdom experience, see Andrew Burrows, *Thinking About Statutes: Interpretation, Interaction, Improvement* (Cambridge, Cambridge University Press, 2018) ch 3.

[4] Checklists of these kinds may be useful in relation to more technical aspects of law-making – for example, drafters often use checklists to ensure that technical matters such as savings and transitional provisions, and consequential amendments, are not overlooked.

[5] The confidence of the original legal designers is however rarely dented: the failures are explained on the basis of flawed implementation (by others) or unpredictable supervening events.

[6] Daniel Kahneman, *Thinking, Fast and Slow* (New York, Farrar, Straus and Giroux, 2011). References are to the Penguin Books edition of 2012.

[7] Daniel Kahneman, Olivier Sibony and Cass R Sunstein, *Noise* (New York, Little, Brown Spark, 2021).

[8] ibid, 12. The aphorism was first proposed in Daniel Kahneman et al, 'Noise: How to Overcome the High, Hidden Cost of Inconsistent Decision Making' (*Harvard Business Review*, October 2016) 36–43, available at: www.hbr.org/2016/10/noise.

[9] Kahneman, *Thinking, Fast and Slow* (n 6) 14.

[10] ibid, 212–16, discussing studies of trading by investors and his own analysis of bonus payments to investment advisers at a firm providing financial advice and other services to wealthy clients. Comparing results and bonuses earned between years, he found no evidence of persistence of skill – the results 'resembled what you would expect from a dice-rolling contest, not a game of skill'.

[11] ibid, 222 ff, referring to the work of Paul Meehl and others, and in particular, Paul Meehl, *Clinical Versus Statistical Prediction: A Theoretical Analysis and a Review of the Evidence* (Minneapolis, MN, University of Minnesota Press, 1954).

[12] Philip E Tetlock, *Expert Political Judgment: How Good Is It? How Can We Know?* (New Jersey, NY, Princeton University Press, 2005).

[13] Kahneman, *Thinking, Fast and Slow* (n 6) 219–20, referring to Tetlock (n 12).

[14] For a sobering discussion of the extent to which people, including public figures and business leaders, operate on the basis of a wide range of misconceptions about the world we live in, see Hans Rosling, *Factfulness: Ten Reasons We're Wrong About the World – and Why Things Are Better Than You Think* (New York, Flatiron Books, 2018). And for persistent misconceptions about human nature, and human responses to catastrophes, see Rutger Bregman, *Humankind: A Hopeful History* (London, Bloomsbury Publishing, 2020) prologue and chs 1–2.

[15] Kahneman, Sibony and Sunstein (n 7) ch 8.

[16] Cass R Sunstein and Reid Hastie, *Wiser: Getting Beyond Groupthink to Make Groups Smarter* (Boston, MA, Harvard Business Review Press, 2015).

[17] ibid, 99.

[18] This phrase is generally attributed to the statistician George Box, who made observations to this effect on a number of occasions. A paper he wrote in 1978 contained a section headed 'All models are wrong but some are useful', which read:

> Now it would be very remarkable if any system existing in the real world could be exactly represented by any simple model. However, cunningly chosen parsimonious models often do provide remarkably useful approximations. For example, the law PV = RT relating pressure P, volume V

and temperature T of an 'ideal' gas via a constant R is not exactly true for any real gas, but it frequently provides a useful approximation and furthermore its structure is informative since it springs from a physical view of the behavior of gas molecules.

For such a model there is no need to ask the question 'Is the model true?' If 'truth' is to be the 'whole truth' the answer must be 'No'. The only question of interest is 'Is the model illuminating and useful?'

See GEP Box, 'Robustness in the Strategy of Scientific Model Building' in Robert L Launer and Graham N Wilkinson, *Robustness in Statistics* (New York, Academic Press, 1979).

[19] See NASA, 'Basics of Space Flight', available at: www.solarsystem.nasa.gov/basics/chapter3-2/:

We learn from Einstein's special theory of relativity that mass, time, and length are variable, and the speed of light is constant. And from general relativity, we know that gravitation and acceleration are equivalent, that light bends in the presence of mass, and that an accelerating mass radiates gravitational waves at the speed of light.

Spacecraft operate at very high velocities compared to velocities we are familiar with in transportation and ballistics here on our planet. Since spacecraft velocities do not approach a significant fraction of the speed of light, Newtonian physics serves well for operating and navigating throughout the solar system. That said, navigational aids such as the fleet of Global Positioning System, GPS, spacecraft do require special-relativity calculations in order to provide accurate position determination. Also, accuracies are routinely enhanced by accounting for tiny relativistic effects. Once we begin to travel between the stars, velocities may be large enough fractions of light speed that Einsteinian physics will be indispensable for determining trajectories.

[20] Philip E Tetlock and Dan Gardner, *Superforecasting: The Art and Science of Prediction* (New York, Broadway Books, 2015).

[21] ibid, 18.

[22] Kahneman, Sibony and Sunstein (n 7) 234, and see generally ch 18 on 'Better Judges for Better Judgments'.

[23] Tetlock and Gardner (n 20) ch 9. See also Kahneman, Sibony and Sunstein (n 7) ch 21.

[24] Tetlock and Gardner (n 20) 19.

[25] Painting by John William Waterhouse, *The Crystal Ball* (Public Domain, 1902), available at: commons.wikimedia.org/w/index.php?curid=1173516.

[26] Tetlock and Gardner (n 20) 31–32.

[27] Kahneman, Sibony and Sunstein (n 7) 140, and see generally ch 11 on 'Objective Ignorance' and ch 12 on 'The Valley of the Normal', exploring why people 'maintain an unchastened willingness to make bold predictions about the future from little useful information'.

[28] Kahneman, Sibony and Sunstein (n 7) 144.

[29] Duncan J Watts, *Everything is Obvious: Once You Know The Answer* (New York, Crown Business, 2011); Nassim Nicholas Taleb, *The Black Swan: The Impact of the Highly Improbable*, 2nd edn (London, Penguin Books Ltd, 2008). See also Nate Silver, *The Signal and the Noise: The Art and Science of Prediction* (London, Penguin Books, 2013). My essential reading list for legal designers is set out in Appendix 2 below.

4

How Humans (Including Legal Designers) Actually Make Decisions

This book is not the place for a complete account of the insights into human decision-making provided by the work of behavioural economists, or even for a detailed summary. There is no substitute for actually reading *Thinking, Fast and Slow* and *Noise*: these two books are essential reading for anyone involved in the business of making laws. A helpful summary of some of the most significant heuristics and biases that researchers have identified can be found in another excellent book that features on my essential reading list: *Nudge: Improving Decisions about Health, Wealth and Happiness* by Richard Thaler and Cass Sunstein.[1] *Nudge* also explores in more detail one of the central themes in this book: the importance of default settings for how people actually behave.

However some of the concepts at the heart of behavioural economics play an important role in explaining why legal designers should adopt an approach along the lines I sketch out in later chapters of this book. And it doesn't seem reasonable (or realistic) to ask you, the reader, to put this book down and go off to read a couple of other (much longer) books before continuing with this one. So in this chapter I provide a very brief and incomplete summary of some of the patterns in human decision-making that Kahneman and others have identified over the last few decades. This chapter is a bit more technical and abstract than other parts of the book. Bear with me: the insights this material provides are worth the journey.

Over-Confidence

Kahneman's best-known work was the product of his long collaboration with Amos Tversky. One of the first studies this extraordinary pair worked on together looked at whether people are good intuitive statisticians, in particular how good a job they do of intuitively estimating the reliability of statistical results based on small samples. People, it turns out, do this really badly. Even statisticians are bad statisticians, when they use their intuition instead of doing the mathematics. Anyone who has worked on public policy issues will immediately recognise this problem: a level of confidence based on a small sample, maybe even just a handful of anecdotal discussions, that is wholly unfounded. ('What You See Is All There Is!') Many politicians operate on this basis, reaching firm conclusions about what is happening in a society based on a handful of media reports about a topic. So do many of their advisers.

More generally, there is a vast literature that confirms the human tendency to reach confident conclusions based on wholly inadequate information, without paying sufficient (or any) attention to the gaps in our knowledge. The psychological processes that produce this over-confidence are outlined in *Noise*. With the benefit of hindsight, we construct narratives about particular events that make those events seem entirely predictable. We think we understand the causes of those events, based on the narrative we have constructed. But this causal thinking is an illusion, that ignores all the many ways in which events could have turned out differently. It fails to take into account all the cases we are not aware of where the same 'causes' we identify are present, but the outcome is different. This causal thinking comes naturally to us. More effortful statistical thinking – which pays attention to the wider universe of similar cases, and the outcomes in those cases – does not.[2]

Substitution

One mental shortcut that affects many of our intuitions and judgements is *substitution*. Where we cannot quickly find a satisfactory answer to the question we have been asked, our minds find a related question that is easier and answer that question instead. Hard questions – for example, about the likely future performance of a prospective employee – are replaced by simpler questions – do I like this person? Did they interview well? We deploy our answer to the easier question as if it is an answer to the harder question. This is one of the reasons that interviews are a poor tool for recruiting new employees, unless those interviews are carefully structured, the weight given to them is modest, and a person other than the interviewer makes the final decision. Kahneman puts forward a conjecture for which he says there are solid grounds, though the evidence is fragmentary: where the interviewer makes the final decision, conducting an interview is actually likely to diminish the accuracy of a selection procedure. The interviewer will be overconfident in their intuitions (which may well be the product of substitution – do I like this person? Do I agree with this person's views on issue X?), and as a result will tend to give too much weight to their personal impressions and too little weight to other information.[3]

The Availability Heuristic

A major source of distortions in the policy process is the *availability heuristic*. People are inclined to predict the relative likelihood and importance of an issue based on how easily examples come to mind. The easier it is to retrieve examples of an event from one's memory, the more common and the more significant such events seem. The ease with which issues come to mind is strongly influenced by media coverage, including social media. And the topics the media focus on are in turn influenced by what they believe people are interested in. Unusual events attract greater media attention than commonplace events – and are in turn perceived as more common than they really are. The emotional impact of an event also contributes to its salience – and thus to the ease with which it is remembered, and to the frequency with which it is perceived as occurring. Thus for example Kahneman cites one study finding that tornadoes were seen by participants as more frequent killers than asthma, although asthma actually caused some twenty times more deaths.[4] The availability heuristic is a form of substitution – the question 'how readily do examples of this come to mind?' is substituted for the question 'how frequently does this occur?'.

The availability heuristic leads to widespread and systematic misperceptions of risk on the part of the public and lawmakers. It distorts private and public decisions about investment in precautions to manage risks. People spend much more on insurance against earthquakes, and put more time and effort into earthquake-proofing their homes and offices, in the immediate aftermath of a major earthquake in a nearby city. The Christchurch earthquakes in New Zealand in 2011 prompted many Wellingtonians – my own family included – to belatedly take a range of precautions such as stocking up earthquake kits, and removing brick chimneys and other hazards. But as memories of the event became less immediate, these efforts faded – even though the underlying risk had not changed. When a significant earthquake hit Wellington in 2013, many people's earthquake kits contained food and bottled water that was past its expiry date, having been stored some two years earlier and then forgotten. Fortunately, it was not a major earthquake and the kits were not needed – that time.

In some cases the availability heuristic can lead to what Cass Sunstein and Timur Kuran have called an 'availability cascade'.[5] Unusual or minor events attract media attention which is disproportionate to the frequency and seriousness of the events (think tornadoes, plane crashes, kidnappings). Their emotional impact is amplified by the coverage. The reaction of the public and politicians to that coverage in turn prompts further media coverage, even more widespread public concern, and increasing pressure on government to take action to prevent further occurrences. Priorities are distorted by the attention the events receive, and public resources are diverted from more productive ends.

Anyone who has worked in the field of criminal justice knows just how influential an availability cascade can be. One high-profile event – an especially horrendous kidnapping or murder – can lead to changes in the law that are of doubtful value, or worse still counterproductive, and that divert attention and resources from other more valuable reforms. Politicians in many countries have become skilled at playing the 'law and order' card and campaigning for tougher sentences, tighter bail conditions and harsher prison conditions off the back of a handful of high profile events – lines which resonate with the public in a way that evidence about the futility of such measures struggles to compete with.

The Affect Heuristic

The *affect heuristic* is another common form of substitution: people frequently make decisions and judgements by consulting their emotions rather than searching for and analysing relevant information. The easy questions – 'do I like this?' or 'how strongly do I dislike this?' – are substituted for more difficult questions such as 'do the benefits of this proposal outweigh the detriments?' The intensity of those likes or dislikes is translated across to an assessment of the benefits of the proposal that is wholly independent of the quantity and quality of the information available.

So for example a survey of opinions on a range of technologies (water fluoridation, food preservatives, cars etc) found that assessments of benefits were strongly correlated with views about risks – participants who saw benefits as high saw risks as low, and vice versa.[6] On this simplified world view, few difficult trade-offs involving high benefits and high risks need to be made. Participants were then asked to read brief texts setting out arguments in favour of various technologies. Some texts focused on the benefits of a particular technology, arguing that they were large. Others focused on the risks, arguing that they were low. These texts had an effect on participants' views – after reading them, participants tended on average to see the technologies in question more positively. But – disconcertingly – the views of participants on both benefits and risks tended to shift in tandem even though each participant saw a text focusing on only one of those dimensions. People who saw arguments about the benefits of the technology saw it as more beneficial – and also saw it as less risky than before, even though they had been given no new information at all about risk. Those who saw information about risk that led them to adjust their view of risk downwards also adjusted their views of benefits upwards – even though they had no new information about benefits. In each case, if they liked the technology more as a result of what they had read then benefits were seen as greater and risks as lower – despite having no evidential basis for adjusting their views on one of those dimensions. Emotion trumped evidence.

The Anchoring Effect

Another well-documented feature of human decision-making is the *anchoring effect*. Many studies show that where a person considers a particular value for an unknown quantity before estimating that quantity, the estimates stay close to the number that was first considered. The effect of considering a number before making an estimate is significant even if the number has no bearing at all on the subject of the estimate, and the person making the estimate knows this. As Kahneman and Tversky showed in one of their experiments, the answers given by study subjects to a range of questions can be influenced by asking those people to spin a 'wheel of fortune', and observe the number the wheel lands on, before they answer those questions. The spin of a wheel of fortune could not possibly be relevant to the questions put to participants (for example, the percentage of African nations among UN members). If asked, any study participant would be certain to say 'of course the outcome of that spin of the wheel is irrelevant – and has no bearing on the answer I give'. But the number that was shown on the wheel had, on average, a significant influence on the answers given – that is, the number acted as an 'anchor'. This is a striking illustration of 'noise' – random factors affecting the decisions people make.

The anchoring effect is not confined to answers given by non-experts, or to answers given to questions about which a person has no other available information. The power of anchors has, as Kahneman explains,

> been demonstrated in some unsettling ways. German judges with an average of more than fifteen years of experience on the bench first read a description of a woman who had been caught shoplifting, then rolled a pair of dice that were loaded so every roll resulted in either a 3 or a 9. As soon as the dice came to a stop, the judges were asked if they would sentence the woman to a term in prison greater or lesser, in months, than the number showing on the dice. Finally, the judges were instructed to specify the exact prison sentence they would give to the shoplifter. On average, those who had rolled a 9 said they would sentence her to 8 months; those who had rolled a 3 said they would sentence her to 5 months.[7]

The anchoring heuristic extends beyond quantitative estimates. It also applies to plans and predictions for the future. If we already have a plan, that plan tends to operate as an anchor and affect forecasts of what is likely to happen in the future. Even if there is reason to be sceptical about the likely success of the plan, the mere fact that it has been articulated tends to result in subsequent forecasts which are closer to the plan than they would otherwise be. What this means in policy processes is that the form of an initial proposal can have a significant influence on subsequent debate. Care is needed to manage the risk of a single option operating as an anchor for stakeholders, and for decision-makers. That risk can be reduced by presenting a wide range of options at an early stage in a policy development process, to avoid any one option acting as an anchor and distorting subsequent discussion and analysis. (Adoption of a plan at an early stage can also distort decision-making as a result of unjustified optimism about the implementation of the plan – this heuristic, often referred to as the *planning fallacy*, is discussed below.)

The anchoring effect can affect the design of legislation in many ways. Some anchoring effects – like the dice-rolling example described above – are essentially random (or would be, if the dice were not rigged). A chance conversation with an angry constituent shortly before a critical meeting may shape a minister's view of an issue. Anchoring effects of this kind are a source of noise in the legal design process. At other times, the anchoring effect leads to a reluctance to depart substantially from the status quo, which itself operates as an anchor. Or the anchoring effect results in the approach contended for by a stakeholder having an impact on the policy debate that is disproportionate to the reliability and relevance of that stakeholder's case. A sophisticated lobby group can consciously exploit the anchoring effect by arguing vociferously for a particular result in the expectation that even if that outcome is not achieved, it will operate as an anchor in discussions of the issue. This happens in commercial negotiations all the time – one party puts a figure on the table with the aim of having it anchor future discussions. It is also a very common tactic in policy processes.

The Representativeness Heuristic

The *representativeness heuristic* is another cause of distortions in decision-making: people judge the probability of an event by how similar the subject is to other representative examples they have in mind. As Kahneman explains, the errors induced by the representativeness heuristic are twofold: a failure to pay attention to base rates – how common an outcome is overall – and insensitivity to the quality of the available evidence. So for example many studies show that people often assess how likely a political candidate is to be a good leader by how closely that candidate physically resembles their mental image of a good leader. There is no reason to think that how much a person physically resembles past leaders provides useful information about their likely performance as a leader. Or that a candidate's appearance provides any useful evidence at all on that score. To the contrary, a focus on representativeness is likely to distort decision-making, as it perpetuates long-standing biases in many societies, including gender and racial bias.

The representativeness heuristic often distorts policy decisions and the design of legislation. All too frequently we design a law to focus on a representative example of the people or the issue we are concerned with (criminal laws that are designed to respond to the most serious crimes, committed by the most culpable offenders; family laws that are designed to work for middle-class heterosexual married couples), and fail to consider the full range of people and circumstances to which the law will in fact apply. The result is that the law works badly in many scenarios that differ in important ways from the representative example we had in mind when the law was designed. Criminal laws designed with the most serious offenders in mind produce unjustifiably harsh outcomes for less serious offenders, and may sweep up in their net people whose conduct falls well short of what most would regard as criminal.[8] Family laws designed with relatively well-off middle-class heterosexual couples in mind can be difficult to apply to the many couples whose circumstances differ from that stereotype, and may as a result produce unfair outcomes for those couples. These family laws are also often prohibitively expensive to access for the many couples who are less well off than the 'representative' couple for whose needs they were designed: for that large section of society, the law ends up being of little practical relevance.

Another way in which the representativeness heuristic distorts decision-making is the tendency many decision-makers and advisers have to assume that the lives of others are similar to their own. In *The Blunders of Our Governments* Anthony King and Ivor Crewe devote a whole chapter to what they call 'cultural disconnect' – cases where 'the assumptions that politicians and civil servants make are radically wrong, when men and women in Whitehall and at Westminster unthinkingly project onto others values, attitudes and whole ways of life that are not remotely like their own'.[9] This factor looms large in a number of the blunders the authors describe, many of which would be funny if they were not so tragic. It is especially problematic where there is a lack of diversity among decision-makers and their advisers, and a failure to engage effectively with the full range of people who will be affected by a proposed law.

Confirmation Bias

The errors caused by the heuristics outlined above are exacerbated by *confirmation bias*.[10] People seek out and pay attention to information that is compatible with the views they already hold, and tend to disregard information they receive that is inconsistent with those views. Two people with diametrically different views on an issue, who read a short paper on that topic, will often both conclude that the paper supports their original view. This is another common pitfall in legal design work – new information is seen through the lens of a pre-existing view about what will or will not work.

Loss Aversion

A factor that drives the design of many laws – including the grandparenting of existing practices, which is a common cause of 'backfires' – is *loss aversion*. People dislike losses much more intensely than they like corresponding gains. If a person already enjoys a benefit of some kind, they will object to having it taken away much more strongly than they would press to obtain it in the first place. And they will want much more compensation for giving up that benefit than the amount they would be prepared to pay to obtain the same benefit if they did not already have it. Politicians and their advisers are very familiar with this dynamic – it is highly controversial to deprive people of benefits (property or legal entitlements or privileges) that they already have, even where there is a compelling policy case for doing so. Achieving this may be costly, if the price for achieving support for the policy is payment of sufficient compensation to satisfy the losers. The path of least resistance is often to preserve the status quo, and make changes prospectively only. People can continue to drive their polluting vehicles. Existing uses of land that are inconsistent with new planning regimes are permitted to continue. But the risk of adopting this approach is that the law becomes a damp squib, or even that it backfires.

Status Quo Bias

I have already mentioned the anchoring effect of the status quo. There is another way in which the status quo for individuals has a powerful effect on their decision-making. The *status quo bias* leads people to stay with their current situation rather than make the effort to change it. This is partly a function of cognitive laziness – it is easier to repeat what you have done before than to make a fresh decision. It is partly a function of the comfort many of us feel with things (situations, places, people) that are familiar. It can also be the result of what Thaler and Sunstein call the 'yeah, whatever' heuristic: having made a choice, many people simply cannot be bothered revisiting it and making a change.[11]

The Framing Effect

Another important feature of human decision-making which contributes significantly to noisy decision-making is the *framing effect*. How a question is put – or how information is framed – has a significant effect on how people respond. Many studies show that people will make different choices when confronted with the same options, depending on how those options are framed. A person is much more likely to agree to a medical procedure if they are told that 90 out of 100 patients survive than if they are told that 10 out of 100 die. And they tend to make different decisions if information is presented in the form of statistics (x per cent suffer serious adverse reactions) than if that same information is presented in terms of representative groups of people (x out of 100 suffer serious adverse reactions).

One example of framing that Kahneman and Tversky wrote about, which is directly relevant to legal designers, is known in the academic literature as the 'Asian disease problem'.

Imagine that the United States is preparing for the outbreak of an unusual Asian disease, which is expected to kill 600 people. Two alternative programs to combat the disease have been proposed. Assume that the exact scientific estimates of the consequences of the programs are as follows:

If program A is adopted, 200 people will be saved.

If program B is adopted, there is a one-third probability that 600 people will be saved and a two-thirds probability that no people will be saved.

A substantial majority of respondents choose program A: they prefer the certain option over the gamble.

The outcomes of the two programs were framed differently in a second version of the survey question:

If program A' is adopted, 400 people will die.

If program B' is adopted, there is a one-third probability that nobody will die and a two-thirds probability that 600 people will die.

A large majority of people preferred program B' – the gamble – to program A'. But if you compare the two versions of this question you will see that the consequences of programs A and A' are identical, and the consequences of programs B and B' are also identical. People tend to make different – and inconsistent – choices depending on how the issue is framed, and in particular whether it is framed in terms of good outcomes or bad outcomes. Where outcomes are good, people tend to prefer the certain outcome to the gamble – that is, they are risk averse. But where both outcomes are bad, people tend to prefer the chance of avoiding the bad outcome altogether to the certainty of a somewhat bad outcome. Kahneman reports that his colleague Amos Tversky tried this problem on a group of public health professionals, and found that they too were influenced by the framing of this question. Deploying his characteristic understatement, Kahneman describes this result as 'somewhat worrying'.[12]

Social Influences

Social influences also play an important part in human decision-making.[13] What we do is influenced to a very significant extent by what we see others around us doing, and what they believe. Social norms shape human behaviour in many ways. We seek the approval of the people we like and respect, and we generally aim to avoid their disapproval. We use their choices as proxies for what will work for us – if our friends behave in a particular way, it is simpler to follow their lead than it is to think the issue through ourselves. We listen to the music they listen to; we go to the places they like to go to; we are more likely to wear seatbelts if they do so; and we are less likely to drive after drinking alcohol if they do not do so, especially if they express disapproval of people who drink and drive.

Legislation is less likely to be effective where it runs against the grain of well-established social norms: additional measures are likely to be needed to achieve the desired outcomes, and (over time) shift those norms. So for example simply passing a law prohibiting entrenched forms of discrimination will not make that discrimination go away: clear leadership and effective public education over an extended period are essential to achieve changes of that kind. Conversely, laws can shape social norms in ways that enable their goals to be achieved with limited investment in enforcement by providing information about what behaviour is seen by that society as appropriate, and what is inappropriate (and likely to trigger disapproval from other members of that society). Legislation is most likely to work in this way where people are well informed about the law, and are predisposed to be sympathetic to its goals. Good legal design pays close attention to social norms, and their likely impact (supportive or otherwise) on behaviour in response to a law change.

We also see social influences at play in legal design and policy processes. There are often strong institutional norms that encourage team members to go along with an approach favoured by colleagues, in particular senior colleagues. It's hard to rock the boat, and most people prefer not to. But the result is often that key information is overlooked, and concerns are not squarely identified and addressed. Legal design processes need to be structured to encourage team members to overcome these tendencies, and share relevant information and concerns. That is one of the purposes of the checklists discussed in part III.

The Planning Fallacy

Another human tendency that frequently trips up decision-makers, including legal designers, is excessive and unfounded optimism. Kahneman and Tversky came up with the term *planning fallacy* to describe plans and forecasts that are unrealistically close to best-case scenarios, and that could be improved by consulting the statistics of similar cases.[14] As anyone who has renovated their kitchen knows, estimates of how much building work will cost are almost always undercooked. And the work almost always takes much longer than your builder's original estimate. The pervasiveness of the planning fallacy is borne out time and time again, in many different contexts. It shows up in legal design processes in many forms: over-optimistic forecasts of how long the reform project will take to complete; over-optimistic forecasts for implementation time frames; and – most problematically of all – over-optimistic forecasts about how the legislation will operate in practice.

There are ways to mitigate the planning fallacy. Paying attention to the 'outside view' – distributional information from other similar exercises – is the most important. Carrying out a *premortem* – imagining that some time in the future (say three years out) your plan has failed disastrously, and you are writing a history of how and why it failed – is another practical way to mitigate overconfident overoptimism. One of the central purposes of this book is to help legal designers take an outside view, by providing a structured way to think about the various ways in which other laws have failed, and whether your project risks failing in one or more of those ways.

The Impact of Bias and Noise in Legal Design

The heuristics that influence human decision-making, and the pervasive presence of both bias and noise in the decisions we make, need to be factored into the models that lawmakers deploy when they design legislation that depends for its operation on the decisions that people make. Which is pretty much all legislation.

The impact of bias and noise also needs to be factored into how lawmakers approach the legal design process. As Tversky's 'somewhat worrying' experience with the public health professionals illustrates, none of us – policy advisers, officials, lawmakers – is immune from these tendencies. Noise and bias are unavoidably present when we exercise judgement in our legal design work. There are ways in which we can mitigate the impact of these distortions in our decision-making. Some of these are explored in more detail below. But the central lesson for legal designers is that relying on intuition is quick, easy, comfortable – and in the policy space, very likely to be wrong. The approach mapped out in this book seeks to replace intuitive judgement on big picture questions ('should the law change from X to Y? Of course – that would be much fairer!') with slow, careful, fact-based analysis of a number of more focused questions. Analysis that seeks out and draws on information held by many different stakeholders. Analysis that is realistic about the limits of the information we can gather, and about the uncertainties of our predictions. Quite often the result will be that we come to fewer conclusions than we could if we deployed our intuition alone – and that we have less confidence in the conclusions that we do reach. That sounds like a pretty disappointing outcome – we work harder to 'know' less, and to know it less surely. But human societies are complex and unpredictable. If our legislative design work pays more attention to these important features of the world we live in, it is much less likely to go off the rails.

---

[1] Richard H Thaler and Cass R Sunstein, *Nudge: Improving Decisions about Health, Wealth and Happiness* (New Haven, CT, Yale University Press, 2008) ch 1. Another excellent summary is found in ch 3 of Sunstein's wonderful short book: Cass R Sunstein, *Simpler: The Future of Government* (New York, Simon & Schuster, 2013).

[2] See Daniel Kahneman, Olivier Sibony and Cass R Sunstein, *Noise* (New York, Little, Brown Spark, 2021) ch 12.

[3] Daniel Kahneman, *Thinking, Fast and Slow* (New York, Farrar, Straus and Giroux, 2011) 225. See also 229–33 for Kahneman's account of the evaluation mechanism for recruits that, as a young lieutenant, he developed for the Israeli army.

[4] ibid, 138.

[5] Timur Kuran and Cass R Sunstein, 'Availability Cascades and Risk Regulation' (1999) 51 *Stanford Law Review* 683.

[6] Kahneman (n 3) 139–40, referring to studies described in Paul Slovic et al, 'The Affect Heuristic' (2007) 177 *European Journal of Operational Research* 1333, 1342–44.

[7] Kahneman (n 3) 125–26.

[8] The representativeness fallacy is a common and practically significant source of distortions in criminal justice policy: see Rachel Elise Barkow, *Prisoners of Politics: Breaking the Cycle of Mass Incarceration* (Cambridge, MA, Belknap Press, 2019) esp ch 1 on 'Misleading Monikers'.

[9] Anthony King and Ivor Crewe, *The Blunders of Our Governments* (London, Oneworld Publications, 2013) ch 16.

[10] Kahneman (n 3) 80–81.

[11] Thaler and Sunstein (n 1) 37–38.

[12] Kahneman (n 3) 369.

[13] There is an excellent summary of the impact of social influences on human behaviour in Sunstein (n 1) 65–68. For a more extended discussion of this important aspect of human behaviour see Duncan J Watts, *Everything is Obvious: Once You Know The Answer* (New York, Crown Business, 2011) chs 3–4.

[14] Kahneman (n 3) 249 ff.

PART II

Lessons for Legal Designers

5

Adopting a Structured Approach to Designing New Laws

The Importance of a Structured Approach

Many of the failed laws that I described in chapter two were the result of failure to gather relevant information, failure to ask relevant questions, and failure to recognise and provide for uncertainty. Their framers relied too heavily on their intuition to answer big picture questions – can legislation help to advance this policy goal? What should the legislation look like? They told themselves (and others) stories about the ease of collecting a tax based on how many windows a house has; or about the impact of a bounty on cobra (or rat, or wild pig) numbers; or about the benefits of a 'global best practice' competition law. Stories that seemed plausible and appealing. But things did not play out in the way the framers of those laws and their advisers expected.

Often, of course, we cannot anticipate future developments – unknown unknowns can sabotage the best laid plans. But in a significant proportion of the cases of failed laws that I described, the eventual outcome should not have been a surprise. Asking some basic questions would have exposed gaps in information and flaws in assumptions about likely responses. Exposing those flaws would have enabled the proposed laws to be better designed, or abandoned as unworkable in practice.

So the first lesson from these failures is that when working on new laws we should be wary of ready answers provided by our intuition (or the intuitions of others) about the current state of play, the problems we face, and likely 'solutions' to those problems. We need to test those ready answers by breaking the project down into more manageable sub-topics, and tackling each of those topics in a structured way. We need to work systematically through our legal design toolbox to choose the tools that have the best prospect of delivering the desired outcome. We need to ensure that we – and others involved in the project – engage System 2.

Chapters six to ten of this book are designed to help lawmakers who are thinking about whether legislation is an appropriate tool to advance a policy goal, and what any such legislation might look like, to identify the key questions they need to ask along the way. Questions about the current position; the problem that the legislation seeks to address; what success would look like; and how the law can change the behaviour of relevant groups to achieve the desired outcome. Simple questions of profound importance to the design of a law, and to whether it succeeds or fails.

Responding to Uncertainty: Adaptive Legislation

Sometimes asking those questions will produce clear and reliable answers. But all too often the problems that proposed legislation is intended to address will be complex, and relevant information will be scarce. That in itself is an important thing to know, which can and should be taken into account in designing the proposed law. Chapter eleven explains the concept of adaptive legislation: legislation that is deliberately framed so that the way it works can be adjusted in response to further information as and when it becomes available, and to unforeseen changes in the environment in which that legislation operates.

Chapters twelve and thirteen focus on two specific areas where adaptive legislation plays an important role: the implications for law-making of new and emerging technologies, and cross-border issues.

Some Tools to Improve How Legislation Works

Chapters fourteen and fifteen address two related issues that have a significant impact on how effective legislation is in advancing its goals while avoiding undesired outcomes: adjusting default settings, and reducing complexity.

In part III I summarise the issues addressed in part II in the form of a set of checklists. These checklists are intended to be a tool which helps to ensure that the critical issues that are relevant to the success or failure of your legislative projects can be identified and addressed in a systematic way.

Who should do the Legal Design Work?

This book is concerned with law-making generally, at every level of government. Different countries, and different levels of government, will have different institutional arrangements for carrying out legal design work. My focus is on how that work should be approached, rather than on who should do it.

So for example I do not discuss which law reform projects are best undertaken in central government agencies, and which are best undertaken by independent law reform agencies such as the Law Commissions found in the United Kingdom and a number of other Commonwealth countries. Plainly this is a very important choice, which will have a significant bearing on the background and skills of the team that carries out the work, the resources available to support that work, and the way in which the exercise is approached.[1] I have already mentioned the importance of putting together an appropriate team to carry out each legal design project, with a mix of relevant backgrounds and skills. But for present purposes, I will take this choice as a given: my aim is to provide some useful insights and process suggestions that are relevant whichever agency (or agencies) may be doing the work.

Three Concerns

Some readers may be sceptical about whether a more structured approach of the kind I have outlined can make a meaningful difference to the quality of legal design. Discussions with colleagues working at the policy coalface suggest three main concerns that might be raised about the practical relevance and likely impact of the approach outlined in this book. I touch on each of them briefly.

First, legislation is often one of the tools deployed to address complex and intractable social problems to which there is no 'right answer' – poverty, homelessness, poor educational outcomes for disadvantaged groups, persistent discrimination on racial and other grounds, to list just a few.[2] Most societies have made modest progress at best towards solving these so-called 'wicked problems', despite investing large amounts of time and money in research and analysis and interventions of various kinds. Many of the challenges in these fields involve predicting how interventions will affect outcomes. So, it might be objected, the approach suggested in this book is a chimaera – it calls for insights that simply are not likely to be achievable.

I readily acknowledge that nothing in this book will solve these long-standing social issues. That would be a wildly optimistic and implausible aspiration. Rather, the approach outlined in this book comes into play if it is suggested that one element of the policy response to a wicked problem of this kind in your society should be legislation. The key questions for the designer of that legislation will then be what the legislation is intended to achieve – how it is intended to contribute to the overall policy response – and whether it is capable of achieving that goal, or is likely to fail to do so. The approach suggested in this book remains squarely relevant to addressing those questions. Suppose for example that a government decides to seek to improve educational outcomes for disadvantaged groups by permitting the establishment of not-for-profit 'charter schools', and providing for public funding of students at those schools. Nothing in this book will help to answer the controversial question of whether charter schools (or any other intervention, for that matter) can help to improve educational outcomes. But the approach outlined can help to ensure that the legislation will enable charter schools to be established as inexpensively and swiftly as possible, will facilitate schools receive the funding for which they qualify, and will put in place effective safeguards in relation to the operation of the schools (curriculum approval powers, premises requirements, inspection regimes etc).

Nor should it be forgotten that a great deal of legislation is concerned with matters that are not especially complex from a policy perspective, where the real challenge lies in effective implementation. Yet all too often the legal machinery for dealing with those matters does not work well – for example, because it is unnecessarily complex or difficult to implement. The approach set out in this book should help to ensure that this legal machinery is designed to work efficiently and effectively.

Second, limited time and resources. Some officials with whom I discussed the ideas in this book expressed concern that my approach may be an unattainable counsel of perfection. In the real world of finite human and institutional bandwidth, and funding constraints, there are limits on the time and money that can be spent working through all the issues I identify in a structured way.

It seems to me that even the most rushed law-making process needs to pay attention to the risk of failure. It is easy – but unreasonable and irresponsible – to simply assume that a proposed law will succeed in achieving its goals, especially if those goals have never been clearly articulated. As a bare minimum, it is necessary to have some idea of the current position, and what change the proposed law is intended to achieve. Some thought then needs to be given to whether the legislation is in fact likely to bring about that change, and to the risk of other undesired consequences. This may have to be done fast, and with few resources. A checklist to ensure that no key issues are completely overlooked seems likely to be valuable in that context. Some understanding of gaps in the available information, and what that means for the confidence with which predictions can be made about the operation of the law, is essential: experience teaches that a common cause of failure is design of laws on the basis that 'What You See Is All There Is'. And the suggestions I make below about adaptive legislation, including mechanisms to enable the law to adapt as new information becomes available further down the track, will be of particular importance where initial information- gathering has been curtailed.

Third, politics. In most if not all societies, law-making is a political process – the stuff of compromises, trade-offs and fudges. How can a structured approach of the kind suggested in this book work in the messy world of politics?

It would be foolish to ignore the important – and sometimes decisive – role that political considerations play in the law-making process. But a scan of the statute book in any of the countries with which I am familiar confirms that a great deal of legislation has limited political salience, and is likely to attract limited political debate. Where proposed legislation does attract significant political attention, the political debate tends to focus on a limited number of high-profile issues. In my experience a great deal of the detail of any legislation is seen by politicians as 'mere machinery', and passes below the political radar, even though that machinery will have a significant impact on the success or failure of the law in practice. This book aims to ensure that the machinery works.

Even on issues where politics loom large, advisers to the politicians promoting legislation need to be able to identify risks that the legislation will not deliver the desired result, and give robust advice about those risks. Many politicians are concerned about the workability of their legislative proposals, as well as their immediate political impact. Indeed the two may be linked – some failures are sufficiently swift and embarrassing that they have political consequences for their proponents.

More generally, the risk that advice will not be taken, or will be superseded by pragmatic compromises and trade-offs, is not a reason to give up on providing high-quality advice. A key audience for this book is responsible legal designers who aspire to provide high-quality professional advice, while understanding that for a range of reasons their advice may not be taken. And on some occasions, may even be unwelcome. But that does not mean the advice should not be given.

Each of these three concerns injects an important note of realism into our discussion. But these concerns need to be kept in perspective: they are not reasons to abandon seeking to understand why laws fail, and how we can reduce the risk of such failures. Of course we will not eliminate that risk. Laws will continue to fail, for a range of reasons. Those failures are likely to be especially acute where laws seek to tackle difficult problems, and are developed under significant time constraints. The political process can lead to compromises and trade-offs that result in legislation failing to achieve its goals. (Conversely, of course, the political process can strengthen and improve legislation by ensuring that it reflects a wider range of information and perspectives, and has broader support from key stakeholders.) But there is every reason to think that better legal design can make a significant difference to how often, and how seriously, laws fail in the various ways I described above. In the coming chapters, I explain how that might be done.

---

[1] For some of the factors relevant to choice of an appropriate institutional home for a law reform project, see G Palmer, 'The Law Reform Enterprise: Evaluating the Past and Charting the Future' (2015) 131 *LQR* 402; Matthew Dyson, James Lee and Shona Wilson Stark (eds), *Fifty Years of the Law Commissions: The Dynamics of Law Reform* (Oxford, Hart Publishing, 2016) esp chs 1, 2, 6, 7 and 40.

[2] See Richard R Nelson, *The Moon and the Ghetto* (New York, W Norton & Company Inc, 1977); Richard R Nelson, 'The Moon and the Ghetto Revisited' (2011) 38 *Science and Public Policy* 681.

6

What is the Current Position?

What is the Current Law? How Does it Operate in Practice?

A confession: I have a terrible sense of direction. I'm actually not too bad at reading maps. But that doesn't usually help me navigate my way to where I want to be, because there's a more fundamental problem: I can't figure out where I am now on the map I'm carefully studying. Google Maps has changed my life – I get lost much less often. That's mainly because the app tells me where I am now. If I don't know that, navigation is pretty much impossible. When I do know my current location, however, I can begin to find my way to my ultimate destination.

Legislating is much the same. It's impossible to figure out how legislation should be framed to change behaviour until you know what the relevant people are currently doing.

So the first task in any legal design exercise is to capture as rich as possible a description of where we are now. In the law-making context, that has two main dimensions: the relevant law, and the factual context within which that law operates – or fails to operate.

It is standard practice for legal designers to identify and describe the existing law in the field in which new legislation is proposed. It is rare for this step to be omitted. A more common omission, however, is to fail to describe that law in its wider legal context. No legislation operates in isolation: there is a backdrop of relevant laws, which may be found in specific legislation or in general codes or (in common law countries) in case law. It is essential for the framers of legislation to have a good understanding of the legal context in which the proposed legislation will operate: how will it relate to existing laws? Thus for example credit laws need to be set in the wider context of contract law; search and seizure laws in the wider context of human rights law and public law generally. Laws that confer rights that are enforceable in civil proceedings before courts need to be read in the context of the law (and procedural rules) governing those court proceedings – including the rules about who pays the costs of court proceedings, and laws governing access to any public funding (legal aid) available for such claims. A good understanding of the legal context in which proposed legislation would operate will shed light on the nature of any 'gap' in the law – and on whether there is in fact a gap, or whether (as is often the case) the real issue is institutional capacity to administer the existing laws. And it will shed light on how the law can be expected to operate in practice, when it comes to be applied in that wider context.

Another very common – and highly problematic – omission in legal design projects is ensuring we have a good understanding of the institutional framework in which the laws operate, and of what people actually do in practice. If we don't understand this, then we understand very little about the way the law works. And if we don't understand how the law works in practice now, then we are flying blind when we come to consider the impact of changing the law.

The Gap between the Law on Paper and the Law in Operation

The gap between the law on paper and the law in operation can be large. Many years ago when I was giving some advice on company law in Samoa, I began by reading the legislation. There were no surprises there, as it was based on a New Zealand statute (since repealed) that I knew well. The regime for registration of core company information, to ensure that it would be available to the public, looked basically fine – maybe a little updating was needed, but no fundamental changes seemed necessary. Then I visited the companies registry. It was a paper-based system: for each company there was a paper file on which documents were supposed to be placed in chronological order. However there was a large filing basket on the registrar's desk full of documents that had been delivered to the registry, but not yet added to the relevant companies' files: so a review of a file would not find any documents filed in recent weeks, or perhaps even months. I reviewed a sample of company files, and it quickly became apparent that many documents had been misfiled – so you could not find them on the file of the company which you were searching. Some files had not had any documents added for many years: it seemed that the requirement in the legislation to file annual returns was honoured more in the breach, and my enquiries revealed that no enforcement action in relation to annual returns had been taken for many, many years.

The morning I spent in the registry combing through a selection of files taught me several important things. First, any effective reform would need to have as its primary focus the operation of the registry and compliance and enforcement mechanisms, rather than the content of the law on paper. Second, we could not take the existing register as a starting point for any new regime – it was hopelessly inaccurate and out of date. There would need to be a mechanism for capturing up-to-date information about all registered companies that were in fact still operating. Third, we would need to make it much easier for companies to comply in the future – for example, by sending out annual summaries of the information the registry held, and asking recipients to either confirm the accuracy of that information or update it and send it back.

Another of my favourite examples of the gap between laws on paper and the operation of those laws in practice also comes from the field of company law – this time, in Sri Lanka. The English company law that was copied with minor modifications in Sri Lanka and many former British colonies in the late twentieth century provided for companies to file notices of all securities over company property at the companies registry. The idea was that a person dealing with the company, for example by purchasing assets or taking security over assets, could ascertain whether any prior ranking securities existed in respect of those assets. If the required notice was filed, that amounted to notice to the world of the existence of the security interest, and the security interest would generally prevail over interests subsequently acquired by a third party. If the required notice had not been filed, and a third party acquired an interest in the relevant assets, the third-party's interest would generally prevail over the earlier security interest. This regime worked reasonably well in countries with adequately resourced and well-run registries.[1] But I vividly remember, on my first visit to Sri Lanka some 20 years ago, being taken to a dark damp room full of piles of paper in no discernible order and informed that this was where notices of security interests were stored. They could not be reviewed in any way. Their existence was not even recorded against the name of the relevant company. It would be difficult (perhaps impossible) to locate a particular notice even if you knew it existed. And, the registrar told me mournfully, many of the older notices had been eaten by rats. A system that treats the world as being on notice of, and bound by, information contained in a document that cannot be located – and that may well have been eaten by rats – is unlikely to achieve its policy objectives.

As these examples illustrate, laws that look identical on paper can operate very differently in different countries with different institutions and different social and economic settings.

More generally, a legal right that cannot be enforced in a meaningful time frame, at a realistic and proportionate cost, is of little use in practice. Likewise, a legal obligation that is very unlikely to be enforced will have little or no effect on how people behave. We cannot understand how law works in practice simply by reading the law on paper – or even by reading textbooks and journal articles that are focused on the substantive content of the law.

Gathering Information about How Laws Operate

How, then, do we gather information about how laws work in practice? Quantitative data are valuable, where they are available. Every effort needs to be made to identify and obtain any relevant data that may be held by government agencies or the private sector. But all too often, quantitative data are scarce. Their accuracy may be doubtful. Important things are often difficult to measure, or simply have not been measured.

Another valuable source of information comes from analysis of interactions by citizens and stakeholders with government agencies, and with the courts. For example, the New Zealand Law Commission recently undertook a review of New Zealand's laws governing how couples divide their assets on separation.[2] One way in which a review of this kind can seek to understand how the existing law in this field operates in practice is to read decisions of judges applying that law. This is an essential step. But it is also hopelessly incomplete and potentially misleading. In almost every sphere of social and economic activity, most of the action takes place out of sight of government agencies and courts. The division of assets by couples post-separation is no exception. Only a fraction of couples who separate seek legal advice. And only a fraction of those couples end up filing court proceedings. Most of those proceedings settle. The disputes that end up as the subject of a final court decision represent a tiny percentage of the cases in which this important practical problem has to be solved. And they will almost certainly not be representative – they will be the most contentious cases, involving an atypically wealthy (and combative!) subset of individuals who can afford the significant cost of litigation, and who choose to go down that path. We need to read the existing legislation and read the relevant court decisions. But in the case of division of assets on separation, as in many other fields, that exercise sheds no light on what the vast majority of people do. It tells us nothing about whether the law influences what they do, or how it does so. As a result it tells us very little about how just or unjust our society's current arrangements for the division of property are from the perspective of the vast majority of citizens. That is not a sensible starting point for an attempt to design more appropriate and more effective legislation.

The only way that lawmakers can build a rich and accurate picture of how people currently behave – and why they do what they do – is by getting out and talking to those people. And to the people who deal face to face with those directly affected by the law: professional advisers, community support groups, front-line service providers in government agencies, among others. Soliciting submissions from stakeholders is not enough: most people will not respond, and the responses that come in tend to be much less informative than the results of a number of well-structured interviews with a wide range of people involved in the relevant field. The focus of those interviews should be very practical – what do you do in practice, step by step? How do you decide what steps to take (or whether to take any action at all)? How long does each step take? How much does it cost? What hurdles and obstacles do you encounter? The closer the interview can be tied to actual decisions made by the interviewee, and the details of those decisions, the better.

The stories people tell about their experiences are a rich source of qualitative data. Working through some illustrative fact scenarios can also improve the focus of the interview, and the quality of the information that you will gather.

Those interviews need to extend to individuals and groups who might in theory be expected to engage with the system, but who do not. Why don't some business owners register their businesses? What might change that? Why do so few couples in countries like New Zealand or the United States enter into 'pre-nups' – agreements to govern how their property will be divided if their marriage fails – even though studies suggest that most people in these countries are aware that a large proportion of all marriages end in divorce?[3]

In a study I carried out in Bangladesh many years ago, looking at the legal environment for doing business, the enquiries I made that taught me the most about the practical operation of the legal system were prompted by my attempts to understand why banks did not make unsecured loans to consumers or to small businesses, and why there was no local plant hire industry. Enquiries about things that were *not happening*, directed to the people one might have expected to be engaged in those activities.

Interviews with stakeholders need to explore what they do, what they do not do, and the reasons for those patterns of behaviour. In detail – generalities are unhelpful, and often misleading. If you are looking at the laws governing business registration, find out exactly how long it actually takes to register a business, rather than simply being told repeatedly that it is too slow. Go to the registry and ask to be taken through the process step by step, and to be shown a range of recent files which illustrate the process. Review those examples and study them closely. Cross-check what you are told by business owners with what you are told by professional advisers such as lawyers and accountants. And with what the registry officials tell you (the front-line staff, as well as the senior managers). And with a review of a cross-section of primary records.

Suppose for example that it becomes apparent that there is widespread non-compliance with the current law. Why is that? Are the relevant people not aware of the law? Why not? Is it too difficult for people to work out what they need to do in practice to comply with a law expressed in general terms? Are they unwilling to comply – and if so, why? Are they attempting to comply, but on the basis of a misunderstanding of the law? Does non-compliance pay? The reasons for non-compliance matter: the design of a more effective replacement regime will differ depending on the extent of non-compliance with the current law, and the factors driving that non-compliance.

The reasons that people give for their actions need to be scrutinised with some care. As discussed above, people are good at constructing plausible narratives, and it is rare for anyone's own narrative to cast its author as a villain rather than as the victim of the sins or omissions of others (or better still, as a superhero battling against immense odds). Nonetheless, legal designers can do better by asking these questions, and paying intelligent attention to the answers, than by making up explanations of their own based on a handful of anecdotes (or media stories) and their own intuitions.

It is better to do some interviews than none, though obviously the smaller and less representative the class of interviewees, the less reliable the overall results. Even a few dozen interviews will enable you to build one of the key tools for a legal designer – a 'decision map' which identifies what decisions are made, and by whom, in the field at which the proposed legislation is aimed. The terrain that you map will depend on the scope of the reform – it should be at least as broad as the field that is under review. The resolution of the map – the amount of detail – will depend on the nature of the review. The more granular the decision map you build, the better placed you are to describe what people currently do, the factors that influence those choices, and how the proposed legislation might change that behaviour. The decision map can be a text document or a flow diagram, or some hybrid of the two.

An example of a decision map that provides a high level 'helicopter' view of the process for division of a couple's property following separation in New Zealand is set out below. A focus on specific issues that arise in the context of division of property – reasons for departing from equal sharing, how the family home is treated, how economic disparity between partners is addressed – would require a more detailed map that zooms in on that issue, and how it affects the steps shown below.

This example of a decision map is based on my own review of official statistics that shed light on marriages, civil unions, divorces and household structures in New Zealand; information in a recent New Zealand Law Commission review of the law relating to relationship property; and discussions with a number of practitioners and judges. The figures for costs are very approximate. I was not able to come up with even very approximate percentage figures for the number of couples taking various different paths to resolve their post-separation property issues – more extensive research would be needed to produce useful estimates. But even with those gaps, the decision map is useful. It clarifies some issues. In particular, it indicates that around 1.5 per cent to 2 per cent of property divisions actually end up being determined by a judge: my rough estimate is that there are somewhere between 10,000 and 15,000 separations per year, but only on average around 200 Family Court judgments each year that finally determine the division of relationship property. So a reform that focuses on fairer outcomes in court proceedings would risk failing to address some 98 per cent of the situations in which this issue arises. The map also squarely identifies some issues about which we do not have any useful information, discouraging unfounded assumptions about those issues and highlighting where more research may be desirable.

Figure 6.1 Decision map – relationship property division

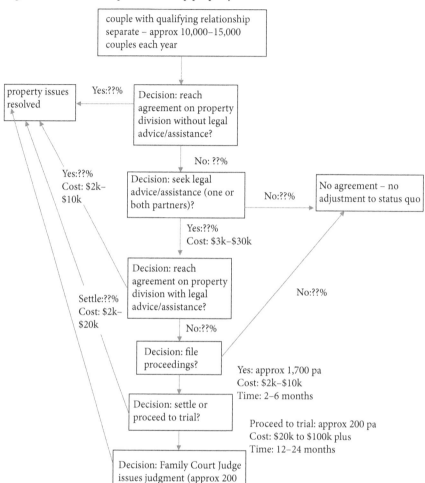

If the goal is to paint a reasonably complete picture of how people act in practice, and the impact (if any) of the law on their actions, then it will usually be necessary to seek professional assistance to design and conduct effective interviews with an appropriately selected representative group of interviewees. Returning to the issue of division of property following separation, a reasonably accurate understanding of why people don't enter into property agreements, or of how people actually do divide their assets following separation, can only be obtained by engaging directly with an appropriately selected sample of individuals who have gone through that experience.[4] Designing and conducting a high-quality study of this kind often involves considerable time and expense. But the alternative of risking failure of the proposed reforms, because the starting point for those reforms has not been accurately identified, is more problematic still.

Recent developments in technology offer some hope that we can gather information about what people actually do in some contexts more easily and more accurately. It is possible to engage with large numbers of people faster and at lower cost than ever before. The 'internet of things' also holds the promise of real-time data about a wide range of human behaviour. In some fields, 'big data' relevant to policymaking are already available as a result of government data collection, and widespread use of social networks and search engines. In his fascinating book *Everybody Lies: Big Data, New Data, and What the Internet Can Tell Us About Who We Really Are* Seth Stephens-Davidowitz, an economist and data scientist, draws on Google searches and other online data to shed light on a wide range of social phenomena.[5] (A simple experiment you can try at home is to type 'is it normal' into the Google search engine, and let the autocomplete function tell you what the most common queries of that kind are in your part of the world today: I guarantee you will learn something new about the preoccupations of your neighbours.[6]) His book provides an intriguing window into the views, preferences and choices of users of digital technology. He provides new information and insights about global and national phenomena, and illustrates how we can use big data to zoom in on variations in behaviour between particular localities or groups. The book also highlights the differences between what people say in public and are willing to disclose in response to surveys, and the information they are willing to share anonymously with Google and other online service providers. Interviews and surveys will often be the best tool available for gathering information about the operation of the existing law: but in many fields we need to be aware of the risk of systematic distortions in the responses provided. If there are ways of cross-checking the responses against other data sources, that will assist in identifying and adjusting for distortions of this kind.

It seems likely that data scientists will be increasingly important members of legislative design teams in the future, to enable us to access these insights into 'who we really are', as Seth Stevens-Davidowitz aptly puts it.

Even with access to abundant data, there is no substitute for making sure that the team working on the legislation has engaged effectively with the people whose daily lives involve dealing with the issues that the legislation seeks to address. They will have a rich understanding of what happens on the ground, and why. They will have views on the strengths and weaknesses of the current arrangements. They will be well placed to shed light on what will happen in practice – what they and the people around them are likely to do – if the rules are changed. If they have been genuinely and effectively engaged in the process of identifying where the existing problems lie, and in developing solutions to those problems, those solutions are much more likely to be relevant. And, critically, those solutions will be much more likely to have a measure of buy-in from the people on whom they will depend for their effectiveness.

---

[1] Though it has since been replaced with different and more effective personal property securities regimes in many common law countries, including Canada, New Zealand and Australia.

[2] See Law Commission, 'Review of the Property (Relationships) Act 1976', available at: www.lawcom. govt.nz/our-projects/review-property-relationships-act-1976.

[3] For a discussion of why there are so few prenuptial agreements, and survey evidence on awareness of marriage breakdown statistics, see Heather Mahar, 'Why Are There So Few Prenuptial Agreements?' (2003) John M Olin Center for Law, Economics and Business at Harvard Law School Discussion Paper Series 436, available at: www.lsr.nellco.org/harvard_olin/436. Mahar's paper concerns the United States, where the chance of a marriage ending in divorce is close to half. In New Zealand, the chance that a marriage will end in divorce is lower (just over one-third). Nevertheless, it is a commonly accepted 'fact' in New Zealand that half of all marriages end in divorce.

[4] Ian Binnie et al, *Relationship Property Division in New Zealand: Public Attitudes and Values. A General Population Survey* (Wellington, Michael and Suzanne Borrin Foundation, 2018).

[5] Seth Stephens-Davidowitz, *Everybody Lies: Big Data, New Data and What the Internet Can Tell Us About Who We Really Are* (New York, HarperCollins, 2017).

[6] ibid, 110–11.

7

What is the Legislation Aiming to Change?

Once we have described the current position, we come to the next key question: what do we want to change about that current position? And how do we want to change it?

All too often the goal of legislation is described in terms of changing the law: 'Why is this statute being enacted?'; 'To change the law from X to Y'. The answer (let's change the law to provide for Y) comes first; the analysis comes later.

But no one (except perhaps for a few nerdy lawyers) cares about the law in the abstract. Nor should they. Law is an instrument for achieving social outcomes, not an end in and of itself. The first step in designing legislation that works is to identify and describe the relevant *social* problem, and the desired *social* change. In order for this exercise to be meaningful, the focus needs to be on the behaviour of the relevant people and institutions: what is it about what certain people do now (whether out of choice, or because they have no choice) that is problematic? What change in their behaviour are we trying to bring about? What will the world look like – in terms of how people behave – if this reform is successful?

Let's return to my example of the division of property by couples upon separation. Often we see the goal of law reform exercises in this field described in terms of making the law fairer. But that formulation misses the point. How fair the law looks on paper tells us little or nothing about what happens in the real world; a world in which most couples have little in the way of assets and struggle to afford legal advice, let alone litigation. The goal of a law reform exercise should always be framed in terms of outcomes in the real world.

For example, the goal of a review of New Zealand's law governing division of property post-separation might be framed in terms of the vast majority of separating couples dividing their assets in a manner that is fair to both. This reformulation matters, because it drives all the subsequent analysis. We are now squarely focused on what a fair regime would look like in terms of how people would behave, rather than the more abstract and much less important question of what a more just written law might look like. Our attention is concentrated on how the law operates in practice – on access to fair outcomes for the majority of people who confront this issue – rather than on designing an ideal regime that may only be accessed by a very few. If we then pay attention to the information available about household net worth – in 2018 for example, some 30 per cent of households in New Zealand had net wealth of less than $100,000, and the median net household wealth was $340,000 – we will need to confront the need for the law to be accessible and inexpensive if it is going to be relevant to anyone apart from a wealthy minority.[1] That practical issue moves from the periphery to the centre of our enquiry. As it must, if the reform is to be meaningful.

Notice also that in my example the goal is not expressed in terms of outcomes for the few that do currently engage with the court process. This is another common way of framing the purpose of a law reform project: to deliver fairer outcomes from the court process. But this formulation also largely misses the point. The goal of a review of relationship property law should not be thought of in terms of changing outcomes for the tiny number of people who already go to court: that may well be desirable, but it ignores the way the law operates (or fails to operate) for the 98 per cent of couples (on my rough figures) whose property division is not decided by a court. Some of the couples who do not go to court will bargain in the shadow of the law: the law also influences the outcomes they reach.[2] But for many couples, the cost of litigating is prohibitive and neither party can credibly threaten to go down that path: the law's 'shadow' does not reach them.

I cannot stress too strongly the importance of keeping the frame wide, and focusing on outcomes for all the people who encounter the issue that the law addresses. If the law is about division of relationship property, then the frame for identifying the desired change in outcomes should be all the people who need to divide their relationship property. That doesn't mean setting unrealistic goals. If it is impossible for the law to reach every affected person, as is usually the case, then we need to face up to that. A more realistic goal might be to secure just outcomes for a substantial majority of separating couples. Even that may be ambitious. But it seems reasonable to be ambitious when it comes to basic rule of law goals: striving to ensure that all members of our society enjoy the protection of the law. If we take rule of law values seriously, we should be reluctant to frame the policy goals of legislation in a way that fails to reflect those values. And ambitious goals can be a spur to the search for creative solutions.

The answer to the question posed in this chapter will drive everything else you do. It needs to be expressed in practical terms that describe the concerns about the status quo that have prompted the law reform exercise, and that describe in as much detail as possible how people will behave, and the outcomes you will see, if the reform succeeds. It should be framed widely, to describe the outcomes you are aiming to achieve across the entire class of people who experience the issues that the law addresses. It is worth spending some time thinking carefully about how the goal of the project is formulated, testing that formulation with others, and ensuring it is understood by everyone involved in the project. As you work on the project you will find yourself referring back to it frequently.

As I said earlier, this book is focused on designing legislation that works to achieve its policy goals, not on the broader question of what those policy goals should be. But the process of translating broad policy goals into a clear statement of the current problem, and of what behaviour would need to change in order to achieve those policy goals, is a shared responsibility for policymakers and legal designers. Legal designers cannot do their job without clarity on these basic points, even if they do not have primary responsibility for setting policy. Either they need to develop the answers to this question in consultation with policymakers, or they need to insist that the policymakers provide a clear answer to this question. If this critical question is not squarely addressed, the prospect that the law will succeed in advancing its policy goals is low.

---

[1] Statistics New Zealand, 'Household Net Worth Statistics: Year ended 30 June 2018' (14 December 2018), available at: www.stats.govt.nz/information-releases/household-net-worth-statistics-year-ended-june-2018. See also, Statistics New Zealand, 'Wealth of Top 20 Percent Rises by $394,000' (14 December 2018), available at: www.stats.govt.nz/news/wealth-of-top-20-percent-rises-by-394000.

[2] The phrase 'bargaining in the shadow of the law' originates from a seminal paper about settling disputes post-divorce: see Robert H Mnookin and Lewis Kornhauser, 'Bargaining in the Shadow of the Law: The Case of Divorce' (1979) 88 *Yale Law Journal* 950, available at: www.jstor.org/stable/795824.

8

Who are the Audiences
for the Legislation?

The process of identifying the change in social outcomes that we want proposed legislation to deliver, and the people whose behaviour would need to change in order for us to see those outcomes, leads logically into the next question: to whom will the legislation be addressed? Who needs to be aware of and act on the proposed law, to achieve the desired outcome? How will this come about?

Plainly the legislation itself needs to be accessible. In most countries today that is a given, thanks to the ease of publishing laws online. Twenty-five years ago when I was working on a project in Bangladesh and needed copies of some statutes, I had to go down to the court building in Dhaka, locate the street vendors in the plaza outside the courts who had copies of the specific statutes that I wanted, and haggle with them to buy each one. Now I can access those same laws online from anywhere in the world, at no cost. It's a less colourful process, but a much more efficient one.

Making the text of the law accessible online is just a beginning when it comes to communicating the law to its various audiences. As we saw when discussing why laws fail, one significant cause of failure is that the people to whom the law is addressed are not aware of it, or don't understand what it requires of them. Or what it enables them to do, which they could not do before. If the law is directed to all citizens, or to a particular group of citizens, how will they learn that it exists? How will they obtain information about it? Most people do not find out what the law requires, or what benefits it can provide to them, by reading legislation. (When did you last read the legislation that governs how much tax you pay, and when you need to pay it? The road traffic legislation that governs how you drive on the roads? The privacy legislation that provides for how government, and businesses, handle your personal information? Thought so.) How will the vast majority of the people to whom the law is addressed – who will never read the legislation itself – find out about the implications for them of this particular law? And comply with it, if it imposes obligations; or take advantage of it, if it provides them with benefits?

A study of health and safety regulation in England by Hazel Genn, a pioneering sociolegal scholar, found that large companies got information about their obligations from a number of sources – specialist safety personnel, and internal and external lawyers.[1] But small businesses struggled to keep up with the evolving laws in this field. She asked one small business owner 'How do you keep up to date on changes in regulation?' His answer: 'I don't'. And when she asked how many different sets of regulations there were that applied to his business, his answer was 'God only knows'. This business owner was in the core audience for the applicable health and safety regulations – but laws that he did not know about, and could not even count, were not going to change his behaviour.

If the effectiveness of the law depends on its administration by public authorities, then it is also essential to consider how those public authorities will be informed about what the law requires of them. The more numerous and disparate the authorities to whom the law is addressed, the greater the investment that will be needed to ensure that the law is effectively communicated and explained. Thus for example a building law amendment that requires a large number of local government agencies to change how they administer a building approval process will need to be communicated to all of those agencies in a way that their staff can understand and act on. (And those agencies will need to have adequate staff, with appropriate skills and training, and the necessary resources to do their job: I return to these essential prerequisites below.)

One mechanism for making law more accessible to users is to draft that legislation, and present it, in a way that facilitates understanding and applying that law. A great deal of work has been done in some countries on enhancing the ease of use of legislation. Plain language drafting is becoming more common – and is especially important where the law's audience is broad and non-expert. Publication of legislation on the internet has undoubtedly broadened the direct audience for legislation.[2]

Conversely, where the audience for the legislation is highly specialised – think securities regulation – it may be more helpful to use well understood technical language and terms of art, rather than attempt a plain language paraphrase. A clear focus on the audiences for the particular law, and how they will use that law, sheds light on where that particular law should sit on the spectrum from contemporary plain language to technical language.

Another promising approach to enhancing the usability of legislation is the use of examples and illustrations in the text of the legislation itself.[3] This can clarify the intended operation of the law and enhance its accessibility for both specialist and general audiences.

One good example of drafting to facilitate the use of laws by non-experts is found in the codes drafted for use in India in the era of the British Empire, many of which were retained post-independence and are still in force (with some modifications) in India, Pakistan and Bangladesh today. The English civil servants who were dispatched to administer the colonies, a role which often included dispensing justice in the regions to which they were posted, were almost all generalists with no legal training. Professional legal advice was not readily available to them. Law libraries were few and far between – and of little use to the non-lawyers performing these functions in any event. It seems that whatever their blind spots, the officials responsible for colonial administration must at least have appreciated that the audience for the colonial laws they were framing consisted of generalists, not qualified lawyers. Traditional English methods of 'doing law' – in particular, reliance on case law – simply would not work in this context. The response of the colonial administrators was to codify a number of areas of law – criminal law, contract, trusts – that were governed by case law in England. The Indian Contract Act 1872, drafted by Sir James Fitzjames Stephen, is a good example. It sought to codify (with a few clarifications and minor reforms) the English common law of contract. As well as setting out operative provisions, this code contained both explanations and illustrations. It is much easier to understand and apply than many modern statutes.[4]

However, as I said earlier, despite increasing use of online legislation by the public it is rare for individuals or businesses to get information about the law that applies to them by reading the legislation itself. How will they get that information? By seeking legal advice from lawyers? That may work if the law is addressed to a small and well-resourced group – for example, large corporations with significant market power. They can be expected to seek legal advice about how laws prohibiting the misuse of market power will apply to their business. Similarly, corporations offering investment products to the public can be expected to seek advice on how to comply with securities market laws – so the audience for those laws is primarily lawyers and other expert advisers. But if the audience for a law is the public at large, or small businesses, that answer is unrealistic. Other mechanisms need to be found to facilitate access to the law, and make it easier for the relevant audiences for that law to understand how it is relevant to them. The user interface for the law is critical to its effectiveness.

The appropriate mechanisms in any given case – the appropriate user interface – will vary depending on the nature of the legislation, and who the audience is for that legislation. There is room for creativity here. Some of the more common options that deserve to be considered include:

- Public information campaigns after the law is made. These may involve a mix of written materials, online materials, training for administrators, and training for professional advisers and/or community groups.

- Guidance on the operation of the law issued by a regulator or government agency. The guidance may be for information only, or the legislation may provide for guidance with authoritative legal force. Various approaches to authoritative guidance are possible – for example, a government agency can be given the power to issue guidelines which provide a safe harbour for complying with the law, but which do not limit other options for achieving compliance.

- Requiring information to be provided orally in real time to the person affected. Many countries' laws require a person who is being arrested to be informed at that time of the reason for the arrest, their right to remain silent, and that they are entitled to seek legal advice.[5]

- Providing for 'signposts' that communicate what the law requires in the context where it is immediately relevant – road markings and road signs; notices in restaurant bathrooms reminding employees to wash their hands; the warnings about severe penalties for drug smuggling that cabin crew are required to read out before your plane lands in Singapore. Signposts reduce complexity for the audience for the law in question, and increase the salience of the legal requirement.[6]

Figure 8.1 No need to read the legislation …[7]

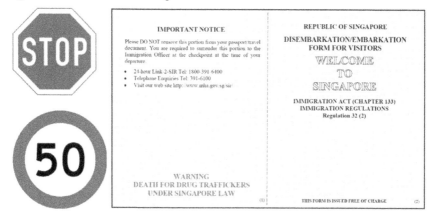

- Implementation mechanisms that involve expert non-governmental actors who can be expected to understand, communicate and monitor compliance with the law – for example, auditors who are required to report on compliance with the law by the businesses they audit.

- Interactive technology that provides information about the operation of the law – for example, websites that enable users to enter relevant information and obtain guidance on how the law applies to them. Some tax administrations provide interactive websites that apply complex tax rules and associated formulae to calculate the amounts of tax that a particular taxpayer must pay, or the deductions that an employer is required to make from an employee's wages. Other government websites calculate the amount of child support that one parent must pay another if they live apart. 'Event-based' websites that focus on significant life events such as the birth of a child, pulling together in one place relevant practical and legal information and links to multiple agencies, promise to significantly improve access to relevant laws and the effectiveness of those laws.[8] An emerging technology that holds considerable promise is the use of chatbots to provide basic information and advice about the law in response to plain language enquiries. There are already some impressive examples of use of technology of this kind in a handful of countries.[9]

- Interactive technology that actually applies the relevant law, removing the need for most users to access and understand the legislation. If users can apply for a licence – or a passport, or a visa, or a benefit – online, and the application is determined by an automated process, then the law will be much more accessible in practice. And its administration is likely to be swifter and more efficient. Again, there are already impressive examples of the use of technology in this way, and more on the horizon.[10]

- Building awareness of the proposed law, and of its policy goals, through the consultation process that precedes and accompanies the legislative process.
- Facilitating access to relevant background materials – law reform reports, relevant international instruments, and any authoritative decisions interpreting and applying the law. Ideally online, in one readily accessible place.

Mechanisms for making it easier for audiences to understand the implications of legislation, and obtain benefits under that legislation or comply with it, are discussed in more detail in chapters eighteen and nineteen below.

Identification of the audiences for the proposed legislation, and how those audiences will be informed about the law, is an essential early step in the design of that law. If these issues are not addressed, the law will almost certainly fail to achieve its intended goals. This item on the checklist cannot be left until after the law is enacted, to be dealt with if and when time and resources permit. Some of the most effective options for communicating how a law works to users will require changes to the content of the law itself. For example, legislative authority may be needed for the use of signposts; for the development and implementation of online mechanisms for applying the law; or for the issue of authoritative guidance. If we identify in advance that there is a real risk of serious difficulties in communicating some aspects of the law effectively, that may require those aspects of the law to be redesigned. Advisers need to understand the overall package of steps involved in making the legislation effective, to ensure that the advice they give takes proper account of the costs and risks of different options. Responsible legislators will also want to understand these trade-offs.

---

[1] Hazel Genn, 'Business Responses to the Regulation of Health and Safety in England' (1993) 15 *Law & Policy* 219.

[2] A survey undertaken in 2012 by the 'Good Law Initiative' of the United Kingdom Office of Parliamentary Counsel in cooperation with the National Archives identified three main groups of users of legislation published by the government on the website legislation.govt.uk: lay persons seeking information on their rights and obligations, including self-represented litigants (about 20%); non-lawyers who need to use legislation for work, such as law enforcers, human resources professionals and local council officials (about 60%); and lawyers and judges interpreting and applying the law (about 20%): see Alison Bertlin, 'What Works Best for the Reader? A Study on Drafting and Presenting Legislation' (2014) *The Loophole* 27, available at: Loophole_-_2014-2__2014-05-09_-What_works_best_for_the_reader.pdf (publishing.service.gov.uk); Helen Xanthaki, 'Emerging Trends in Legislation in Europe' in Ulrich Karpen and Helen Xanthaki (eds), *Legislation in Europe* (Oxford, Hart Publishing, 2017).

[3] See, eg, Personal Properties Securities Act 1999 (NZ); Fisheries (Amateur Fishing) Regulations 2013 (NZ), sch 4; Unit Titles Act 2010 (NZ), s 9 and sch 1. For a discussion of the use of examples in legislative drafting see Ross Carter, 'Statutory Interpretation Using Legislated Examples: Bennion on Multiple Consumer Credit Agreements' (2011) 32 *Statute Law Review* 86; Ross Carter, *Burrows and Carter – Statute Law in New Zealand*, 6th edn (LexisNexis NZ Ltd, 2021) 154–57.

[4] The Indian Contract Act 1872 is available at: www.liiofindia.org/in/legis/cen/num_act/ica1872152/. See, eg, s 20 on void agreements:

20. Agreement void where both parties are under mistake as to matter of fact

Where both the parties to an agreement are under a mistake as to a matter of fact essential to the agreement, the agreement is void. *Explanation.–* An erroneous opinion as to the value of the thing which forms the subject-matter of the agreement is not to be deemed a mistake as to a matter of fact. *Illustrations* (a) A agrees to sell to B a specific cargo of goods supposed to be on its way from England to Bombay. It turns out that, before the day of the bargain, the ship conveying the cargo had been cast away and the goods lost. Neither party was aware of the facts. The agreement is void. (b) A agrees to buy from B a certain horse. It turns out that the horse was dead at the time of the bargain, though neither party was aware of the fact. The agreement is void. (c) A, being entitled to an estate for the life of B, agrees to sell it to C. B was dead at the time of the agreement, but both parties were ignorant of the fact. The agreement is void.

[5] See, eg, New Zealand Bill of Rights Act 1990 (NZ), s 23; Canadian Charter of Rights and Freedoms, s 7; *Miranda v Arizona* 384 US 436 (1966).

[6] For a helpful discussion of the importance of salience, see Cass R Sunstein's book *Simpler: The Future of Government* (New York, Simon & Schuster, 2013) ch 6.

[7] Road signs, available at: File:Vienna Convention road sign B2a.svg – Wikimedia Commons; Government of Singapore, available at: commons.wikimedia.org/w/index.php?curid=6816602.

[8] See, eg, SmartStart, 'Find the Right Services For You and Your Child', available at: www.smartstart.services.govt.nz/, a website that provides information for parents expecting a child, and parents with new babies, and enables parents to register the birth of a child and apply for financial support, among other services.

[9] See, eg, the New Zealand government's trial of an artificially intelligent 'bot' for honey exporters – see Richard MacManus, 'Meet Tai: The AI Bot For Honey Exporters' *Newsroom* (Auckland, 27 November 2018), available at: www.newsroom.co.nz/2018/11/27/334181/the-governments-ai-bot-for-honey-exporters.

[10] For one ambitious cross-agency project, see: /businessconnect.govt.nz/.

9

What Institutions will the Legislation Depend on? Do they have the Capacity to Play their Role?

In my early teens I came across a book on my parents' bookshelves called *Twisted Tales from Shakespeare*.[1] It retold some of Shakespeare's most famous plays, briefly and with lots of terrible jokes. I loved it – especially the terrible jokes. (My children would tell you that I still love terrible jokes.) In the course of summarising the play 'Othello', the book refers to Desdemona's famous 'Willow' song and says 'She even sings the part that is plainly marked "Refrain"'. When I was 14, I thought this was hilarious. (Actually, I still do.)

My refrain in this book (and yes, I'm going to keep singing it) is that it is impossible to design laws without paying close attention to the institutions that administer them. They are inextricably linked. The *Twisted Tales from Shakespeare* also contains parodies of essay questions for students about each play. One of the questions on Hamlet is 'How long can you discuss Rosencrantz without mentioning Guildenstern, and vice versa?' It's pretty much impossible, of course – they enter, exit and act throughout as an inseparable pair. But when it comes to laws and the institutions that implement those laws, people seem strangely able to discuss one without the other, at great length. This is more worrying than funny.

As I said in the introduction to this book, laws are like the code running in the background on your computer or your phone. The institutions that implement the law are the hardware and user interface through which we interact with that code. Good code is code that is optimised for the environment in which it will run – and achieving that may require changes to the code, changes to the hardware, or both. It would be absurd for a programmer writing an app for a smartphone to ignore how the users will experience the app on their devices, focusing instead on the elegance and purity of the underlying code. It is equally absurd to focus on the law on paper, and ignore the institutions through which it will be encountered by users.

Identifying the Relevant Institutions

The first step in thinking about the interplay between a proposed law and the institutions that will administer it is to identify those institutions. Does the law allocate functions to government officials? Existing agencies? New agencies? Does it need to be enforced through the courts? Here also it is helpful to prepare a decision map, which shows the roles each relevant institution is intended to play in the operation of the law.

Do those Institutions have the Capacity to Play their Intended Role?

Once the relevant institutions have been identified, we can consider how well placed each one is to perform the functions allocated to it. Does each relevant institution already exist, and have the capacity and the resources needed to play its intended role? The willingness to play that role? Wishful thinking (sometimes verging on wilful blindness) often comes into play here. But if the effectiveness of the legislation depends on institutional actors, it is foolish – indeed, negligent – not to tackle this issue head on. The law will not serve a useful purpose if the 'user interface' – the institutions through which it operates – does not work.

If an institution lacks the capacity to administer the law, then it is very likely that the law will be a damp squib: it will fail to achieve its policy goals. Worse still, an institution that lacks the capacity or the will to administer a law in a way that gives effect to its goals can produce all manner of perverse outcomes – nasty surprise failures.

A couple of quick examples: first, the damp squib. The contract laws of New Zealand and Bangladesh are very similar, reflecting their common English law heritage. But when I spent some time in Bangladesh in the 1990s, I learned that the lengthy delays in the courts meant that even the simplest claims could take many years to be determined. A creditor who finally obtained a judgment, years down the track, could then expect to encounter all sorts of obstacles in enforcing that judgment. The courts almost never awarded interest on money due, and inflation was high. So even if you got a judgment, and even if you could enforce it, the amount you ultimately recovered would be a fraction of what you were owed in real terms. In this setting there were strong incentives for debtors to delay paying their debts, stringing their creditors along indefinitely. The only constraint was reputation. And for many, that constraint was weak. The result was that unsecured lending by banks, or through other formal channels, was virtually non-existent. By contrast in New Zealand a summary judgment claim for a debt could be pursued through to judgment in a few months, and the judgment could readily be enforced. Interest would be awarded as a matter of course. Because enforcement of judgments in New Zealand is quick and easy, it is hardly ever needed – most debtors who can pay will do so voluntarily rather than wait to be sued, with all the additional costs that involves. The differences in practical outcomes could not have been more stark, despite the similarity of the substantive law. In Bangladesh, contract law simply did not work. The words on paper were essentially irrelevant.

Changing the substantive provisions of the contract legislation would not make any difference at all – we would simply be replacing one non-operational regime with another.

Another damp squib, this time from New Zealand – wealthy countries are by no means immune from this phenomenon. In 2001 New Zealand amended its law governing the division of property when couples separate to give the courts the power to make orders directed at disparity caused by the division of roles within a relationship, as a result of which the human capital and earning capacity of one partner (almost invariably the man) were enhanced, and the human capital and earning capacity of the other (almost invariably the woman) diminished. This is a significant factor in the substantial economic disparity that often arises between men and women after a relationship ends. At the time of the reform the Family Court Judges expressed concern about this proposal, saying it would create a huge amount of extra work which would require another six judges to be appointed just to deal with it.[2] But experience has been very different. The courts have decided only a handful of claims under the provision in the 20 years it has been in place. No new judges were needed to handle this very modest workload. Why? Because the provision was expressed in very general terms. The generality of the provision made it complex to interpret and apply in practice.[3] The courts required the applicant to provide extensive evidence – including expert evidence about their actual and 'counterfactual' (ie, without the division of roles) earning potential. Running an economic disparity case would typically cost the claimant tens of thousands of dollars, and would take several years to resolve. Outcomes were uncertain – the court was given a broad discretion – and the judges took a cautious and conservative approach to their new powers. So in most cases an economic disparity claim either was not made at all, or was settled on a highly discounted basis in the context of the overall division of property. The new provision made almost no difference. The cost of accessing the relevant institution – here, the court – was such a significant barrier that the vast majority of the people who were intended to benefit from the law could not afford to pursue their new rights.[4] This much-debated reform achieved almost nothing in practice.

The UK has had its fair share of damp squibs in recent decades. The failed laws described by Anthony King and Ivor Crewe in *The Blunders of Our Governments* include the 1991 child support legislation that left children no better off, and arguably worse off; the 2002 proceeds of crime legislation that established an Assets Recovery Agency that recovered minimal assets – less than its operating costs – before it was abolished in 2008; and the enactment of the Identity Cards Act 2006 which was repealed in 2010 with the handful of cards that had been issued – some 15,000 against an original target of around 60 million – all being cancelled.[5] The common theme in each of these failures was a lack of institutional capacity to implement the law. The law established a new agency or conferred significant new functions on an existing agency, without any reason to expect that this would work. Little or no thought was given to what the institution would need to do in order to make the law work, and whether this was realistically achievable.

Second, nasty surprises. We've already seen an example of this – the newly established competition regulator with no competition expertise that used its powers to block the sale of a state-owned business to the highest bidder despite the absence of any plausible competition concern. Whether this outcome was the result of incompetence or corruption, it was certainly undesirable and inconsistent with the policy goals of the shiny new 'global best practice' competition law.

Another nasty surprise caused by institutional capacity issues was what came to be known as New Zealand's 'leaky building crisis'. In the early 1990s, New Zealand's highly prescriptive building regulation regime was replaced with new 'performance-based' regulation. Instead of specifying what materials had to be used to build a house, and exactly how it should be built, the new regulatory regime required buildings to achieve performance standards on various dimensions – including structural stability, durability and weathertightness. This approach was seen as consistent with an international trend towards performance-based regulation in many sectors. A building designer could select any design, materials and construction techniques that would achieve the prescribed performance standards.

After the new regime had been in operation for about 10 years, widespread issues became apparent in relation to weathertightness of homes and other buildings. Many factors contributed to the leaky building crisis.[6] But the most significant were lack of capacity in the industry and in its regulators. The New Zealand construction industry was largely made up of small firms that lacked the knowledge and expertise to assess whether new designs and new materials – in particular, monolithic face-fixed cladding – would comply with performance-based standards. The legislation conferred responsibility for day-to-day administration of building standards on local government agencies, which lacked the resources and expertise needed to carry out their regulatory functions effectively: their role changed significantly from assessing compliance with highly prescriptive standards for houses built using standard techniques and materials, to assessing new techniques, new materials and what performance outcomes were likely with those techniques and materials. Their existing personnel, systems and information-base simply were not up to this new task. The central government agency that was supposed to support local authorities in the performance of their functions, as well as performing a range of other regulatory functions, was hopelessly under-resourced. Many houses were built using designs and materials that were poorly suited to New Zealand conditions, and the building work was not properly executed. The regulators did not detect these problems – they approved the relevant designs, and issued certificates for the completed buildings confirming (incorrectly) that they complied with the new performance-based building code. Remediation and replacement of 'leaky buildings' became a major social and economic issue, with costs estimated to be well in excess of $10 billion (a huge figure for a small country with a population of around four million at that time). This was a very expensive nasty surprise caused by a failure to identify significant institutional capacity deficiencies, and to address those deficiencies in a timely way.

Performance-based regulation provides flexibility, and encourages innovation and adaptation. But as this example illustrates, it will not work unless all the institutions on which it depends have the capacity to carry out their functions effectively.

Addressing Concerns about Institutional Capacity

If each relevant institution already exists and already has the capacity, resources and will to perform the role envisaged for it then you can move on to the next issue. But if that is not the case, then there are three broad options that you will need to consider:

a.   Find ways to reduce the dependence of the proposed reform on that institution.
b.   Take action to address those institutional capacity issues.
c.   Review the viability of the proposed reform.

One option for addressing institutional weakness that is too often overlooked by legal designers is reframing the proposed legislation to reduce dependence on a weak institution, or on a proposed institution that it may not be feasible to establish. Is the involvement of that institution necessary? Can default rules be changed to reduce the frequency with which it needs to be involved, or to reduce the impact of failure? Can the legal framework be adjusted so that the institution does not need to make a decision in all cases, but only in a subset of cases where the default setting under the legal framework gives rise to concern? The importance of default rules in the context of institutional capacity is discussed in more detail in chapter fourteen below.

Another option may be to reduce the complexity of the decisions that the institution is required to make. The institution may not have the capacity to administer complex tests for eligibility for a benefit, for example. But it may have the capacity to administer a simpler test that would also be consistent with the project's policy goals. Some options for reducing complexity are outlined in chapter fifteen below.

If a particular decision-making role is indispensable, another way to reduce dependence on a weak existing institution is to allocate the role to another institution. Are there other existing institutions that can play the relevant role, with better prospects of success? Should a new institution be established, which can start with a clean slate in terms of systems, personnel and culture? Is there scope for collaboration with other jurisdictions to establish shared institutions with greater capacity than any one jurisdiction could achieve alone (for example, the Caribbean Court of Justice, the EU Patent Office, Food Standards Australia New Zealand)? Can online systems or other forms of logistical support be provided by another country's corresponding institution, or by a private provider (for example, the online companies registries of Niue and Tonga, which are operated on behalf of those small Pacific countries by the New Zealand companies registry)?

Another option is to take action to address the institutional capacity issues that might lead to failure: work out what is needed to ensure that the institution can play the envisaged role, and provide it. In some cases this can be achieved by the simple mechanism of providing adequate funding for the task (though this is often politically difficult, in a world of constrained public budgets). More often there are concerns about the institution's systems, and the skills and experience of the people in the institution, that need to be identified and tackled. This may involve introducing new systems, or training, or recruiting new people with the relevant skills, or some mix of these.

But strengthening an existing institution to the point where it can administer the law effectively may not be possible, or may be a long-term project that is unlikely to address the issues in a way that adequately reduces the risk of failure in the short to medium term. Building institutional capacity is usually a slow and difficult task.

Ensuring institutional capacity to implement proposed legislation can also be challenging where a new institution is being established for that purpose. The necessary capacity has to be built from scratch. Many significant failures – both damp squibs and nasty surprises – are the result of unfounded optimism about the process of establishing a new institution, and its ability to implement new legislation. Establishing a new institution to implement legislation requires more than the normal level of planning and analysis, not less. Pilots and dry runs can be valuable: I return to this in the next chapter. An establishment unit with lead responsibility for the establishment of the new institution is often essential. It is a high-risk strategy to leave detailed work on institutions until after the legislation has been adopted. At best, delays are likely. You may discover that the legislation needs amendment in order to be implemented successfully. Or that the problems run so deep that the legislation cannot be implemented successfully in anything like its current form.

It is all too common for the designers of a legal framework to acknowledge that there are institutional capacity issues, and that an institution will need to be strengthened or established for the legislation to work as intended – and then move on, satisfied that they have identified a task for someone else to address at some other time. That is not a satisfactory response: the role of the legal designer is to design a regime that works in practice, not just in theory. If there is no assurance that a weak institution can be strengthened within a reasonable time frame, then the designer needs to go back to the drawing board and look closely at how to design a law that will work despite the institution's weakness. If it is not possible to strengthen an institution that lacks the capacity or the will to implement proposed legislation within a reasonable time frame, and if it is not possible to redesign the legislation to reduce dependence on that institution, then there is every reason to expect the legislation to fail. Likewise, if a new institution is proposed, and the necessary work has not been done to ensure that the new institution can be set up in time and will be able to perform its role, then there is every reason to expect the legislation to fail.

If there is no sound basis for expecting that key institutions will be able to perform their role in implementing the legislation, serious thought needs to be given to whether it is sensible to proceed with the legislation. Will it do any good at all? Or is it just a pointless charade? Worse still, might it have undesired adverse consequences? The country I mentioned above that enacted a shiny new 'best practice' competition law would almost certainly have been better off without that law, however impressive it looked on paper, in the absence of an effective and competent agency to administer it. The UK would have been much better off if it had never enacted its 1991 child support legislation, which established a new Child Support Agency that was such a disaster that its acronym – CSA – was often mockingly referred to as standing for 'Complete Shambles Agency'. The UK would also have been better off if it had never enacted its 2006 identity card legislation, rather than enacting the law first, then turning attention to implementation and discovering that the logistical challenges and costs of implementing that law made it completely unworkable. In the absence of concrete plans for implementation of proposed legislation by the relevant institutions, based on a realistic assessment of their existing or future capacity, the risk of failure is likely to be unacceptably high.

---

[1] Richard Armour, *Twisted Tales from Shakespeare* (New York, McGraw-Hill, 1957).

[2] (29 March 2001) vol 591 NZPD 8627.

[3] Complexity – and how to reduce it – is discussed in ch 15 below.

[4] See Claire Green, 'The Impact of Section 15 of the Property (Relationships) Act 1976 on the Vexing Problem of Economic Disparity' (PhD dissertation, University of Otago, 2013).

[5] Anthony King and Ivor Crewe, *The Blunders of Our Governments* (London, Oneworld Publications, 2013) chs 6, 11 and 15.

[6] See Peter Mumford, 'Enhancing Performance-based Regulation: Lessons from New Zealand's Building Control System' (PhD thesis, Victoria University of Wellington, 2010); Brent Layton, 'A Case of Regulatory Failure' in Susy Frankel (ed), *Learning From the Past, Adapting for the Future*: *Regulatory Reform in New Zealand* (Wellington, LexisNexis, 2011) 311; James Zuccollo, Mike Hensen and John Yeabsley, 'Weathertight Buildings and Performance-based Regulation: What Lessons can be Drawn from a Complicated and Evolving Situation?' in Susy Frankel and Deborah Ryder (eds), *Recalibrating Behaviour: Smarter Regulation in a Global World* (Wellington, LexisNexis, 2013).

10

How will the Legislation Change Behaviour? How might that go Wrong?

How will the Legislation Change Behaviour?

In the course of tackling the questions outlined in chapters six to eight above, we should develop a reasonable picture of how the relevant stakeholders currently behave; our concerns about the status quo; and how we would like to see the behaviour of those stakeholders change in order to achieve the policy goals of the proposed reform. In chapter nine we went on to consider the institutions that will play a role in implementing the legislation, and their capacity to perform that function.

That brings us to the next and hardest issue: identifying whether, and how, legislation could contribute to the desired changes in behaviour in our own society. Remember King Canute: simply issuing orders, or passing legislation, won't magically translate into change in the real world. What is the pathway by which legislation can bring about the desired change in behaviour, or contribute to that change? At what cost? If other steps need to be taken in tandem with passing the legislation, in order for the legislation to be effective, what are those other steps? And what will they cost? In light of those answers, is legislation desirable? And what should it look like?

The decision map that I suggested in chapter six is an indispensable tool when it comes to developing a 'theory of change'. How is the legislation expected to change that map? Why will each relevant decision-maker change their behaviour as a result of the proposed legislation? How is their behaviour likely to change? What barriers are there to the desired changes in behaviour? How can those barriers be eliminated or reduced – is it possible to make it easier for decision-makers to do the right thing?

Analysing these issues requires us to make medium to long-term predictions about how people will respond to the proposed legislation. This is difficult, as discussed above. Often it cannot be done perfectly or with a high degree of confidence: the world is too complex and uncertain, and the resources and bandwidth of those involved are limited. But it can be done much better than most law reformers currently do it. Diverse perspectives from within the team, and from engagement with stakeholders, are important when it comes to gathering the relevant information and understanding its implications. Experience in other societies is an important input, as discussed in more detail below. The analytical insights of economists, social psychologists and other relevant experts will help to ensure that you are using models that are 'fit for purpose' to explain and predict behaviour in the field that you are tackling.

Your theory of change should pay careful attention to the incentives that each relevant audience will face if the legislation is adopted. As we saw in chapter two, many legislative failures result from paying insufficient attention to the changes in behaviour that a new law will encourage. People do respond to incentives, even if that response does not always line up perfectly with what a classical economic model might predict. You should consider whether your theory of change is based on a good understanding of the incentives that the members of each audience will face, and is consistent with a rational response by them to those incentives in both the short term and the medium to long term. How will behaviour change over time? How might people seek to circumvent the law change? Or exploit it for their own benefit?

As we saw in chapter four, recent work in behavioural economics reminds us that human decision-making does differ in some important respects from the classical economic model. You should consider whether your theory of change harnesses deeply ingrained tendencies in human decision-making – for example, by making the desired behaviour the default outcome for most people, so inertia is your friend. Conversely, if your theory of change assumes that people will take active steps to gather information and to depart from the status quo where it is in their best interests to do so, you should give careful thought to just how likely that behaviour really is. And you should consider whether it is possible to adjust default settings to avoid this potentially significant barrier to success.

There is an increasingly rich body of studies that shed light on important questions such as the impact of paying for blood donations on the willingness of people to donate. For example it appears, contrary to what one might expect based on a simple classical economic model of human behaviour, that paying for blood donations can reduce the willingness of many people to give their blood – and in particular, to give blood without payment.[1] The studies that show that more parents will pick their children up late from day care if there is a financial penalty for doing so – because they perceive themselves as paying for a service, rather than breaking a social norm – cast significant doubt on the use of financial penalties in some other contexts. Many studies show that making it easier for people to comply with bail conditions (for example, sending texts to remind them of reporting obligations and court dates) has a large impact on compliance.[2] Predictions about how people will behave if the law changes are more likely to miscue if they are made without taking into account the work done over the last few decades on how humans actually make decisions.

The central lesson that behavioural economics provides is that we should be cautious about any overly deterministic abstract model of human behaviour. People are much more complicated and much less predictable than most models assume, and their behaviour changes (or fails to change) in ways that are often difficult to predict in advance. So perhaps the most important question in this context is whether your theory of change has been tested in the real, complex, messy world. If so, how did that go? You can be much more confident in your theory of change if it has been tested, and has worked in practice. There are two main ways in which a theory of change can be tested in practice: by looking to experience in other societies, and by conducting trials or pilots in your own society.

Has this been Tried Elsewhere?

It is common for proponents of law changes to point to other countries (or states, or cities) as precedents for their proposed change. Look, they say, this has been done elsewhere – we should follow their example.

Comparative analysis forms an important part of any well-run legal design process. Legal designers look to the laws of other similar societies to see if what has been proposed has been done somewhere else. If it has, that is seen as providing both a level of comfort about the proposal, and a useful model for how to implement a change of that kind.

It makes good sense to avoid reinventing the wheel if it has already been invented successfully elsewhere. In particular, if there is a relevant international model or a clear trend towards a particular model in similar societies, legal designers can and should take that model as their starting point. Adopting a proven international model greatly simplifies the legal design process. It also facilitates cross-border dealings and governmental cooperation. In the regulatory sphere, it can significantly reduce barriers to trade. The OECD recommends that members should, 'in developing regulatory measures, give consideration to all relevant international standards and frameworks for co-operation in the same field and, where appropriate, their likely effects on parties outside the jurisdiction'.[3]

Two Critical Questions

However I am constantly surprised by how frequently legal designers who look to legislation in another country as a model for their own reforms fail to go on to ask two critical questions:

a.   If this has been done elsewhere, was it a success there? How do we know?
b.   If it was successful there, will that success translate into our setting?

The mere fact that something has been tried elsewhere tells us almost nothing. It suggests that other societies saw the initiative as worth trying – but it may have been a failure, perhaps even a spectacular failure. The French proponents of the window tax could point to England as a precedent, and probably did just that. But the result was replication of a flawed and in many ways harmful innovation.

In an ideal situation you will have two societies (A and B) that are similar on all relevant dimensions, that start with identical laws and institutions, with society A changing its law in the very respect that you – an adviser in society B – are now considering. Time passes. Nothing important changes as between the two societies on any other dimension. Society A conducts a rigorous evaluation of the effect of the change. That evaluation is able to identify the impact of the change after allowing for all other relevant factors, and identify whether or not it was a success. Unfortunately, in more than 30 years of legal design work I have never yet had this ideal experience. There are always confounding factors, and there is usually only limited (and frequently, contested) information about the impact of the reform in society A.

In some countries the constitutional division of law-making responsibility between different levels of government facilitates natural experiments in which one jurisdiction tries something, and other similar jurisdictions can watch and learn. The famous American legal scholar and Supreme Court Justice Louis Brandeis observed in one of his opinions that: '[i]t is one of the happy incidents of the federal system that a single courageous state may, if its citizens choose, serve as a laboratory; and try novel social and economic experiments without risk to the rest of the country'.[4] Indeed the diversity of solutions at state and city level produced by the normal political process will often result in natural experiments that test the outcomes of different legal frameworks without the need for the explicitly experimental courage that Brandeis referred to. But an experiment is worthless unless we can track its outcomes – and understand what other factors may be influencing the outcomes we observed. It is often difficult, if not impossible, to identify the other factors in play that produced the observed result. And even more difficult, in many cases, to understand whether there are relevant differences between the social, economic or institutional environments of the other jurisdiction and our jurisdiction that cast doubt on whether the experience in one will translate to the other. Which takes us back to the two questions identified above.

How does the Law Operate Elsewhere? Is it a Success?

The first question that needs to be asked is how the proposed law operates in the other society. Sometimes it is possible to get some basic information about how the law works – the volumes of decisions made, and the experience to date in terms of outcomes, time frames and costs. Surprisingly often, even this level of information is not available. Where it is available, basic information of this kind can be helpful. Comparisons with other similar societies can be helpful for ruling out extreme predictions made by some stakeholders: if the sky has not fallen when the law was changed in this way in society A, it is unlikely to fall when the law is changed in the same way in (similar) society B.

But in many cases a change will be too recent, or no data will have been gathered, or other changes in the social context or in the law at around the same time make it impossible to disentangle the effect of the law change from other factors. We need to be careful about adopting an oversimplified narrative in which change X occurred, some good things happened, so change X must have caused those good things. Or, of course, vice versa. It is rare to have good quality evidence about the outcomes of law changes in the other societies that are identified as precedents for a proposed reform.

Sometimes – and I emphasise, sometimes – quantitative analysis can help us to disentangle the effect of the reform in society A from the effect of other factors. I never cease to be amazed by how often meaningless statistics are bandied about to support – or oppose – proposed reforms. A basic level of rigour is essential if a study is to be anything more than a quantitative anecdote. And even the most sophisticated quantitative studies are not magic bullets. The confidence with which we can rely on the results of such studies depends on the quality of the data and the appropriateness of the model used to analyse it. Remember the aphorism that all models are wrong, but some models are useful. Is the model deployed in the quantitative study useful for the purpose for which you are seeking to rely on it? There is abundant room for disagreement about the design of such studies, and about the inferences that can reliably be drawn from them, just as there is in relation to qualitative studies. Legal designers should pay careful attention to analysis of this kind, especially where there is an extensive literature that reaches consistent results over an extended time frame. But they should not be overawed by the apparent precision of quantitative methods.

Will Success Elsewhere Translate into Your Society?

The second question is whether the law's success in the other society will translate into your own society. The greater the social and institutional differences between the two societies, the less confident we can be about that prospect.

The single factor that has the greatest bearing on how a legal regime translates from one society to another is, in my experience, differences in the institutions responsible for administering the law. We have already seen the huge difference between how virtually identical contract laws operate in Bangladesh and New Zealand. The institutional differences in that case were stark. But even quite modest differences in institutional capacity, resources and culture can produce very different outcomes. This is an especially important factor to bear in mind when asking if success elsewhere will translate into success in your society.

Summary: Precedents are Useful but Caution is Needed

In almost every law reform exercise in which I have been involved, an understanding of how the issue is tackled elsewhere has played an important role in identifying the range of available approaches and in understanding, at a basic level, how those approaches might play out. The same concerns that we have about a proposal will often have been identified elsewhere. The approaches others have adopted to address those concerns are at the least a source of ideas to consider as we design our law, and in some cases we will be able to observe how those approaches have worked in practice. Where difficulties have been encountered elsewhere, we can learn from them, and avoid repeating the same mistakes.

So we should always look to the experience of other comparable societies which have laws similar to what is proposed for our society. We should always try to gather as much information as possible about the operation of the relevant law in those other societies. If a particular model has been widely adopted in similar societies, that in itself provides some comfort that it has been seen as success-ful. And as noted above, there are significant advantages in adopting international standards and frameworks. But we should remain clear about what we can, and cannot, reliably conclude based on the experience of other societies. We should avoid substituting the easy but largely irrelevant question (is there a precedent for what we are proposing?) for the much harder questions that actually matter: if something similar has been done elsewhere, was it a success? How confident can we be that this success would translate into the social and institutional setting of our society? What would we need to do to make it work here? Are we both able and willing to do this? Our answers to these questions are critical factors in decid-ing whether following a precedent from elsewhere is likely to contribute to the desired policy outcomes.

Is a Trial/Pilot an Option?

The best way to test the likely impact of a law change in our own society is to try it. Not in the traditional way – change the law for the entire society, then argue incon-clusively and at great length about whether or not that made a difference – but as a controlled experiment in which the law change applies to a representative subset of the population, but not to others. If this is feasible, it is far and away the most effective method to obtain genuine insight into the likely consequences of a law change, as Philip Tetlock reminds us in the passage quoted in chapter three above.

Sometimes there will be ethical objections to this approach – obviously we can't just decide to send a randomly selected group of people to prison for twice as long as the control group, and see how that plays out. But often there are several different reasonable ways to tackle an issue: a trial of a possible new approach while maintaining the status quo for everybody else may be both morally accept-able and practically workable.

There is a small but growing body of high-quality trials of policy proposals in a handful of countries around the world. There is an entire movement – sometimes referred to as the 'what works' movement – focused on evidence-based policy design.[5] Evidence that an initiative has been tried elsewhere and has worked in practice is always valuable. Conversely, if an initiative has been trialled elsewhere and has failed to achieve its goals, that makes a pretty compelling case against repeating that failure. Their experience may also shed light on what went wrong, and on how our proposal might be modified to avoid the same pitfalls.

And as we saw earlier, in some contexts we can learn from a 'natural experiment' where the proposal that we are considering has been implemented in another society that is similar to ours on relevant dimensions.

But no two societies are identical, and there are limits on what we can infer from even the best controlled experiments that have been conducted in different social and institutional settings. The 'gold standard' for testing the effect of a law change is a randomised controlled trial in our own society, administered by the same institutions that would administer any wider roll-out of the proposed reform.[6]

Where the outcome of a law change is uncertain, and there are no directly comparable natural experiments to look to, legal designers should consider the possibility of a trial of that law change. A small scale trial is much less costly than wholesale change. A trial is much easier to abandon or modify if it is not successful – both because of its scale, and because it is explicitly labelled as a trial so fewer expectations are engendered and less face is lost if it is abandoned. It is still rare to see trials of initiatives involving law changes, for a mix of practical reasons and reasons of principle. But where the likely outcome of proposed legislation is difficult to assess, and there are no conclusive objections to adopting different approaches for different people for a limited time, more thought should be given to the potential for a trial that enables an initiative to be tested, assessed and rolled out more widely if and only if it is a success.

It may be possible to conduct a trial without the need for specific legislative authority. In some contexts, the existing law is sufficiently flexible to enable the agency that administers that law to make rules, or grant exemptions, in order to test alternative mechanisms for giving effect to the law's core objectives. So for example a securities market regulator may be able to make rules that permit use of novel products, services and market structures, with a view to informing future rule changes.[7]

In other cases, a proposed trial will be inconsistent with the existing law and legislative authority will be needed for that trial. The practical realities of the legislative process will usually preclude legislating for a trial, then seeking further legislation if the trial is successful. There may be space in the legislative programme for one legislative vehicle, but not for two in short succession. But that is not fatal to the use of trials. One option to enable both trials and subsequent roll-outs is to introduce a new, more flexible law that delegates rule-making to the executive or an agency. The rule-maker can then make rules that permit trials, and modify the generally applicable rules in light of those trials if they are successful.

Another option may be to develop a law that provides for both a trial and a full roll-out, with flexibility for the executive to design and implement the trial and to authorise a full roll-out. If the decision to roll the initiative out more widely is seen as requiring the approval of the legislature rather than the executive, options for seeking legislative approval that fall short of going through the complete legislative process may be available in some systems. Thus for example the law might provide for an executive decision to proceed with a roll-out to be tabled in the legislature, and be subject to disallowance by resolution; or to require approval by resolution. Conversely the legislation could mandate a general roll-out by a specified date unless the executive recommends not proceeding, based on the trial results, and that recommendation is approved (or is not disapproved) by the legislature.

Different legal frameworks in different settings will require different approaches. But it seems hard to argue that it is always (or even generally) better to apply an untried and potentially ineffective initiative to an entire society than it is to run a trial of that initiative that affects only some members of that society. In some contexts, one or more trials will make good sense. Ideally randomised controlled trials; but if that is unworkable it may still be better to run a trial on some other basis (for example, a pilot in one city or region), before proceeding with broader implementation.

In other contexts, trials may be ethically dubious, unworkable in practice, or politically infeasible. There will be no directly relevant natural experiments to draw on. Even if a trial has been conducted, it may prove inconclusive, or the potential for a successful trial or pilot to scale up to an entire society may be uncertain. For any or all of these reasons, we may well be left unsure about whether, and how, the behaviour of key actors will change. Assessing the significance of that risk is an important, and often overlooked, component of a well-managed law reform project.

Assessing the Risk of Failure to Achieve the Desired Change

Having developed a theory of change, the next step is to assess the risk that the world will not conform to that theory. How confident can you be – based on experience elsewhere, or on trials or pilots in your own society, or on appropriate models of human behaviour – that things will go as planned? Is there a risk that the legislation will not deliver (much) change at all – that it will be a damp squib? Is there a risk that some decision-makers will act in ways which lead to an over-shoot? Is there a risk that some decision-makers will act in ways that lead to nasty surprises, or backfires? What can be done to address those risks?

There are a number of ways to tackle this question. My preferred approach is to begin with the different ways in which legislation can fail, and consider which are the most likely causes of your project failing, and what can be done to avoid the risk of each of those different forms of failure. This is a form of 'pre-mortem': an exercise I describe in more detail below.

It can be difficult for people who are close to a project to identify risks of failure. People are usually over-confident and over-optimistic about their plans.

They often do not have all the information needed to identify what could go wrong in practice with their elegant scheme. And they are not sufficiently alive to this lack of information, and its implications – remember Daniel Kahneman's 'What You See Is All There Is!' This is another stage in the law-making process at which consultation with stakeholders is essential. Proposals should be exposed to the critical scrutiny of the people who will be affected. Formal consultation processes – 'discussion papers' outlining policies; consultation drafts; the US 'notice and comment' regime for making rules under certain federal statutes – all serve to gather dispersed knowledge about the ways in which a proposal could go wrong, and to identify what might be done to avoid that outcome.[8]

Formal processes of this kind should be coupled with proactive informal engagement with a range of stakeholders, including interviews along the lines discussed in chapter six above. Interviews of that kind are especially important to ensure that you are aware of the likely impact of the proposed law on groups that are not well served by the existing law due to information and resource constraints. Those groups are often best placed to understand the practical impact of the proposed changes. But they are also less likely to engage with formal consultation processes. So more effort needs to be put into seeking out the information and views that they can contribute to the law-making process. The benefits checklist and the compliance checklist set out in chapters eighteen to nineteen below underscore the critical importance of such engagement.

A Pre-Mortem for the Legislation

A time traveller returns from the near future, say five years hence, and tells you that unfortunately your legislative project has failed. How will it have failed? Is it possible that the legislation turned out to be a damp squib? And if so, why might that have happened? As we saw in chapter two, common causes of the 'damp squib' variety of failure include:

- Lack of awareness/understanding of the legislation on the part of those to whom it is addressed – the public and/or relevant institutions.
- The people who are intended to benefit from the legislation lacking the resources, knowledge and skills to be able to invoke the law in practice.
- Relevant institutions lacking the capacity to implement the law, or the will to do so.
- Social beliefs and practices that are inconsistent with the outcomes the law seeks to bring about.
- The gains from non-compliance exceeding the expected cost of sanctions: so not complying with the law is a rational strategy.

Few if any projects are immune from these risks. Spend some time working out which ones loom largest for your legislative project: which ones the returning time traveller is most likely to identify as the icebergs that sank your proposal.

If there are good reasons to expect the proposed law to change behaviour in a way that is consistent with the goals of the reform, and avoid the peril of being a damp squib, then we can move on to the next stage of the pre-mortem and consider the other ways in which laws fail – overshoots, nasty surprises and backfires. Is it possible that the time traveller will tell you that the law has failed in one or more of these ways? If so, how will that have come about – what are the factors that could lead to these outcomes? As we saw above, common causes of overshoots, nasty surprises and backfires include:

- Failing to pay sufficient attention to the long-run incentives created by the law – for example, the window tax, the Mexico City carless days scheme, grandparenting existing vehicles or factories when adopting new pollution standards, and the cobra effect more generally.

- Failing to pay sufficient attention to institutional arrangements, and the capacity of the relevant institutions to implement the law – for example, the newly established child support agency that lacks the personnel and IT systems needed to implement ambitious child support legislation; the building regulators who lack the skills and resources to implement a performance-based regulatory scheme; or the competition regulator that lacks the necessary expertise to make the law work as intended, but which misuses its merger-blocking powers for other purposes.

Once you have identified the most likely causes of failures in the context of your project, you can move on to consider how best to reduce the risk of such failures. Some options for managing those risks are discussed in chapters eleven to fifteen below.

---

[1] Michael J Sandel, *What Money Can't Buy: The Moral Limits of Markets* (London, Penguin Books Ltd, 2013) 119 ff.

[2] Brice Cooke et al, 'Using Behavioral Science to Improve Criminal Justice Outcomes: Preventing Failures to Appear in Court' (University of Chicago Crime Lab / ideas42, January 2018).

[3] See OECD, Recommendation of the Council on Regulatory Policy and Governance 2012, Recommendation 12.

[4] *New State Ice Co v Liebmann* 285 US 262, 311 (1932) (Brandeis J dissenting).

[5] Ron Haskins and Greg Margolis, *Show Me the Evidence: Obama's Fight for Rigor and Results in Social Policy* (Washington DC, Brookings Institution Press, 2015); Michael Howlett, *Designing Public Policies*, 2nd edn (Abingdon, Routledge, 2019) 64–66.

[6] See Cass R Sunstein, *Simpler: The Future of Government* (New York, Simon & Schuster, 2013) 186–89.

[7] An approach that is sometimes referred to as a 'regulatory sandbox'. For an overview of the regulatory sandbox operated by the United Kingdom Financial Conduct Authority, see: www.fca.org.uk/firms/innovation/regulatory-sandbox.

[8] For an insightful discussion of the origins and value of notice and comment rule-making, see Cass R Sunstein, *The Cost–Benefit Revolution* (Cambridge, MA, MIT Press, 2018) esp 83–91.

11

Adaptive Legislation

The Need for Adaptive Legislation

Legislation is not inscribed in stone forever. Laws can be amended or repealed. But the process of making new laws, especially in national legislatures, is often complex and slow. Legislative agendas are crowded – a law-making body has only finite time, and typically has many issues clamouring for its attention. And law-making should not be rushed, if it is to be done well and with appropriate public participation. It is not realistic to expect lawmakers to engage in a constant process of fine-tuning legislation as and when issues arise. If there is a significant change of policy direction – new goals, or significant changes in how those goals are pursued – then that can and should be dealt with by the legislator. Basic constitutional and democratic principles require decisions of that kind to be made by the legislator with the legitimacy to make, and political accountability for, those decisions. But in many cases, a legislative scheme will require more modest adjustments from time to time in order to achieve its existing goals. For all the reasons explored above, we should expect this to happen quite often.

The greater the uncertainty about the way in which the law will play out, and the longer the period for which the law is expected to operate (for most laws, there is no expiry date), the more likely it is that adjustments will be required.[1] If it is necessary to go back to the legislator to achieve this, however, then it may take a very long time to make those adjustments – or they may not happen at all. Meanwhile, the legislation will not be advancing its goals as effectively as it could be. What are the alternatives?

Fortunately there are many ways of building into legislation mechanisms for adapting the way it operates as information becomes available about how it is working in practice, and as the environment in which it operates changes: *adaptive legislation*. I describe some of the more important forms of adaptive legislation below. These approaches make it possible for the legislative scheme to be adjusted over time. But they do not guarantee that those adjustments will happen, or that they will succeed. That requires monitoring, and review against the policy goals of the legislation. I will come back to that later.

Uncertainty about the Status Quo

The first question to ask yourself in this context is whether there is a real risk that the project has not been able to gather comprehensive and accurate information about the current position. Have all stakeholders been able to contribute their perspectives on the issue? Have all available sources of relevant information been tapped? Are there significant gaps in the available information that it has not been possible to fill?

The less time and resource you have been able to commit to developing a detailed map of the status quo, the greater the risk that the proposed legislation has been developed on the basis of incomplete or inaccurate information about how people currently behave, and about the drivers of that behaviour. And the greater the likelihood of relevant information about the status quo emerging down the track, after the legislation has been adopted. The more significant this risk, the more important it will be to ensure that the legislation incorporates mechanisms for continuing to gather relevant information about the status quo, and for adapting to reflect that information.

Thus the less we know about the status quo, the more essential it is that any legislation be adaptive. In practice, as discussed below, this is likely to require the legislation to be framed in terms of goals to be pursued, or principles or standards that must be complied with, rather than detailed prescriptions. Detailed provisions in primary legislation about processes to be followed, or tests to be applied, are difficult to modify if it becomes apparent that they are problematic. The more likely it is that adjustment will be needed, the more desirable it becomes to exclude details of this kind from the primary legislation. Rather, that legislation should be confined to setting goals for decision-makers to pursue, standards that the relevant actors must comply with, or some combination of these. This approach to primary legislation can be coupled with a number of different mechanisms for filling in the details – for example, in delegated legislation – as discussed in more detail below.

Where some form of adaptive legislation is adopted, it is especially important to ensure that there are institutions that are capable of gathering additional background information over time, and assessing the implications of that information, to enable the adaptive process to work in practice. The decision map for the proposed legislation should include this information-gathering function, and identify which institution(s) will be responsible for that role and how their work will translate into adaptations to the legal framework.

Uncertainty about the Effectiveness of the Legislation Over Time

It is normal, indeed inevitable, for there to be some uncertainty about the likely effectiveness of proposed legislation. But the degree of uncertainty will vary from project to project. How much do you know about the likelihood that the legislation will produce the desired changes in behaviour over time? If there have been successful trials in your own society, or if the legislation follows a widely adopted and successful international model, the risk of not achieving the desired outcomes may be modest (it will never be zero, if only because of social factors and institutional arrangements which can change over time). At the other end of the spectrum, if the legislation is a rushed response to a crisis, is novel, and has not been tested in any way, then the risk of a damp squib or of nasty surprises is much higher. The risk of failure is also higher where the legislation will operate in a field where there is likely to be significant social or economic change during the life of the legislation – it is much more difficult to aim at a moving target.

The less we know about the mechanisms by which the legislation is expected to produce the desired outcomes, and the less we know about the likelihood of that happening, the more important it is to have institutional arrangements in place for regular review of the effectiveness of the legislation. And for adapting the legal framework in light of the feedback from that process.

In this context also, high levels of uncertainty are best managed by ensuring that primary legislation is framed in terms of goals for decision-makers and/or obligations expressed in terms of principles or standards. These approaches ensure that the implementation of the legislation can be adapted to take into account new information about its practical operation. Again, these approaches can be coupled with various mechanisms for filling in the details.

The greater the level of uncertainty about the effectiveness of the legislation to achieve its goals, the more important it is to ensure that there are institutions that are capable of monitoring outcomes over time, and assessing the implications of that information, to enable the adaptive process to work in practice. The decision map for the proposed legislation should include this monitoring function, and identify which institution(s) will be responsible for that role and how their work will translate into adaptations to the legal framework.

The Implications of Changing Technology

If there is one constant in the law-making environment today, it is the fast pace of technological change. This presents both opportunities and challenges. You should identify foreseeable changes in relevant technology, and consider the implications of those changes for your project. You should strive to avoid framing legislation in ways that are tied to (or that assume) particular technologies: rather, legislation should wherever possible be designed to be technology neutral. That approach reduces the risk of failure as a result of changes in technology that render the legislation irrelevant, and maximises the scope for taking advantage of new technologies in the implementation of the legislation. The implications of technological change are discussed in more detail in chapter twelve below.

Designing Adaptive Legislation

That brings us on to the practical question of how laws can be framed to adapt to take into account additional information about the environment in which those laws operate, about changes in that environment, and about how the law is operating. What does adaptive legislation look like in practice?

Delegated Rule-Making

One common form of adaptive legislation is to set out the core of the legislative scheme in the primary legislation, and delegate the making of more detailed rules to the executive or to an executive agency. Those detailed rules can then be modified from time to time by their maker. There may be one or more layers of delegated rule-making. In New Zealand, for example, some primary legislation provides for regulations to be issued by the executive government and for rules to be issued by a specified minister or agency or official.[2]

The rationale for a legislative structure which provides for rule-making often focuses on the level of detail required in the rules, and the impracticality of the primary lawmaker engaging with that level of detail. But this approach also has the significant advantage of accommodating the need to review the details of the workings of the scheme over time, and adapt it in light of new information, unexpected challenges and changing circumstances.

There are variations on the delegated rule-making theme. The primary legislation may impose general obligations which are themselves enforceable, and provide for rules to be made that clarify what people must do in order to comply with those general requirements, or that prescribe processes to be followed (for example, to obtain permits, or to verify compliance, or to apply for some benefit). I give some examples of the various ways in which that can be done below. Alternatively, the primary legislation may not itself contain any directly enforceable obligations. Instead, it imposes an obligation to comply with rules made by the executive, or by an executive agency, and prescribes the goals that the rule-maker must seek to achieve through those rules. Many significant US regulatory regimes take this form.[3]

In some countries, including New Zealand, concerns are often raised about the overuse of delegated legislation. There is a particular sensitivity to delegating the ability to modify the scope of application of primary legislation, for example by providing for the executive to make rules granting broad exemptions from that legislation, or rules which modify core substantive requirements. This is driven by an understandable concern about the constitutional implications of leaving matters of substance to the executive. But the reality is that this ship has already sailed: legislatures in New Zealand and other similarly situated countries have consistently enacted broad statutory powers which allow for delegated policymaking, and that delegated legislation has consistently been used to deal with matters of substantive policy. It is unlikely that this will change any time soon, particularly given the demands on parliamentary time. Nor should it: if we are modest about our ability to predict the future, and realistic about the prospect of needing to adjust laws to reflect new information and changing circumstances over time, the ability to adapt the operation of primary legislation through use of delegated legislation is a crucial tool. The answer to concerns about the appropriateness of delegated legislation is not to curb its use; rather, the answer is to provide adequate accountability mechanisms to ensure that the executive does not abuse its powers.

In saying this, I am not advocating the uncritical and widespread use of so-called 'Henry VIII clauses', which give the executive a broad power to make rules which prevail over primary legislation. Powers of this kind can raise significant concerns in terms of constitutional legitimacy and accountability. A power to make rules under a particular statute should normally be confined to fleshing out general provisions in that statute, and should not extend to modifying the substantive policy of the statute. A power to make rules that modify matters of detail in the primary legislation is less problematic – but calls into question the desirability of putting those matters of detail in the primary legislation in the first place. It is especially problematic to confer powers under one statute to make substantive modifications to other statutes: where trade-offs must be made between different legislative schemes, it should generally be the legislator that makes that decision.[4] The broader the delegation of power, the clearer the justification for that delegation needs to be.

Legislating Principles

Another common form of adaptive legislation is to express the law in general terms – setting standards or principles that must be complied with by the relevant actors, rather than detailed rules. The agencies responsible for administering the law, and the courts, are left to work out the implications of those principles over time. That approach can also accommodate changes in circumstances: the principles will be applied to the circumstances as they exist from time to time.

However this approach provides much less guidance to people affected by the law. That uncertainty comes at a cost in terms of ease of access to the law, and ease of compliance with the law. The significance of that cost is very dependent on the circumstances: how widely the law applies, how frequently it must be applied, and the sophistication and resources of the people to whom it applies. The more frequently the law has to be applied, and the wider the range of people affected, the less satisfactory a principles-only approach is likely to be. Where a law applies to many people of limited means – for example, laws on division of property by a couple following separation – legislating at a level of principle, without any mechanism to fill in the detail, virtually guarantees failure measured by reference to outcomes for the people affected by the law. The cost of arguing about what a principle such as 'fair division' means, and the inevitable variation in how different judges will answer that question if it comes before them, will mean that access to the law is too slow and too costly for a very large percentage of the population. A just principle on paper will translate into widespread injustice in practice.

The difficulties caused by legislating at a level of principle can be mitigated in a number of ways. The choice between these options should be driven primarily by a careful analysis of the practical implications of each option, having regard to the frequency with which the issue will arise; the time and cost involved in invoking and applying the law; the acceptability (and practical implications for the way the process operates) of significant variations in outcomes; and whether there are certain types of error that are less acceptable than others.[5]

Some Hybrids

There are also many hybrid approaches that combine standards and rules in different ways. One option is for the primary legislation to be expressed at a level of principle, coupled with delegated legislation in the form of rules specifying a 'safe harbour' for compliance. So for example consumer credit legislation could require that the break fee payable under a consumer credit contract for early repayment of a debt must be set out in the loan agreement, and must be 'reasonable'. The legislation could then go on to provide that the executive, or a regulatory agency, can issue rules that specify an approved method for calculating a reasonable break fee. If the break fee is calculated in accordance with those rules, it is deemed to be reasonable: that is, it is deemed to comply with the relevant principle. A structure of this kind makes it easier for lenders who want to comply with the law to do so by choosing to adopt the pre-approved safe harbour approach; makes it easier for many debtors to obtain advice on whether the provision in their loan agreement is reasonable and thus enforceable; enables the safe harbour provision to be modified with relative ease if market practices change in a way that makes the detailed rules in that provision less relevant or less appropriate; and still leaves room for innovation, by permitting lenders to adopt different approaches that can be shown to be reasonable.[6]

Hybrid approaches of this kind are especially important where, consistent with modern trends, regulatory regimes focus on performance standards rather than design standards. For many years the laws governing construction of buildings in New Zealand, as in many other countries, set detailed requirements for the designs, materials and construction techniques that could be used. This approach stifled innovation, and increased the cost of building homes and other buildings. As I mentioned earlier, reforms in the early 1990s replaced this prescriptive approach with performance-based regulation. In addition to providing for a building code that would set out the relevant performance standards that a new building must meet, the legislation contemplated the issue of 'acceptable solutions' – detailed specifications for ways of achieving compliance with the building standards. These operated as safe harbours: if the building complied with an acceptable solution issued in relation to a standard, then it complied with that standard. This is an increasingly common regulatory model internationally.

There are many other hybrid approaches that combine generally applicable standards or principles with delegated rule-making, or authoritative application of those principles in a particular case. Consider the following approaches to a law setting requirements for the habitability of rental accommodation:

a.   The legislation prescribes a broad standard: the dwelling must be reasonably habitable. Landlords and tenants need to work out what this requires on various dimensions – structural soundness, weathertightness, plumbing, sanitary fixtures, services, cooking facilities, washing facilities and so on.

b.   The legislation prescribes a broad standard and also provides a 'safe harbour': the dwelling must be reasonably habitable, and is deemed to comply with this requirement if it meets more specific requirements set out in the legislation or in rules issued by a regulator. This approach provides landlords with more predictability about what they must do to comply, and tenants with more predictability about what they are entitled to. But it may give rise to a risk of failing to achieve the policy goal if some feature (or combination of features) of a dwelling that are not addressed in the detailed requirements mean it is not reasonably habitable. That risk is greater if the detailed rules are set out in the primary legislation and cannot be replaced or supplemented with rules made by a regulator as new information is obtained, and as circumstances change.

c.   The legislation prescribes a broad standard coupled with minimum requirements: the dwelling must meet certain specific requirements set out in primary or secondary legislation, and must also comply with the broad 'reasonably habitable' standard. This gives landlords greater predictability about what they must do to comply, and tenants more predictability about what they are entitled to. It retains the ability to deal with unanticipated issues by identifying further requirements that must be met for some or all types of dwelling to be reasonably habitable. But the flip side of retaining this flexibility is that any incremental requirements are less predictable for all concerned, and give rise to greater complexity if they are invoked at the enforcement stage. The more territory that is covered by detailed rules, the less significant this 'residual complexity' concern becomes.

d.   The legislation prescribes a broad standard, and provides for a regulator to issue guidance: the dwelling must comply with the broad 'reasonably habitable' standard, and a regulator is authorised to issue guidance on what this requires in practice. If the guidance is given authoritative force, then this looks like option (c). If the guidance has no authoritative force, and is given little or no weight when the law is applied in particular cases, this approach looks more like option (a) but with the costs of seeking advice reduced somewhat for both landlords and tenants. If the guidance is given some weight in deciding what the standard requires – failure to comply with the guidance is likely to be seen as a breach, and compliance with the guidance is likely to be seen as meeting the standard – then you end up somewhere in between.

e.   The legislation prescribes a broad standard, and provides for the regulator to issue binding rulings in advance about whether a specific dwelling meets those requirements, or (if not) what needs to be done to bring it into compliance. The ruling provides guidance and certainty to the landlord and the tenant in that dwelling. But inspecting individual dwellings is likely to be costly. Depending on the cost, and who is required to bear it, there is a risk that few rulings will be sought in practice;

f.   The legislation prescribes a broad standard, and requires each landlord to obtain a licence (or permit) from a regulator before letting a dwelling. The licence translates the broad standard into specific requirements tailored to that dwelling. This approach provides a high level of certainty for landlords and tenants. But the cost involved in licensing each and every dwelling seems likely to be prohibitive. An approach of this kind, in which broad standards are translated into specific requirements for each affected person, is more likely to be workable in other contexts where there are fewer licensees (for example, under a regime for licensing banks and other financial institutions).

g.   The legislation prescribes a broad standard, and requires each landlord to submit a 'compliance plan' detailing how they will meet that standard in relation to particular dwellings. The plans, or a subset of them, are audited by the regulator. As with the licensing approach described above, the compliance plan translates the broad standard into specific requirements tailored to each dwelling. The costs incurred by the regulator are reduced, and there is likely to be more scope for flexibility and innovation. But landlords incur the cost of preparing a compliance plan, and have less certainty as they may discover after the event that their compliance plans do not meet the broad standard, so they are in breach of their obligations. The entitlements of tenants will be less clear, as in some cases it will be necessary to look beyond the compliance plan to the underlying standard. And (depending on the frequency of audits) there is a greater risk that the policy of the law will not be achieved;

h.   The legislation provides for a regulator to issue rules setting out specific requirements designed to ensure that a dwelling is reasonably habitable, with a direction to the agency to keep the rules under review to ensure that they continue to achieve this goal. The legislation requires landlords to comply with the rules, but does not itself prescribe any substantive requirements. This approach achieves a high level of predictability for both landlords and tenants at any given time. It is a form of adaptive legislation: new rules can be issued as new information is obtained, or as circumstances change. This approach risks failing to give effect to the policy behind the law if the detailed rules are out of step with that policy – if they do not go far enough, or go too far and overshoot. But they can be brought back into line with the policy prospectively.

i.   Detailed requirements are set out in the primary legislation. This approach provides a high level of predictability for all audiences. It reduces dependence on a regulator when it comes to formulating detailed requirements. But it risks failing to give effect to the underlying policy if those detailed requirements fail to take account of relevant factors, or if circumstances change.

j.   Detailed requirements are set out in the primary legislation, as with approach (i). The regulator is given a power to grant exemptions from those detailed requirements where the dwelling meets a broad standard of habitability despite not meeting one or more of those detailed requirements. This approach provides a high level of predictability for all audiences, while reducing somewhat the rigidity of approach (i). How different this is from approach (i) will depend significantly on the cost and time involved in seeking an exemption, and who bears that cost, among other factors.

Many of these options on this spectrum (all but (a) and (i)) are hybrid approaches that combine standards and rules. The choice between these options will affect how complex the law is in practice for its users. And it will affect the extent to which the underlying policy is likely to be achieved. But – to echo my refrain once again – this will depend as much on the relevant institutions as it will on what the law says on paper.

There are other ways in which hybrid approaches combining standards and rules can be incorporated in primary legislation. For example, rather than simply setting out a broad principle to be applied in all cases, the legislation can set a bright-line rule coupled with a 'safety valve' where applying that rule would be inconsistent with the policy goals of the legislation. This is how the law in relation to division of a couple's property following separation is structured in New Zealand and in many other countries. The law provides for equal division of property acquired during the relationship. But it also provides for departure from equal division in certain specific cases (for example, if one partner has deliberately destroyed property) and gives the court a general discretion to depart from equal division if that would result in a serious injustice. The higher the threshold for applying the 'safety valve' provision, the stickier the default rule – and the smaller the number of cases in which parties need to go beyond the bright-line rule and consider the implications of the broad principle for their case. This approach makes the law simpler to understand and apply, reducing complexity and cost for many users, while still preserving flexibility to deal with hard cases in a principled way. It is especially useful where there will be a significant number of cases, or multiple decision-makers (and a resulting risk of inconsistency and unpredictability in applying a broad standard), or where end users have limited resources and cannot be expected to engage in an open-textured process involving significant costs, or where speed of decision-making is important.

In some law reform projects in which I have been involved, it has been suggested that legislation expressed in terms of broad standards is workable, indeed desirable, because it couples initial flexibility with the ability to obtain more concrete guidance over time from decisions of regulators or courts in particular cases. We can learn from experience. That is true to some extent, in some fields. But significant time may pass before a useful body of guidance develops. The nature and value of that guidance will depend on what cases happen to come before the relevant decision-maker. If the decision-maker is a regulator, then the extent to which previous decisions provide useful precedents may be limited – especially if the regulator does not issue public reasoned decisions. If the decision-maker we are relying on to provide guidance in the future is a court, then there are other concerns. Courts are not generally well placed to determine policy issues involving multiple factors and multiple interests.[7] The parties usually do not have the resources – or, often, the incentive – to put all relevant considerations and all relevant evidence before the court. Other people and groups who are affected by the outcome may not be entitled to participate in the court hearing: so their voices are not heard, and the additional information they could contribute is not taken into account. The court may not have the institutional expertise to make what is in effect a forward-looking policy choice. Courts in most countries cannot limit their decisions on what the law requires to apply prospectively only, or allow for a transition period. And the resulting court decisions are unlikely to be as accessible as the legislation itself. Lawmakers should not see the potential development of a body of precedent applying a legislative standard as a panacea for a lack of predictability in the application of such standards.

The choice between the many possible approaches to combining standards and rules depends on context. It depends on identifying the audiences to whom the legislation is addressed, and the implications of the different approaches for the behaviour of those audiences. It is necessary to consider, in context, the benefits of each approach – and in particular, how it will contribute to achieving the policy goals of the legislation – and the costs of that approach. Careful attention needs to be paid to institutional arrangements for each approach in order to predict both likely benefits and likely costs.

Express Provision for Reviews?

In some countries, it is becoming more common for laws to provide that their operation must be reviewed after a prescribed interval that is long enough to gather meaningful experience of its operation. So for example New Zealand's legislation providing for compliance with legal requirements for writing and signatures using electronic means contained a list of exceptions, and provided for a review of those exceptions within two years of the legislation coming into force.[8] Provisions of this kind should rarely be necessary if it is standard practice for laws to be actively monitored and kept under review by the agencies responsible for their operation: an approach that has been labelled 'regulatory stewardship'.[9] But where that is not the case, or where the legislator recognises that there is a high level of uncertainty about some aspect of a new scheme and wishes to ensure that a review focusing on that issue is prepared and published within a prescribed time frame, provisions of this kind can be useful.

Express Provision for Experiments?

In some contexts where different approaches are available and their effectiveness is uncertain, a trial will be the best way to figure out what will work. The importance of trials – and in particular, randomised controlled experiments – for reaching confident conclusions about the effect of different approaches was discussed in chapter ten above. It may be possible to implement a trial before making any changes to the law, to inform the law reform process. But if the trial involves applying the law differently to different groups, then legal authority will probably be needed for the trial itself.[10]

Suppose for example that the law imposes a substantial penalty for failing to file a tax return on time. A proposal is made that this should be replaced with a regime under which late filers receive a reminder that their return is overdue, and are told that if they file within the next 30 days the penalty will be waived. In some contexts, the tax agency will have sufficient flexibility in administering the law to conduct a trial of this proposal without the need for specific legal authority. In other contexts, it may be necessary to amend the law to provide the tax agency with the authority to waive the penalty, and to undertake a trial in which some people will be offered the waiver option while others will not.

If specific legal authority is needed for such a trial, the law could be amended for that limited purpose. But then it would be necessary for further legislation to be passed if the trial is successful, and the government decides to go ahead with rolling out the new approach. A more efficient approach would be to amend the legislation to provide more flexibility to the tax agency generally, so it can conduct the trial and – if successful – adopt this approach more widely. That approach will also enable other trials to be conducted in the future. If that approach is not seen as acceptable, another option may be to authorise the trial and also authorise, in the same law, rolling out the new approach if the trial confirms that it works. As discussed above, this can be done in a number of ways. The simplest is to include in the legislation provisions that would apply the new approach across the board, and give the executive the power to bring those provisions into effect if the executive is satisfied that it is desirable to do so having regard to the outcome of the trial.

The Need for a Baseline, and for Monitoring and Review

Whichever of these adaptive approaches is adopted, the best way to reduce the risk of the law failing in one or more of the ways identified in chapter two is to have a clear baseline and to measure outcomes.

The baseline should not present too many difficulties – if the current position has been mapped with reasonable accuracy, as contemplated in chapter six (and in item 1 of the checklist in chapter seventeen), that map of the status quo can serve as the baseline for evaluating the success of the legislation.

Monitoring and evaluation of outcomes pose a greater challenge. This isn't standard practice in most countries, for a mix of reasons.[11] As the UK House of Lords Constitution Committee observed in a report on the legislative process, 'Post-legislative scrutiny appears to be similar to motherhood and apple pie in that everyone appears to be in favour of it. However, unlike motherhood and apple pie, it is not much in evidence'.[12]

The most common reason for this gap is that resources are limited, and there are many other claims on those resources.[13] A focus on new projects tends to squeeze out monitoring and data gathering in relation to legislative projects that have been 'completed', in the sense that the legislation has been passed and has come into force. So the data needed for a meaningful evaluation often are not available. And the criteria for evaluation need to be clear, relevant and systematically applied: all too often the evaluation process falls victim to the same decision-making frailties that we observe in the initial legal design process.[14]

The result is that in most countries I am familiar with, there is no systematic monitoring and evaluation of the outcomes of legislation. Where ad hoc reviews are carried out, the process adopted and the criteria applied are of variable quality. There are three problems with this. First, without ongoing monitoring we will struggle to know if the law has in fact succeeded, or if it is failing in one or more ways. Second, we lose the opportunity to take steps to avoid or mitigate failure – for example, by making adjustments to the way the law is administered to respond to unexpected adverse outcomes. New Zealand's 2013 bail law change provides a good example of the sort of modest practical steps that can significantly reduce unexpected and undesired outcomes – in that case, a significant overshoot – if we have good information about what is happening on the ground. Third, we lose the opportunity to learn for the future, and improve our approach to design of new legislative proposals based on reliable information about how previous approaches have – or have not – worked.

If data about the operation of a law are gathered systematically, periodic reviews can be conducted using those data, coupled with the other information-gathering techniques discussed under item 1 above. The success or failure of the law can be assessed, and any necessary changes made. This is what Cass Sunstein calls, in his recent book *The Cost–Benefit Revolution*, retrospective review.[15] Sunstein also holds out the possibility of harnessing technology to implement a new approach that he calls *measure and react*.[16] 'The basic idea', he says, 'is that it is increasingly possible to measure, in real time, the effects of policies and thus to learn, by December, how they worked in November'. As he notes, such approaches often are not feasible – 'but they are the most promising of all, and we will eventually see far more use of them'.[17]

We would not tolerate an approach to public health measures, or to design and construction of high-rise buildings, that paid so little attention to outcomes – and in particular, adverse outcomes. We should be equally intolerant of law-making that involves a high risk of failures that may go unnoticed and unremedied for lengthy periods. Bad law-making may be cheaper initially – but it is a false economy that comes at a high cost to the society that tolerates it. Technology makes it ever easier and cheaper to capture and aggregate data about how laws are performing. There is a strong case for treating this as a basic cost of making laws of acceptable quality.

I suspect that in many cases another reason that ongoing monitoring of laws is not undertaken is the confidence of their makers that those laws will certainly work. Why waste time and money on tracking a sure thing? But as we've seen, confidence of this kind is almost certainly misplaced. We need to move beyond this unjustified hubris.

Wilful Blindness

Finally, there may be cases where a lawmaker is not merely indifferent to tracking the success of an initiative, but is positively hostile to doing so. If the proposed legislation is intensely political, and if the prospect of its success is open to doubt, then the last thing its proponent may want is a reliable and neutral way of tracking its results. This is an essentially political issue. No amount of earnest technocratic advice can help to resolve it.[18]

The best long-term solution to challenges of this kind may be to institutionalise independent and apolitical tracking of legislative outcomes: make it a default approach, so any proposals to depart from that approach attract attention and heightened scrutiny. Some countries have generally applicable laws or directives providing for independent reviews of the costs and benefits of significant regulatory proposals, or of certain government spending proposals, or of election manifesto policies. It may be easier to persuade legislators to subject all future initiatives to a generally applicable regime for independent scrutiny, whether those initiatives are their own or come from their political opponents, than it would be to persuade them that a particular initiative should receive special scrutiny.

---

[1] On the importance of planning for surprises see, eg, Philip E Tetlock and Dan Gardner, *Superforecasting: The Art and Science of Prediction* (New York, Broadway Books, 2015) 242–49.

[2] See, eg, the Gambling Act 2003 (NZ), which confers powers to make regulations on the Governor-General in Council (in effect, on ministers acting collectively), on the Lotteries Commission to make rules governing lotteries, and on a senior government official to make rules governing certain forms of gambling, and to prescribe forms for various purposes.

[3] eg, the Environmental Protection Agency makes rules under a number of environmental laws and Executive Orders including the Clean Air Act 42 USC §7401, the Clean Water Act 33 USC §1251, and the Toxic Substances Control Act 15 USC §2601; the Federal Communications Commission makes rules under laws governing interstate and international communications by radio, wire, satellite and other electronic technologies; the Securities and Exchange Commission makes rules governing the

operation of the securities industry under a number of statutes including the Securities Exchange Act 15 USC §78a. These rules are for the most part made under a process known as 'notice and comment rulemaking': for an overview, see Office of the Federal Register, 'A Guide to the Rule-Making Process', available at: www.federalregister.gov/uploads/2011/01/the_rulemaking_process.pdf. For the objectives of the notice and comment process, and some challenges in meeting those objectives, see Cass R Sunstein, *The Cost–Benefit Revolution* (Cambridge, MA, MIT Press, 2018) ch 5.

⁴ There are exceptions – as I write this note, for example, I am working at home in New Zealand during the COVID-19 pandemic. In New Zealand, as in many other countries, legislation provides for the executive to make rules modifying the operation of a range of statutes where that is necessary to respond to an epidemic, or to other forms of civil emergency. There is a convincing case for such powers, given the very limited contexts in which those powers may be exercised, the need for a swift response (often, in circumstances where it will be difficult for the legislature to meet), the difficulty of anticipating the nature of that response, and the limited time for which any such rules are likely to operate.

⁵ For an overview of the trade-offs between rules and standards see Daniel Kahneman, Olivier Sibony and Cass R Sunstein, *Noise* (New York, Little, Brown Spark, 2021) ch 28. There is an extensive literature on the subject of rules versus standards: see, eg, HLA Hart, *The Concept of Law* (Oxford, Oxford University Press, 1961) ch 7; Anthony I Ogus, *Regulation: Legal Form and Economic Theory* (Oxford, Hart Publishing, 1994, reissued 2004) chs 6 and 8; Louis Kaplow, 'Rules Versus Standards: An Economic Analysis' (1992) 42 *Duke Law Journal* 557, and the works cited at fn 1 of that article.

⁶ This example is inspired by the New Zealand Credit Contracts and Consumer Finance Act 2003, ss 41–44B and 54.

⁷ Issues of the kind that Lon Fuller described as 'polycentric' in a famous article on the limits of court-based adjudication: see Lon L Fuller, 'The Forms and Limits of Adjudication' (1978) 92 *Harvard Law Review* 353.

⁸ See New Zealand's Electronic Transactions Act 2002, s 35.

⁹ See The Treasury, 'Regulatory Stewardship' (2 December 2020), available at: www.treasury.govt.nz/information-and-services/regulation/regulatory-stewardship.

¹⁰ For a comparative study of the use of experimental legislation in the United States, the Netherlands and Germany, and a discussion of techniques for enacting experimental legislation, see Sofia Ranchordás, *Constitutional Sunsets and Experimental Legislation* (Cheltenham, Edward Elgar Publishing, 2014).

¹¹ See Andrew Burrows, *Thinking About Statutes: Interpretation, Interaction, Improvement* (Cambridge, Cambridge University Press, 2018) ch 3; Geoffrey Palmer, 'Law-Making in New Zealand: Is There a Better Way?' (2014) 22 *Waikato Law Review* 1, 29–30.

¹² Select Committee on the Constitution, *Parliament and the Legislative Process* (HL 2003–04, 173–I) para 165, and see generally ch 5, available at www.publications.parliament.uk/pa/ld200304/ldselect/ldconst/173/173.pdf. For a recent review of post-legislative scrutiny practices with a particular focus on the United Kingdom and Europe, see Franklin De Vrieze and Philip Norton (eds), *Parliaments and Post-Legislative Scrutiny* (Abingdon, Routledge, 2021) esp chs 1 and 3. Even in countries where there is an explicit commitment to mechanisms for post-legislative scrutiny, practice can fall far short of that goal: see Tom Caygill, 'The UK post-legislative scrutiny gap' (2020) 26 *Journal of Legislative Studies* 387.

¹³ Select Committee on the Constitution, *Parliament* (n 12) paras 173 and 182–92.

¹⁴ See Robert Baldwin, Christopher Hood and Henry Rothstein, 'Assessing the Dangerous Dogs Act: When Does a Regulatory Law Fail?' [2000] *Public Law* 282; Robert Baldwin, Martin Cave and Martin Lodge, *Understanding Regulation: Theory, Strategy and Practice*, 2nd edn (Oxford, Oxford University Press, 2013) ch 3.

¹⁵ Sunstein (n 3) 82. See also 92–95 on retrospective analysis of agency rules. See also David de Boer et al, 'Assessing the Stock of Regulation: A Tool For Regulatory Stewards' (2016) New Zealand Institute of Economic Research Working Paper 2016-01); Derek Gill, 'Applying the Logic of Regulatory Management to Regulatory Management in New Zealand' in Susy Frankel and Deborah Ryder (eds), *Recalibrating Behaviours: Smarter Regulation in a Global World* (Wellington, LexisNexis, 2013); Derek Gill and Susy Frankel, 'Learning the Way Forward? The Role of Monitoring, Evaluation and Review' in Susy Frankel and John Yeabsley, *Framing the Commons. Cross-cutting Issues in Regulation* (Wellington, Victoria University Press, 2014).

¹⁶ Sunstein (n 3) 83. Cass Sunstein attributes the 'measure and react' terminology to Duncan J Watts' fascinating book *Everything is Obvious: Once You Know The Answer* (New York, Crown Business, 2011), which is also on my essential reading list for legal designers – see especially ch 8.

[17] Sunstein (n 3) 83, 97–98 and 214.

[18] For a discussion of the resistance of some lawmakers to gathering reliable information about how laws operate in practice, and to acting on that information, see Peter Orszag and John Bridgeland, 'Can Government Play Moneyball?' *The Atlantic* (Washington DC, July/August 2013) 63. See also Peter H Schuck, *Why Government Fails So Often – And How It Can Do Better* (Princeton, NJ, Princeton University Press, 2014) esp ch 6.

12

The Implications of New and Emerging Technologies

In the last few decades new technologies, and new uses of those technologies, have affected almost every sphere of human activity. The pace of change poses a number of challenges for lawmakers. It also gives rise to opportunities to design better laws, and to make those laws work more effectively. This chapter touches, briefly, on some of the key issues that lawmakers need to consider to address those challenges and to take full advantage of those opportunities.

Laws should Adapt to Technological Change

First, the challenges. The core challenge is that in almost every sphere of law-making, we are aiming at a moving target – in the time that it takes to design and adopt a law, and implement that law, technologies change what people are doing, or how they do it, or both. A law that assumes a fixed set of technologies is likely to be irrelevant at best a few years down the track.

In the course of gathering information about the current position (the critical first step discussed in chapter six above) you should develop a reasonably comprehensive picture of what people are currently doing in the relevant field, and how they are doing it. You should also try to paint a picture of where things are heading – what developments are expected in the next few years. But you can be fairly confident that those projections will be proven wrong to some extent – the direction of change, or pace of change, or both, will differ from current expectations. And in many spheres there is the possibility of truly disruptive change, as new technologies emerge and are harnessed in unexpected ways.

Lawmakers have already had to grapple with these issues in many fields. Some attempts have been more successful than others. Two concepts have been at the forefront of effective legal responses to technological change: technology neutrality, and functional equivalence.

These concepts are neatly illustrated by the UNCITRAL Model Law on Electronic Commerce, and the many national laws based on that Model Law.[1] Among the issues addressed in that Model Law are the circumstances in which use of electronic media satisfies legal requirements for writing, or for a document to be signed. The Model Law provides that a requirement that information must be in writing is satisfied if that information is accessible so as to be usable for subsequent reference. A requirement that a 'data message' (defined to include any electronic document or message) must be 'signed' by a person is satisfied if

a.   a method is used to identify that person and to indicate that person's approval of the information contained in the data message; and
b.   that method is as reliable as was appropriate for the purpose for which the data message was generated or communicated, in the light of all the circumstances, including any relevant agreement.

These tests are technology neutral. They do not refer to any particular form of technology. Rather than prescribing particular technologies, they focus on functional equivalence – does the method used to record the information provide the same level of durability and accessibility as traditional hard copy writing? Does the 'signature' identify the person and indicate approval of the content of the information in a reliable way? These tests will work whatever new technologies may emerge for storing or communicating information. They provide an adaptive legal framework for the use of new technology to meet legal requirements that a document be in writing, or signed. They do this by providing for standards that must be met, rather than rules based on particular known technologies. These standards focus on the underlying purpose of requirements for writing and requirements for signature, and ensure that the purpose is achieved by whatever technology is adopted.

Notice also that these tests avoid setting more stringent requirements for new technologies than we apply to familiar technologies. When the Model Law was being developed, some commentators suggested that there should be specific long-term durability and recoverability/legibility requirements for electronically stored information, before it could qualify as 'writing'. But paper is not guaranteed to be durable for a particular period – it can be lost, or destroyed, or rendered illegible when you spill a cup of coffee on it. A paper document does not fail to meet a requirement that it be in writing merely because the writing is very difficult to read, or is written in a language that many people do not understand. It makes no sense to set more prescriptive or more onerous requirements for new technologies than for existing, familiar technologies.

As discussed in more detail in chapter fifteen below, one disadvantage of laws based on standards is that they can be more complex for users to apply in practice because it is necessary for each user to consider whether a particular approach will meet the relevant standard. In some cases that is manageable in practice – there may be some initial uncertainty, but a widespread understanding of what the standard requires in common scenarios quickly emerges. In other cases, where complexity of this kind is more problematic, it can be reduced by providing more detailed rule-based safe harbours that refer to particular technologies, and confirm that the use of those technologies will meet the relevant standard. If this approach is adopted, it will almost invariably be desirable to have a mechanism for adapting or adding to those safe harbours over time without needing to revisit the primary legislation. Putting the standard in primary legislation, and providing for the executive to issue rules setting out safe harbours that are treated as meeting the standard, is often the most workable approach.

Primary legislation should be framed in a way that is technology neutral, in the absence of compelling reasons to adopt a technology-specific approach (for example, where the purpose of the law is to prohibit use of a particular technology).[2] Requirements should not be framed in terms of particular technologies, or in ways that pre-empt the use of technology to achieve functionally equivalent outcomes. If it is necessary to make provision for use of particular technologies – or for specific forms or processes that assume the use of a particular technology – this should generally be done in rules or other forms of delegated legislation that can be modified and updated relatively simply and swiftly. Even in these scenarios, it is preferable to make the provisions non-exhaustive: so for example a prescribed form may be used to provide information to an agency, but the agency remains free to accept the information in other ways, such as direct user input into a webpage.

But framing laws in a way that is technology neutral will not solve all the challenges that evolving technologies pose for the law. An insightful article by Lyria Bennett Moses identifies four ways in which the law might be called on to change in response to changing technology:

> (1) there may be a need to create special rules designed to ban, restrict, encourage or co-ordinate use of a new technology; (2) there may be a need to clarify how existing laws apply to new artifacts, activities and relationships; (3) the scope of existing legal rules may be inappropriate in the context of new technologies; and (4) existing legal rules may become obsolete.[3]

The potential need for laws to adapt to respond to such issues – in particular, issues in the second and third categories – underscores the need for adaptive legislation. Issues that emerge in these two categories do not call into question the principles that underpin a law, but will often require the law to be clarified or adjusted. If primary legislation is needed to achieve this, that may take considerable time. And unless and until amending legislation is passed, difficulties will be encountered in applying the existing law, and the law's effectiveness will be compromised. The law may become a damp squib, if new technology to which the law does not apply can be substituted for existing technologies, circumventing the law. There may be an overshoot, if the law on its face does apply to the new technology, but the rationale for the law does not extend to that technology. The application of existing laws to new technologies can also result in nasty surprises, for example where the law prevents the use of new technology to achieve significant social benefits.

Difficulties of this kind are less likely to arise if primary legislation is framed as adaptive legislation, using the various techniques described in chapter eleven above. And where such difficulties do arise, adaptive legislation that enables the executive to make rules or provide authoritative guidance on the detailed workings of the law will often enable those difficulties to be addressed more promptly.

Finally, another important challenge that new technologies pose for lawmakers is the way in which those technologies erode the practical significance of national borders, and borders of states and other subnational units – the traditional boundaries for the reach of our laws. This very important practical issue is discussed in chapter thirteen below.

Harnessing New Technologies to Make Better Laws, and to Make Laws Work Better

New technologies also provide a range of opportunities to improve the quality of our laws, and the effectiveness of those laws.

In chapter six I mentioned Seth Stevens-Davidowitz's book exploring the enormous quantities of data that are already available about how people live, work and interact, and about their views and their preferences. The scope and quantity of those data are increasing very rapidly. So too is our ability to gather and analyse those data. Lawmakers should do their best to make effective use of this rich trove of information about what is currently happening in relevant domains. A great deal of this information is held by governments, and should in principle be accessible to lawmakers. An increasing share of this information is held by large businesses – some of it accessible to researchers, some not. Access to such data is an issue of growing importance for governments, if they are to do their job well. This is a major topic in its own right, which cannot be tackled here. But even where private sector data are commercially sensitive and are not generally accessible to researchers, governments may be able to reach agreement with the holders of that data to obtain specific information that will be relevant to policy decisions and proposed legislation. There is little to be lost by asking.

Technology also holds great promise for improving the implementation of laws, by putting the users of the law at the centre of the way the law is framed and delivered. New technologies have transformed the user experience for people seeking to buy books or groceries, organise travel and accommodation, choose a restaurant, find a date for the night or a partner for life. They have also begun to transform the user experience of laws in a wide range of fields – applying for a driver's licence, calculating and paying taxes, providing information to regulators, reminding people of court dates and bail reporting requirements, even civil dispute resolution. We have barely begun to tap the potential for technology to improve access to information about legislation, and to make it easier (faster, simpler, cheaper – all things that technology is good at) for the relevant audiences for a law to understand that law and comply with it, or benefit from it. And also, of course, for agencies to implement that law effectively, efficiently and in a way that is consistent with the law's policy goals.

New technologies also hold out the possibility of increasingly tailored laws – for example, variable speed limits that are adjusted depending on traffic and road conditions, and the characteristics of the vehicle and its driver. Law is often a blunt tool – technology holds the promise of a more nuanced, contextual approach to legal requirements without compromising basic rule of law principles. In particular, information-gathering, data analysis and communication technologies may be used to bridge the gap between generally applicable standards, and what those standards require of a particular user in a particular context – in advance, or even in real time.[4]

As I explain in chapter fourteen below, technologies using artificial intelligence (AI) and other forms of algorithm show promise as a method of tailoring default outcomes, removing the need in many cases for the involvement of a human decision-maker.[5] Examples discussed in chapter fourteen include setting an initial amount of child support that one parent pays another, using a 'formula assessment', and the automation of company name approval. In each of these examples, initial decisions were automated, but with scope for a human decision-maker to consider more complex or contested cases where there is dissatisfaction with the result produced by the algorithm.

More generally, the use of technology to resolve some kinds of dispute – online dispute resolution, which may involve human decision-makers, AI, or some combination of the two – holds the promise of real advances in providing access to justice. It is difficult to see any other way in which we can meaningfully address the 'justice gap' for the vast majority of people for whom our current court systems are too costly, too complex and too slow to ensure that rights on paper are realised in practice.[6]

Another area in which there is a real prospect of major improvements in outcomes is the use of AI tools to improve the quality of predictions that are an input into certain types of decision provided for in legislation. A recent study of US data on bail decisions for defendants awaiting trial suggests that AI tools can significantly outperform human judges when it comes to predicting the risk that a defendant will fail to appear at a future court hearing, or will commit further offences if released on bail.[7] A policy simulation incorporated in the study shows crime committed by defendants awaiting trial could be reduced by up to 24.8 per cent with no change in jailing rates, or jail populations of remand prisoners could be reduced by 42 per cent with no increase in crime rates. The algorithm outperformed not only the average judge, but also each individual judge out of the 25 judges in the study with the largest caseloads. The study strongly indicates that the key problem leading to the large underperformance by judges compared with the algorithm is that judges respond to 'noise' (irrelevant factors that are not correlated with the risk of non-appearance or offending) as if it were 'signal' (ie, a source of relevant information).[8] The algorithm performs better as a result of *disregarding* some of the factors that influence judicial decision-making. Far from being a disadvantage, the narrower focus of the AI tool improves the quality of its predictions and would lead to significantly better decisions. That result comes as no surprise in light of the lessons from behavioural economics summarised in chapter four above. As this study illustrates, there are large potential gains from designing laws to provide for greater use of AI in contexts where (high-volume) decision-making depends in whole or in part on predictions made by the relevant decision-makers.[9]

You should consider how technology is being used elsewhere to improve the accessibility and effectiveness of laws similar to the legislation you are working on – in other countries or states or cities, and in other policy contexts that raise similar practical implementation issues. If technology has been used effectively elsewhere, consider whether it can be implemented in similar ways in your environment. Caution is appropriate if there are no precedents for particular uses of technology – going first can be expensive and risky. Many of the most spectacular blunders in the UK that are described in *The Blunders of Our Governments* involved reforms that depended on large-scale, novel, IT systems for their implementation. Pilots or trials are valuable in this context: they enable new approaches to be explored at lower cost and with lower risk.

In appropriate settings – in particular, where a law must be applied frequently and predictably – consideration should be given to developing the law to be machine consumable – 'legislation as code' – or to developing in parallel legislation and code to implement that legislation.[10] The process of developing a law from scratch with both human and computer 'audiences' in mind, ensuring it is comprehensible to both, facilitates use of technology to implement the law and make it accessible to users. It also brings valuable structure and discipline to the design of the law by forcing clarity about inputs and the logic of decision processes. It reduces complexity and uncertainty for users by creating strong incentives to avoid (or limit) the use of imprecise tests or broad discretions that cannot be expressed as code, so cannot be automated.[11]

Even if there is no technology that is immediately available to improve the way in which a particular law operates, it is worth giving some thought to ways in which technology may become relevant in the future. One way of ensuring that laws can adapt to new technology is to make sure that the law does not create unnecessary barriers to use of such technologies. It is also worth considering whether the law should expressly provide for the use of new technologies – for example, by conferring a power on the executive to issue rules providing for the use of a particular technology for the purposes of implementing that law, with the ability to modify certain aspects of the law to accommodate that technology. Even if the law is framed in technology-neutral terms, provisions of this kind may be useful to enable rules to be issued that provide guidance and safeguards for the use of particular technologies.

---

[1] See United Nations Commission on International Trade Law, *Model Law on Electronic Commerce with Guide to Enactment 1996* (New York, United Nations, 1999), available at: www.uncitral.un.org/sites/uncitral.un.org/files/media-documents/uncitral/en/19-04970_ebook.pdf.

[2] For a discussion of techniques for drafting technology-neutral legislation, and some of the challenges this can pose, see Geoff Lawn, 'Achieving technological neutrality in drafting legislation' (2014) *The Loophole* (2014.1) 29, available at: www.calc.ngo/sites/default/files/loophole/jan-2014.pdf.

[3] Lyria Bennett Moses, 'Recurring Dilemmas: The Law's Race to Keep Up with Technological Change' (2007) *University of Illinois Journal of Law, Technology and Policy* 239.

[4] For a discussion of the potential for what the authors term 'microdirectives', which translate broad standards into specific guidance for a person to whom the standard applies, see Anthony J Casey and Anthony Niblett, 'The Death of Rules and Standards' (2017) 92 *Indiana Law Journal* 1401.

[5] See Daniel Kahneman, Olivier Sibony and Cass R Sunstein, *Noise* (New York, Little, Brown Spark, 2021) chs 10 and 26–27. For an overview of the use of algorithms in government decision-making, see Joy Liddicoat et al, 'The Use of Algorithms in the New Zealand Public Sector' (2019) *New Zealand Law Journal* 26.

[6] For a passionate argument in favour of online courts to improve access to justice, see Richard Susskind, *Online Courts and the Future of Justice* (Oxford, Oxford University Press, 2019).

[7] Jon Kleinberg et al, 'Human Decisions and Machine Predictions' (2018) 133 *Quarterly Journal of Economics* 237. See also Kahneman, Sibony and Sunstein (n 5) chs 10 and 26–27.

[8] For an insightful and entertaining discussion of these concepts, see Nate Silver, *The Signal and the Noise: Why So Many Predictions Fail – But Some Don't* (United States, Penguin Books, 2012).

[9] See also Kahneman, Sibony and Sunstein (n 5) chs 9 and 26–27.

[10] For an insightful discussion of the issues raised by machine-consumable legislation, see Tom Barraclough, Hamish Fraser and Curtis Barnes, *Legislation as Code for New Zealand: Opportunities, Risks and Recommendations* (Auckland, 2021) available at: static1.squarespace.com/ static/5ca2c7abc2ff614d3d0f74b5/t/6048527d31390f164856dfe8/1615352459942/Legislation+as+Code +9+March+2021+for+distribution.pdf; See also, 'Better Rules for Government: Discovery Report' (2018), available at: www.digital.govt.nz/dmsdocument/95-better-rules-for-government-discovery-report/html.

[11] Where broad tests (eg, based on reasonableness) or discretions are unavoidable in the context of high-volume decision-making processes, it may still be possible and desirable to provide for those approaches to be applied only at a second review level. The initial decision-making process can be rule-based and machine consumable, with the broader test applied by a human decision-maker in the subset of cases where the initial (automated) decisions are challenged by an affected person.

13

Cross-Border Issues

Cross-Border Issues are Common

'No man is an island', wrote John Donne in one of his most famous poems. 'Every man is a piece of the continent,/A part of the main'.[1] These days, even an island (or group of islands, like New Zealand) isn't an island for many legal purposes. Thanks to the internet, and the ease with which people and money and information can cross borders, every jurisdiction has myriad linkages with other jurisdictions. Some laws do not raise significant cross-border issues – for example, speed limits on local roads. But many laws do raise important and challenging issues about their application to cross-border activities that need to be considered when legislation is drafted.

Consider gambling regulation. If country X passes a law restricting the forms of online gambling that are permitted in that country, where does that law apply? Does it apply to providers of gambling services based in that country, regardless of where the gambler is located? Does it apply in relation to gamblers present in that country, regardless of where the provider is located? If the goal is protection of gamblers, and in particular problem gamblers, then the second of these approaches may seem more attractive to legal designers in country X. But will it work in practice? How will the law be enforced against providers based abroad? If it cannot be enforced against providers based abroad, is there any practical point in regulating the provision of online gambling services by local providers?

Cross-border issues that often arise, and that may be relevant to your project, include the following:

a. Relevant actors outside the jurisdiction.
b. Relevant property outside the jurisdiction.
c. Relevant information outside the jurisdiction.
d. Overlapping laws: the potential for the laws of more than one country to apply to some activities, giving rise to conflicting obligations or complexity or unnecessary duplication.
e. Regulatory gaps, where no country's law both applies on its face and is practically effective in relation to certain actors or activities.
f. The desirability of unilateral or mutual recognition of outcomes (regulatory approvals, court decisions etc) in other countries, to reduce barriers to entry

and regulatory compliance costs, and thus enhance competition in local markets for goods and services.

g.   A need for information sharing and other forms of cross-border regulatory cooperation in order for the law to be effective.

h.   A need for enforcement to take place abroad in order for the law to be effective.

You should work your way through this list, then pause and ask if there are any other ways in which people or events outside your jurisdiction may be relevant to the practical operation of the law. Identifying the range of cross-border issues that are likely to arise is an important first step before you can go on to address those issues.

Addressing Cross-Border Issues

In all but the most obvious contexts, legislation should include an express provision setting out the circumstances in which it applies where there is a cross-border element. This is one facet of the question posed in chapter eight: who is the intended audience for this law? It brings into focus the territorial dimension of the question posed earlier about whose behaviour we are seeking to influence.

It is helpful to frame this question in terms of 'connecting factors' – the relevant links between the legislating jurisdiction, and the people or activities to which the legislation will apply. What are the connecting factors on which the application of the law should depend? Presence in the country? (Whose presence?) Residence? Nationality? Supply of goods or services to a person in the country? One-off, or sustained, business activities in the country? Effects produced in the country? The selection of an appropriate connecting factor raises a number of practical issues. It also raises some more fundamental questions: there are principles of international law that guide the exercise by states of what is sometimes called (rather unhelpfully, in my view) 'jurisdiction to prescribe'.[2]

Thought should be given to the potential for unilateral or mutual recognition of regulatory approvals, licences and other decisions in other countries. Suppose for example that you are reviewing legislation governing electrical device safety. If an electrical device has been approved as safe by a regulator in another country with similar standards to your own, is it necessary for that device to go through any further safety review or approval process in your country, or should the other country's approval be recognised as sufficient? Or suppose you are working on legislation governing the provision of physiotherapy services. A person has been licensed to work as a physiotherapist in another country with comparable standards. Should they be able to register as a physiotherapist in your country without the need for further examinations or approvals? Should they be able to provide services in your country without needing to register in your country in addition to being registered in the other country? What arrangements (if any) are needed with other countries before recognising relevant regulatory outcomes from those countries – for example, arrangements in relation to exchange of information, investigations and enforcement?

Even where specific unilateral or mutual recognition regimes are not on the table at the time the legislation is designed, it can be valuable to include in the legislation a mechanism for implementing such regimes in the future (for example, by means of delegated legislation that identifies recognised equivalent approvals or qualifications).[3] This is a form of adaptive legislation that makes it possible to respond to new information and new developments in the cross-border context.

More generally, the laws of other countries can and will change in ways that are difficult to predict. When you address cross-border issues, you need to consider how your law will interact with the current laws of other relevant countries, and whether it will continue to work effectively if those laws change. Adaptive legislation that can accommodate such changes is highly desirable.

If the proposed legislation deals with civil or commercial law issues – ie, it is not exclusively concerned with criminal, regulatory or revenue issues – then the interface between the legislation and the jurisdiction's private international law rules will also need to be considered. Those private international law rules form an important part of the context in which the legislation will operate. Suppose for example that proposed legislation in country C will provide for certain terms to be implied into contracts of insurance entered into by consumers. Will the standard choice of law rules of country C apply, with the result that the prescribed terms will be implied if and only if the insurance contract is governed by the law of country C? Is the legislation intended to apply despite a choice of foreign law to govern the insurance contract, if the law of country C would apply but for that choice? Or is it intended to apply whenever a consumer resident in country C enters into an insurance contract, regardless of the governing law of that contract? If these issues are not addressed then the legislation will give rise to unnecessary uncertainty, and will as a result be more complex and more costly to apply. The position will at best be clarified over time, through court decisions. But that process can take many years. And, crucially, there is a risk that the answer the courts eventually give will not be aligned with the policy goals of the legislation. It is much more efficient and user-friendly to address these issues expressly in the legislation.

Thought should also be given to how the legislation will be enforced where cross-border issues arise. I have seen many laws that prohibit activities or communications directed to a person in the legislating country, where it seems no thought has been given to how that law will be made effective. The result in some cases has been that the law is wholly ineffective to achieve its policy goals – it is breached frequently, and with impunity, by people and businesses outside the relevant country.

In most countries there are general mechanisms for bringing cross-border civil claims, and for seeking (and providing) cooperation in connection with both civil and criminal proceedings. It is important for legal designers to understand those mechanisms and their limits. In fields where cross-border issues are likely to arise frequently, or to have a significant impact, it may be necessary to go beyond those general mechanisms and consider additional enforcement mechanisms to enhance the effectiveness of legislation, such as:

- Providing for civil claims against a breacher to be brought by (or on behalf of) victims. In some countries it may be necessary to make express provision for the way in which such claims will be brought against people based outside the country. Judgments granted in proceedings of this kind may be enforceable in some other countries: the extent to which that is likely to be the position should be considered before relying on this response.

- Cooperation arrangements with other countries with similar policy concerns and similar legal frameworks.

- Providing for criminal proceedings to be brought against breachers even though they are not present in the country. Practical enforcement is likely to be problematic, if the breacher elects not to participate in the proceedings and chooses not to comply with any sanctions that are imposed. But in some contexts, the reputational impact of criminal proceedings may be effective to encourage compliance.

- Providing for enforcement against firms inside the country that facilitate, or can take action to restrict, the conduct of the breachers outside the country. Are there third parties (banks, advisers etc) who are in a position to identify and hinder the breacher's conduct – for example, by declining to handle payments to the breacher from their customers?

There is an ever-increasing range of important social and economic issues that cannot be effectively addressed by any one country, let alone by separate states or regions within a country. If laws in these fields are to be effective, cooperation is needed in relation to the content of the relevant legal frameworks, or the implementation of those legal frameworks, or both. Arrangements of this kind may be informal, or formal. They may be bilateral – for example, the many regulatory cooperation regimes between Australia and New Zealand; regional – the European Union has extensive arrangements for regulatory coordination and cooperation; or multilateral – for example, the intercountry adoption process provided for in the Hague Conference on Private International Law's widely ratified treaty in this field.[4] International organisations often play an important role in developing arrangements of this kind, and in assisting countries to implement these arrangements.

The design of laws to enhance their effectiveness in an increasingly interconnected world is an important topic which deserves a more extended treatment than this short book can provide. It is a leading candidate for further work, as noted in the introduction to this book.

[1] John Donne, 'Meditation XVII'. John Donne was a barrister, and served as a Member of Parliament, before becoming a cleric. But the poem was intended to make a rather different point from the one I have borrowed it to illustrate.

[2] James Crawford, *Brownlie's Principles of Public International Law*, 9th edn (Oxford, Oxford University Press, 2019) ch 21. For an overview of the implications of cross-border issues for legislation see Legislation Design and Advisory Committee, *Legislation Guidelines: 2021 Edition* ch 10, available at: www.ldac.org.nz/assets/documents/LDAC-Legislation-Guidelines-2021-edition.pdf.

[3] See, eg, the recognition and application regime provisions for cross-border securities offerings in sub-pt 6 of pt 9 of New Zealand's Financial Markets Conduct Act 2013.

[4] Hague Convention on Protection of Children and Co-operation in Respect of Intercountry Adoption 32 ILM 1134 (opened for signature 29 May 1993, entered into force 1 May 1995).

14

Adjusting Default Settings

The Importance of Default Settings

One of the most powerful tools in the legal designer's toolbox is adjusting default settings. It may be possible to change default outcomes under proposed legislation in a way that removes the need for one or more decision-makers to make a decision, or that alters the consequences of a failure to make a decision. Another closely related tool is to adjust the 'stickiness' of the default setting, by making it easier to move away from that default.

These tools are critically important in relation to decisions made by the 'end users' of the legislation – members of the public, or businesses, or whatever other group the law is primarily aimed at. The same tools are also critically important in relation to decisions made by officials and other institutional decision-makers. Nothing changes a decision map as radically as deleting the need for a decision, or changing the default consequences of not making a decision. If getting to the right outcome is automatic – if it happens without the need for a person to give the issue any real thought, or take any active steps – then it is much more likely to happen.[1] Making it easier to depart from a default – reducing the time and effort needed to achieve the right outcome – can have almost as great an impact.

Adjusting default settings is an extremely effective way of reducing the risk of a 'damp squib' failure caused by lack of awareness of the law, or barriers to access to the benefits provided by the law. It can also be a very effective way to address institutional capacity concerns that may give rise to a damp squib failure, or to nasty surprises (including backfires).

One well-known example of the power of changing defaults is enrolment for retirement savings schemes.[2] In New Zealand, and in a growing number of other countries, any time a person begins a new job the default setting is that they are enrolled as a member of a retirement savings scheme unless they choose to opt out. Contributions at a prescribed rate are deducted from their salary, and further contributions are also made by their employer. They can choose a savings scheme. But if they do not make an active choice then they are randomly allocated to a scheme that meets the prescribed criteria. It turns out that a default 'enrol' setting significantly increases the number of people who save for their retirement, and the amount they save, compared with a default setting under which employees need to opt in. Where employees need to take some positive action to sign up for retirement savings schemes a very high proportion fail to do so, even where joining the scheme will entitle them to contributions from their employer or from the government. They simply leave the money on the table, whether as a result of inertia or due to reluctance to make an active choice to reduce their pay cheque by the amount they would need to contribute. If they have to make decisions about how much of their salary to save, and about what retirement scheme to join, that process involves still more time and effort and is even more likely to be left for another day – a day which for many never comes. But if all of this is taken care of by default, then enrolment rates increase dramatically.

Another good example of the importance of default settings is the law governing organ donation. Most if not all countries face an acute shortage of organ donors, and as a result cannot provide much-needed transplants of kidneys, hearts and other organs. The main source of organs for transplants is people who have been declared 'brain dead' – they have suffered an irreversible loss of brain function. Various approaches have been adopted to encourage people to consent in advance to the use of their organs for transplants in such circumstances. In many countries, for example, when you obtain or renew a driver's licence, you can consent to the donation of your organs and that consent is recorded on a central register. In some countries, you are required to make a choice (a 'mandated choice' approach) – if you don't tick the 'consent' or 'don't consent' box, your application cannot proceed.

The single most significant factor affecting donation rates is the default framework set out in the law in relation to consent to the use of organs. Does the law require express consent to the use of organs (opt in), or is consent presumed unless a person opts out? If a person has given their consent, can their family override that consent at the time of their death? In Austria, for example, the law provides for presumed consent subject to the ability to opt out. In neighbouring Germany, the default is that organs cannot be used without the donor's express consent. These different default rules account for a striking difference in donor rates. In Austria some 99 per cent of adult citizens are eligible organ donors, compared with just 12 per cent in Germany. That doesn't mean that changing the default rule is the right solution ethically, or that it is politically viable. Other options such as mandated choice will be preferred in many societies. The options for tackling this important issue are explored in a characteristically insightful way in Thaler and Sunstein's *Nudge*.[3] But what this example vividly illustrates is the significance of the default outcome prescribed by legislation.

Adjusting Default Settings to Make it Easier to Benefit from Legislation

As we saw in chapter two, 'damp squib' failures can result from the people who are intended to benefit from a legal regime being unaware of that regime, or being unable to access it in practice because invoking the law is time-consuming or expensive. The easier we can make it to access legal frameworks that provide benefits such as licences, permits, incorporation of a business, funding for tertiary study, child support payments, or tax refunds, the greater the prospect that the benefits those laws are intended to provide will actually be received by the people who are intended to be able to access them.

There is often a large gap between what the law is supposed to deliver to its citizens, and what it delivers in practice. If a law is intended to protect the rights and interests of individuals, but is so slow or costly to invoke that they cannot use it to solve the problems that it purports to address, then the law is a failure from the only perspective that counts. Legal designers – and the politicians they serve – need to pay much more attention to this issue. It goes to the heart of the rule of law, and equality before the law. It is central to the integrity of the law-making process. Addressing this issue is often difficult, and would involve major changes to legal regimes or significant additional investment in institutions. So all too often we adopt a Nelsonian stance, and put the legal design telescope to our blind eye so we cannot see the problem, while we work on refinements to the law for the few who can actually access it. If we are more honest about this issue, and tackle it head on, what options do we have to address it?

The first and most effective response, which should be considered whenever this issue looms large, is to change default settings so that the people who are entitled to the benefit of the law can obtain that benefit without needing to understand the legal framework or make active decisions, or take action. And without having to engage with slow, costly institutional processes. Can the legislation operate automatically, without the need for positive action on the part of the person who is entitled to benefit from it? Can particular steps be eliminated, so the process is simpler and faster and less costly?

We have already seen the example of retirement savings – automatic enrolment whenever an employee begins a new job significantly increases the uptake of such schemes, and enables employees to benefit from employer contributions and, in some countries, government contributions. This simple change in defaults makes a very big difference to achievement of the policy goals of the legislation.

There are many other contexts in which policy goals can be advanced by changing default options. If the legislation provides for funding for certain medical services, for example, the funding can be paid directly to the provider of those services on the basis of information supplied to the service provider by the ultimate recipient when they seek those services. Many insurance companies make arrangements of this kind for their customers – it should be possible for government funders to be equally efficient and user-focused. Funding for tertiary students who qualify for government support can be paid direct to their educational institution when they enrol in a qualifying course, leaving it to the institution to deal direct with the funder. Tax refunds can be assessed and paid automatically, at least for some categories of taxpayer, without the need for the taxpayer to fill in a tax return.

In many contexts, it will remain necessary for a person seeking to benefit from a legislative scheme to take some positive action. But the simpler, faster and cheaper it is for them to take that action, the more likely it is that they will do so, and that the policy goals of the legislation will be achieved. In particular, we should be slow to make it necessary to go through a protracted and costly court process in order to obtain the protection of the law unless we can be confident that the time frames and cost involved do not represent a significant barrier to the people that the law is intended to protect. Everything depends on context, and the interests of all parties need to be taken into account. Making life easier for claimants at the expense of injustice to respondents is not a satisfactory solution. But we need to be much more flexible and creative in designing processes that provide access to just outcomes and legal protection for most citizens, in place of inaccessible processes that offer a 'Rolls Royce' outcome to the very few.

Consider, for example, the payment of child support by one (liable) parent to the other (caregiver) parent following a separation. In many countries a caregiver parent seeking child support must make an application to a court to obtain an order for the payment of child support. This will normally take a few months at least – and it can take many months, or even years. The caregiver may need legal advice and representation to navigate the court system – which they will often be unable to afford, unless it is funded by the state (and that tends to involve more form-filling and more delay before funding is obtained, and the court application can be made). All the while no child support is provided – the default setting is non-payment unless and until an order is made. Adjusting the process for departing from this default setting can have enormous practical significance. For example, New Zealand's child support laws provide for an initial 'formula assessment' based on a number of relevant factors. This formula assessment can be automated. The formula assessment – which is effectively instantaneous, once the limited information required by the formula has been gathered – results in an immediate obligation on the part of the liable parent to make periodic payments to the caregiver parent of the amount assessed. There is no material cost or delay. Of course there will be cases where the formula produces an inappropriate result, because there are factors it does not take into account that affect the needs of the caregiver parent, or the ability to pay of the liable parent. So the legislation also provides for either parent to be able to seek a review of the amount payable. The review is conducted by an official (or, on appeal, by a court) by reference to a broader set of criteria. But while the review takes place, the liable parent's obligation to pay the sum assessed using the formula remains in place: the assessment is what I term a 'preliminary binding determination'. The default outcome pending any review by an official or a court is that some child support, assessed on an approximate basis, is payable to the caregiver for the benefit of the child.

As this example illustrates, one effective way to ensure that more people can invoke a law that exists for their benefit is to provide a simplified, low-cost mechanism to depart from the 'no outcome' status quo in a way that gets closer to justice in most cases, without incurring the cost and delay associated with a quest for more perfect justice. Paradoxically, introducing an extra step into the legal framework can simultaneously enhance access to justice, and reduce the overall cost of doing justice. The use of simple algorithms, as in the child support example, or of more sophisticated artificial intelligence tools, is an option in some cases. (The ability to go on to pursue the case in the 'normal' way, before a human decision-maker, addresses many of the concerns that are often raised about using technology to deliver justice.) In other cases, it may be worth considering an abbreviated procedure before a neutral human decision-maker that leads to a preliminary binding determination that must be implemented immediately. A party who is unhappy with that outcome can pursue their claim before a court, or in an arbitration, just as they would in the absence of that abbreviated procedure. An approach along those lines has been implemented successfully in the construction sector in a number of countries.[4] There is an initial 'adjudication' process, with strict time limits: an adjudication should normally be completed within a month or two of the process getting under way. The adjudicator's decision must be implemented by the parties. But a party can then go to court, or to arbitration, if they are unhappy with the outcome at adjudication. The vast majority of disputes that come within this scheme are resolved by adjudication – very few go further.[5] A similar approach may be able to be adopted in other fields where legislation currently fails to operate effectively because the time and cost involved in invoking that legislation are unrealistic for many people.

One more example of adjusting default settings in a way that improves access to the law, and can also reduce dependence on weak institutions: this time from the field of company law. In many countries the company formation process takes weeks, while in others it can be carried out online within one working day. In some countries where delay is a problem, a significant cause of that delay has been the company name approval process. The law in those countries typically provides for a broad test for the acceptability of company names – for example, that the name must not be misleading or offensive. A broad test of this kind requires the exercise of judgement. So the application would sit in an official's in-tray until they had time to consider it. And in some countries, how long it sat there was influenced by family or political connections, or by low-level corruption: a small bribe needed to be paid to get your application to the top of the pile in a reasonable time frame.

It turns out there is a relatively simple solution to this problem. The rule requiring a decision in advance about whether a proposed company name is misleading or offensive can be replaced with a rule that does not permit use of near-identical names or of certain prohibited terms when forming a company, coupled with the ability for an official to give notice post-incorporation requiring a name change if concern arises that a name is misleading or offensive. This approach can be implemented by a relatively simple algorithm that enables the name approval process to be computerised, and to be carried out online. Computers do not have overflowing in-trays or influential cousins, or require side payments to do their job. On this approach, only a very small proportion of company names will need to be assessed by an official applying a broad evaluative standard, as and when a concern arises. This approach retains a limited form of advance approval. But by simplifying the test and automating the approval process, the delay involved is eliminated and the cost reduced.

Advances in technology in recent decades have opened up many new ways to modify default rules and simplify decision-making processes. Some approval processes involving relatively simple decision-making criteria can be reduced to an algorithm that is automated and made accessible online. More complex approval processes can be redesigned and split into two stages, as with the company name approval process. An initial simplified approval process is reduced to an algorithm and automated. A second more complex process involving human judgement is triggered only in a limited number of cases where specific concerns arise – ideally, after the event.

There are often ways to simplify a process to reduce the need to engage with slow, costly institutions. It may be possible to design an initial process that is simplified and automated, as with the company name approval example discussed above. It may be possible to have an initial decision-making process that is swifter and less sophisticated, as with construction contract adjudication. It may be possible to provide that certain consequences follow automatically from invoking the procedure, unless someone opposes that outcome and seeks a contrary decision. And even then, it may be possible to provide for an interim pragmatic outcome while a more sophisticated decision-making process takes place. All of these options should be considered whenever the effective operation of the law, and the achievement of its policy goals, is undermined by the time or cost involved in invoking that law.

What all of these options have in common is that they simplify the process by which end users access the benefit of the law, by altering default settings or making it easier to depart from default settings. Put another way, they reduce the complexity of the law as it is experienced by end users. I discuss some other ways of reducing complexity in chapter fifteen below.

Adjusting Default Settings to Address Institutional Capacity Concerns

The default setting also matters a great deal when it comes to decisions made by institutions. Where there are concerns about institutional capacity, or about the cost and time involved in engaging with an institution, the first question to ask is whether the institution needs to be involved at all. If the answer is yes, the second question to ask is whether the institution needs to be involved in all cases before the event, or only in some cases after the event, if and when a problem arises. The third question to ask is what the consequence should be of a failure to act on the part of the institution.

As the company name approval example illustrates, adjusting default rules to remove the need for an institution to make a decision in every case can significantly reduce dependence on institutions that lack capacity, or that are slow or costly to deal with. Reducing the routine workload of an agency by removing the need to make such decisions can also enhance its capacity to perform its remaining functions. Adjusting default settings in this way can reduce the risk of a damp squib, and can also reduce the risk of nasty surprises caused by weak institutions.

I encountered another example of choosing a default setting to address institutional capacity issues in the company law context some years ago, when I was asked to give advice in a developing country on a proposal to introduce a voluntary administration regime for companies in financial difficulty – a similar concept to what is known in the United States as 'chapter 11'. The idea is that the company gets a breathing space from the pressure of claims by creditors, and can trade on while it puts together a rescue package. This can be a useful alternative to moving straight to liquidation of the company, a process which often involves sacrificing employees' jobs and losing much of the value of the enterprise as a going concern. The model we were looking at from another country contemplated a court making an order putting the company into administration and appointing an administrator. This approach had been chosen in that other country in preference to the US approach in which the company's board can trigger chapter 11. It responded to concerns that management might simply use voluntary administration to protect themselves from creditors in circumstances where there was no realistic prospect of a rescue, or where the existing management was a significant part of the problem. The difficulty with adopting this model, as one very experienced local lawyer pointed out, was that the courts in that country were notoriously slow to deal with the matters before them – even urgent matters such as injunctions. Most of the judges lacked expertise in commercial matters, which exacerbated delays: it seemed that many judges were reluctant to make decisions on unfamiliar issues of this kind, and were easily persuaded to adjourn a case in the hope that it would come before some other judge when it was next called. The fate of the company would be long decided one way or another, I was told, before a court decided whether or not to appoint an administrator. So the model we were studying was not workable: in reality the only available options were appointment of an administrator by the company's board, or no (effective) voluntary administration regime. The approach that was ultimately adopted was to allow appointment of an administrator by the board – so urgent action could be taken to initiate a rescue – but with the ability for any creditor to apply to the court to end the administration, or to appoint a different administrator. The court would be involved only in cases where administration gave rise to concerns, rather than in every case. The government understood that this safeguard would be imperfect, because of the slowness and lack of expertise of the courts.[6] But the view that the government took was that it was desirable to have a voluntary administration regime that could be accessed swiftly and easily, despite the risk that it would be overused, and despite the weakness of the courts in constraining misuse.

One more example – this time from the field of occupational regulation. Australia and New Zealand have a mutual recognition regime for registered occupations – for example, nurses, plumbers, lawyers and engineers. A person who is entitled to carry on a registered occupation in one country is entitled to be registered to carry on that occupation in the other country, provided certain basic requirements are met. The bodies responsible for registration of some occupations were not enthusiastic about the proposed introduction of this regime: lawmakers identified a risk of long delays in the registration process that would significantly hinder the practical operation of the scheme. So they switched the default rule. The usual default rule where a person seeks to be registered in an occupation is that they cannot carry on that occupation until their registration is approved. If you apply for registration as a plumber, or a nurse, or a lawyer, you have to wait to be registered before you can begin work in that capacity. But the trans-Tasman mutual recognition regime provides that a practitioner from one country can carry on the relevant occupation in the other country from the time they apply to be registered in that country: they do not have to wait for a decision. And if a decision is not given within the time frames set by the mutual recognition legislation, the person is entitled to immediate registration. There is a power to postpone a decision, but it is time-bounded, and meanwhile the person can carry on the occupation.

This switch in default rules prevents occupational registration bodies from using delay as a tool to frustrate mutual recognition. It means that the scheme works even if a registration body is inefficient or slow. It also creates strong incentives for registration bodies to operate more efficiently, as otherwise they are unable to exercise any of their licensing powers where practitioners from the other country seek registration.

This approach – deeming a licence or approval to be granted if a decision is not made within a specified period – can be a very effective tool for addressing concerns about the capacity or will of an agency to make decisions that are consistent with the law's policy goals in a timely manner. But it is unlikely to be an appropriate approach where a deemed approval would have irreversible consequences, or would affect third-party interests. In those contexts, seeking to strengthen the agency will usually be a more appropriate option.

A Risk of Overshoots?

As I said earlier, changing default rules is a powerful tool. In the voluntary administration example discussed immediately above, choosing 'appointment by the board' as the default, rather than 'appointment by the court', meant that voluntary administration would be a realistic and workable alternative to liquidation. But it also created a risk of overuse, and potential abuse. Careful thought needs to be given to safeguards to ensure that the baby is not thrown out with the bathwater.

The 'overshoot' in relation to New Zealand's 2013 bail law discussed in chapter two above resulted from a failure by that law's framers to identify the risk that changing default rules about bail for defendants awaiting trial would lead to many more defendants being held on remand than the goals of the reform required. The default rule for a significant number of defendants switched from 'bail unless the court is satisfied by the prosecutor that there is a flight risk' to 'remand in custody unless the court is satisfied by the defendant in relation to a number of criteria including their likelihood of offending while on bail, and the appropriateness of their place of residence'. It turned out that even where those criteria could be met, a significant number of defendants struggled to establish this to the satisfaction of the court. And for many other defendants, the criteria could be met provided they received a modest amount of support from social services: but the absence of any way for them to make the necessary arrangements while they were in custody meant they also spent significant time in prison on remand.

What appears to have been overlooked in 2013 was the need to focus on a very practical question: how will the proposed law work in practice? How will an accused held in custody establish that they meet the criteria for bail, or make arrangements for new accommodation that would meet those criteria, or find other forms of support to enable the criteria to be met? Who will fill in the necessary forms for an accused in custody who cannot read or write well enough to do so themselves? Who will make phone calls to social housing providers on behalf of an accused with no access to a phone? These modest practical challenges appear to have prevented many individuals from making the case for a departure from the new default rule of 'remand in custody'.

The lack of understanding of how the law would operate on the ground may have been contributed to by a disconnect between the policy designers and the people with relevant practical expertise. A diverse team with different backgrounds, lived experience and expertise can make a significant difference to the amount and quality of relevant information that is available to shed light on such risks. Cass Sunstein and Reid Hastie's *Wiser* provides valuable insights into how to make the most of the full range of information available to a team, and avoid the risk of 'group think'.[7]

Of course even the most diverse team of legal designers cannot know everything themselves. They need to engage proactively with stakeholders to try to understand the current picture, and how a proposed law change is likely to play out in practice. The further the issues are from the daily experience of the legal design team, the more important it becomes to reach out early to people with hands-on experience of how the system works to explore the likely impact of making changes to that system. Formal consultation mechanisms which leave it to the consultees to take the initiative to engage with the legal design process are unlikely to be sufficient – especially where the affected groups include a significant number of people from disadvantaged communities.

It may not have been possible to predict the consequences of the 2013 bail reforms with any precision, even with good consultation. There were few directly relevant precedents for such a change. A trial was not an option for a change of this kind, as treating some defendants selected on a random basis more harshly than others would be unfair and unjust. But the risk of an overshoot should have been apparent if a detailed decision map was prepared, and the likely behaviour of each of the relevant decision-makers – defendants, prosecutors, judges – was considered. This was the most likely form of failure for a reform of this kind, where the default rule was reversed. Steps could and should have been taken to ensure that the change in default outcome did not also capture defendants who did not pose any real risk, but who lacked the literacy or financial resources or support to establish they should be granted bail. And, most important of all, the practical results of the change should have been carefully monitored in real time to see if the risk of an overshoot materialised, and how significant any overshoot actually was.

New Zealand's 2013 bail reform holds three main lessons for lawmakers considering a change to default settings. First, it is important to do the work needed to understand the practical consequences of a change in default rules. Second, it is important to consider what safeguards (legal or practical) may be needed to avoid an overshoot as a result of the change in default settings. Third, monitoring outcomes is essential to ensure that any overshoot – or other nasty surprise – is identified and addressed sooner rather than later.

---

[1] See Cass R Sunstein, *Simpler: The Future of Government* (New York, Simon & Schuster, 2013) ch 5 for a discussion of the importance of default outcomes, and of making good choices automatic.

[2] See Richard H Thaler and Cass R Sunstein, *Nudge: Improving Decisions about Health, Wealth and Happiness* (New Haven, CT, Yale University Press, 2008) ch 6.

[3] ibid, ch 11.

[4] In the United Kingdom, see the Local Democracy, Economic Development and Construction Act 2009, the Construction Contracts (England and Wales) Regulations 1998, and the Scheme for Construction Contracts (England and Wales) Regulations 1998 (Amendment) (England) Regulations 2011. In Australia, most states and territories have similar legislation – see, eg, the New South Wales Building and Construction Industry Security of Payment Act 1999. In New Zealand, see the Construction Contracts Act 2002.

[5] Peter Rosher, 'Adjudication in Construction Contracts' (2016) *International Business Law Journal* 497, 500; Robert Gaitskell, 'International Statutory Adjudication: Its Development and Impact' (2007) 25 *Construction Management and Economics* 777.

[6] We also explored a number of options for addressing the judicial capacity issue, including requiring all of these matters to be dealt with in the courts in the capital city where judges tended to have more commercial expertise, or establishing a commercial court. As is often the case, these options raised much wider issues about the structure and capacity of the judiciary that could not realistically be addressed in the context of a law reform exercise focused on one area of the country's substantive law. They were pushed off to be dealt with at some later time.

[7] Cass R Sunstein and Reid Hastie, *Wiser: Getting Beyond Groupthink to Make Groups Smarter* (Boston, MA, Harvard Business Review Press, 2015).

15

Reducing Complexity

People have been complaining about the complexity of legislation for a very long time. Back in 1550 King Edward VI wrote a letter to the English Parliament about the work to be done in its next session, in which he said that he

> could wish ... that the superfluous and tedious statutes were brought into one sum together, and made more plain and short to the intent that men might better understand them; which thing shall much help to advance the profit of the Commonwealth.[1]

King Edward was right to focus on the implications of complexity for how easy it is for people to understand the law – including unnecessary overlap in laws, unnecessarily lengthy laws, and other 'tedious' features of laws. He could have gone on to add that as the law becomes more complex, it also becomes harder for people to comply with it, or take advantage of the benefits it provides. And it becomes harder for officials and courts to apply the law – and in particular, to apply it in a way that is consistent with the policy underpinning the law. All too often, the policy is lost sight of as we scramble through the complex maze of interlocking (and overlapping) provisions.

As Cass Sunstein says in another recent book that features on my essential reading list, 'governments can be much better, and do much better, if they make people's lives easier and get rid of unnecessary complexity'.[2] Legislation should be as simple as possible to comply with where it imposes obligations; and as easy as possible to invoke for the people who are meant to benefit from it.

However King Edward wasn't right to equate ease of understanding with brevity – or, put the other way around, to equate complexity with length. It cannot be emphasised too strongly that the complexity of a law needs to be assessed from the standpoint of its users: the various audiences to whom it is addressed. A law that looks very short and simple on paper may be very complex for users to apply, for example if it provides for a broad standard and the practical implications of that standard are not easy to figure out in particular contexts. A law that looks very long and detailed and complicated on paper may be very simple for users to apply if the institutional mechanisms for applying it are user-friendly, just as your smart phone is user-friendly even though there is some very complex code running behind its user interface. Avoiding complexity isn't the same as making the text of the legislation as short or as simply expressed as possible. Rather, the focus needs to be on the day-to-day experience of users of the legislation. And – to echo my refrain from chapter nine – that means looking at the interplay of the legislation and the institutions that administer it, to understand how a user will experience the operation of the law in practice.

Standards, Rules and Complexity

Consider a family business, Bacchus Vineyard Services, that provides maintenance services for small-scale vineyards – pruning, spraying, canopy management and so on. The sprays it uses to control weeds, and to manage vineyard pests, are potentially hazardous if they are spilled or used inappropriately. Most countries regulate the storage and handling of such chemicals.

Legislation on this issue could be enacted at a high level of generality: the law could provide that hazardous substances must be stored, transported, handled and used taking all practicable steps to avoid causing harm to any person or to the environment. A standard of this kind, expressed in general terms, is simple and inexpensive for lawmakers to formulate in advance. But it is complex and costly to apply for all the audiences to whom it is addressed: people using or transporting substances that may qualify as hazardous, enforcement agencies, and courts called on to apply the standard in particular cases. The owners of Bacchus would need to make enquiries about the various sprays they are thinking of using in their business to find out if they are likely to be regarded as hazardous for the purposes of the legislation. That would require them to obtain information about how the standard has been applied in the past, and is likely to be applied in the future, and what that means for various different sprays. They would need to find out about different storage, transport, handling and application methods and work out which ones would be likely to be seen by the enforcement agency, and ultimately by a court, as meeting the 'all practicable steps' requirement. In other words, they would have to translate the broad standard into specific rules that they would then apply in their own business. Many people – farmers, small businesses, large businesses, professional service providers and others – would need to go through a similar process, gathering information of this kind and attempting to put it into practice. They could seek advice from experts. But obtaining expert advice is likely to be costly for the many small businesses and individuals to whom the law applies. There is no guarantee that by consulting an expert they will get a clear-cut and confident answer about what the law requires – reasonable people can and do differ about issues of this kind, so predicting how regulators and courts will apply a standard is often an inherently uncertain exercise. And where reasonable people can differ, they will: different advisers will reach different views. There will be noise – probably, lots of noise.[3]

The enforcement agency will also face a complex task as it seeks to make judgements about what criteria it should apply, and what enforcement action to take, in relation to a wide range of substances. Its decisions – whether to take enforcement action, or to refrain from doing so – are likely to be controversial, and frequently contested. When enforcement action is taken, court hearings are likely to be complex and costly, and will almost inevitably involve expert evidence on one or both sides. There will be a significant risk of error in applying the standard – by users of hazardous substances (who end up taking inadequate precaution and exposing others to harm, and themselves to sanctions, as the result of a good faith mistake, or taking excessive precaution which results in unnecessary costs), enforcement agencies and courts. Different judges will inevitably reach different conclusions about similar fact scenarios. Again, noise.

So this very short provision, although it might have appealed to King Edward back in 1550, would be complex to apply in practice. A law in this form risks being a damp squib, or producing nasty surprises. Or both.

Alternatively, the legislation could be more detailed and prescriptive. It could provide for hazardous substances to be listed – in the legislation itself, or more likely in delegated legislation issued by an executive agency – and categorised by risk profile; and for requirements to be set out for the storage, handling and use of each different category of substances. This information could be made available in a readily searchable form on the internet. 'Compare' features of the kind that many retailers include on their websites could enable users to select, and compare the rules in relation to, different substances that they might consider using. This would involve more work upfront for the lawmakers and the responsible agency. But it would significantly reduce the need for the people to whom the law is addressed to gather information and form judgements about what the law requires.

Enforcement of a law in this form would also be much simpler – for both the regulator and the courts. And the risk of error – people taking too little precaution and causing harm, or wasting resources by taking unnecessary precaution – would be reduced.

A law in this form would be much longer. The detailed provisions could run to hundreds, perhaps thousands, of pages. It could be complex for users to navigate. But – to return to one of my core refrains – that all depends on the institutional arrangements for implementing the law. The longer law can be designed to be much less complex in practice for its users, if there are mechanisms that enable a user to navigate through the lengthy and detailed rules to identify the particular requirements that apply to them. I cannot emphasise too strongly that the complexity that matters is the complexity experienced by users of the law – and this cannot be assessed solely by reference to the length or content of the law on paper.

These approaches can also be combined in various ways. This is not a stark binary choice. For example, detailed rules in relation to listed substances can be coupled with a general principle applicable to all unlisted hazardous substances. The level of detail provided about requirements for storage and handling of listed substances can also be graduated along a spectrum from the very specific to the more general. The many different ways in which standards and rules can be combined were outlined in chapter fourteen above.

Discretion

It is worth adding a word on discretion at this point. The word 'discretion' is used in a number of quite different ways, which can cause confusion. It is sometimes used to refer to an unrestricted freedom for a decision-maker to arrive at whatever result they prefer in each case. Discretions of this kind are not only unusual in the legal context; they are difficult to reconcile with the very concept of law. More commonly, legislation will confer a discretion on a decision-maker in the sense that the decision-maker is authorised to choose between a range of possible decisions by reference to a broad standard, or a policy goal. For example, a court may be authorised to select an appropriate remedy for a breach from a wide set of options, but (either explicitly or implicitly) the remedy must be consistent with the policy of the legislation, and must respond to the wrong that has been done. Or a regulator may be authorised to grant an exemption from certain requirements, but (either explicitly or implicitly) may do so only where that will not impair the policy goals of the legislation.

Discretion in this second sense is really just one way to structure the application of a broad standard or principle – the decision-maker is given express authority to say what that standard or principle requires in practice in a particular case. Understood in this way, legislation that confers a discretion raises the same practical issues as legislation that provides for a standard to be applied. Because an approach conferring a discretion is less certain and predictable than a rule-based approach, there is more complexity for users and for decision-makers.

Various combinations of discretions and rules are possible, as with standards and rules. The combination may be horizontal – with some matters governed by discretions, and others by rules – or vertical, with rules applied to arrive at a default outcome, subject to discretionary review and adjustment where an affected person objects to that default outcome.

The effectiveness of a law that provides for significant exercise of discretion will depend heavily on the capacity and performance of the institution that exercises the discretion. The greater the scope of the discretion, and the more frequently it will need to be exercised, the more critical the role of the institution will be. I return to this below.

Other Options for Reducing Complexity and Increasing Predictability

There are many other ways in which legislation that establishes a principle or standard can be made more predictable in particular cases. Options include:

- Limiting the scope of the inquiry that is undertaken when applying the principle – for example, by limiting the factors that can be taken into account. This approach can reduce the scope of disputes, and so reduce the time and cost involved. But in my experience it is rare for this to make a material difference in practice, and it can limit the flexibility and adaptability of the legislation.
- Providing for an affected person to apply to the regulator for confirmation that the action it proposes to take complies with the law, or will be treated as compliant – a 'clearance' or 'binding ruling'. So for example the law may prohibit

mergers and acquisitions that substantially lessen competition in a market, but provide for an intending acquirer to apply to the competition authority for a clearance for the merger. This approach enables a person affected by the law to obtain a higher level of confidence that they are complying with that law before taking the proposed action. The value of an approach of this kind is very dependent on the time frame and cost involved in obtaining a clearance or binding ruling: if the mechanism is likely to be slow and/or costly, then it will not be used frequently and will be of less practical relevance.

- Setting out a detailed set of requirements – either in the primary legislation, or in rules issued under it – and then providing for an agency to grant exemptions from the detailed requirements in particular cases, where those detailed requirements are inapplicable or serve no useful purpose. The key feature of this approach is that the law's requirements are highly prescriptive, and must be complied with unless an exemption is obtained by refence to the underlying principles of the law. A person cannot simply take a view on whether their proposed action complies with the principle, and act on that. This approach forces a person who considers that their conduct is consistent with the principles underpinning the law, but not with the detailed rules, to approach the agency for an exemption. It may result in a greater number of applications to the relevant agency, with associated costs for applicants and for the agency itself. But it may have the incidental benefit of keeping the agency up to date with market practices and changing circumstances, facilitating periodic reviews of the detailed rules.

- Putting in place a mechanism to provide advance clarification of what the standard requires in particular circumstances. Some licensing regimes work in this way, translating general requirements into specific requirements for each licensed business in the form of licence terms and conditions. Technology holds the promise of translating general standards into specific requirements on a real-time basis in some contexts – for example, variable speed limits on major roads that adjust to reflect traffic volumes and road conditions.

The Importance of Institutions for Making these Approaches Work

All of the approaches identified above depend for their effectiveness on the capacity of the institutions responsible for administering them. Different approaches will depend more heavily on different institutions.

An approach that requires a regulator to make rules will work well only if the regulator has the capacity to make initial rules that are consistent with the law's policy goals, and to update those rules as new information becomes available or circumstances change. Consider the 'reasonable habitability' requirement for rental housing that we looked at in chapter fourteen. If the regulator does not have the capacity to perform a rule-making function that sets detailed requirements for rental properties, there is a risk that the minimum requirements will be set too low and will fail to achieve the policy goal of the legislation – a 'damp squib' outcome. Conversely, there is also a risk that the regulator will set very demanding requirements that go beyond what is affordable for many tenants. That would waste resources, and reduce the supply and increase the cost of rental accommodation to the detriment of the very people the legislation is intended to benefit. So a lack of capacity to make (and update) rules could lead to a nasty surprise outcome, perhaps even a backfire.

An approach that provides for standards that are enforced by a regulator also depends on the capacity of the regulator to develop appropriate enforcement policies and strategies, and take enforcement action. And it depends on the capacity of the courts (or other enforcement institutions) to apply the standard appropriately (ie, consistently with the policy goals) in particular cases.

Similarly, an approach that confers discretion on a regulator or some other institution, or which provides for an institution to grant clearances or exemptions, depends on the capacity of the relevant institution to exercise those decision-making powers in a manner that is timely and consistent with the policy of the legislation. The greater the scope of the discretion, and the more frequently it must be exercised, the greater the risk of noise, and the greater the need for mechanisms to reduce that noise.

All of these approaches also depend heavily on the institutions through which the laws are ultimately enforced, whether those laws prescribe standards or rules or some hybrid of the two. In the rental accommodation example, whether any of the listed approaches will result in meaningful obligations for landlords and meaningful entitlements for tenants will depend on the institutional arrangements for dealing with tenant complaints. If a tenant has to go to court to enforce the relevant requirements – whether standards or rules – then those requirements are likely to be ineffective. The cost will be prohibitive, and the time frames involved are likely to exceed the length of many rental terms. So the law will be a damp squib. Providing an effective, timely and affordable enforcement mechanism is more important than any of the other design choices identified above. This is true in many contexts.

Institutional Arrangements that Avoid or Reduce Complexity

If the institutional arrangements for implementing a law are well designed and effective, on the other hand, then they can actually reduce apparent complexity. In particular, they can make it simple to apply even very lengthy and detailed laws (of the kind that King Edward VI would have seen as extremely tedious). Yet again, the key is how users will interact with the law in practice. Long and detailed laws – such as tax laws in many countries – can be made very simple for most users to apply. The vast majority of taxpayers in New Zealand, for example, do not need to know anything about the tax laws that apply to them in order to comply with those laws. Tax is deducted at source from most sources of income – in particular, wages paid by employers and interest paid by banks and other financial institutions. Most people are not required to file tax returns, because the amounts deducted at source will be close enough to the tax payable that the administration costs of requiring and reviewing tax returns are not justified. Most people can simply ignore the hundreds of pages of tax laws that apply to them, because from their perspective the law takes care of itself. Compliance is automatic.

Where compliance cannot be made automatic, good institutional arrangements can still go a long way to making compliance easier and less complex. One way to achieve this is to design the law and the associated institutions to work in a way that removes the need for the people affected by it to understand the law in any detail – in the same way that the operating system of your computer works invisibly behind the scenes, without you needing to understand the detail of how it works, let alone actually read the code that controls how it works. If the process for invoking a law – be it applying for a building permit or a marriage licence or a divorce or a welfare benefit – is structured to help the user know what information they need to provide, and the conditions that must be met in order to obtain the desired result, then that 'user interface' may convey all of the information about the operation of the law that the users require.

Using appropriate technology to apply the law is one way to achieve this. This option is discussed in more detail in chapter twelve. Well-designed user-friendly information packs and forms can also make a significant difference, especially if the audience is a broad one that includes people with limited literacy. The Criminal Cases Review Commission of England and Wales saw a 74 per cent increase in applications over a two-year period as the result of introducing an 'Easy Read' application form for use by prisoners, coupled with other measures to provide greater access to its services.[4] Agencies with front-line staff who can guide people through a process represent another (typically more costly) user interface option.

One good example of providing information about what the law requires in particular situations is right in front of us every day when we venture out on the roads. In order to comply with the laws governing how you drive, you need a basic level of understanding of the structure of those laws, and of the different kinds of road sign and road marking used where you are driving your car. But you don't need to read the legislation. (How many road users have ever read it? Have you? All of it, all the way through?) The detailed requirements that apply to you – what speed limits apply where; when you are and are not allowed to overtake – are communicated by road signs and lane markings. We don't need to investigate and memorise all the speed limits that apply to different stretches of road between home and Aunt Agatha's house: we just need to know the default rule (for example, a limit of 50 kilometres per hour in urban areas), and that departures from the default will be well signposted. The signs we encounter at regular intervals on the roads advise us of the applicable speed limit, providing easily understood information about what the law requires (and regular reminders in case that information has been overlooked or forgotten).

As mentioned earlier, in some countries technology is already used to set variable speed limits on some roads to reflect current road and traffic conditions: this is an excellent example of real-time translation of standards into specific rules that are communicated to users as and when they are relevant. The signs found above hand basins in toilet facilities in restaurants in some countries, reminding employees that they must wash their hands before returning to work, are another example of reminders of what the law requires that are intended to increase the prospect of compliance. If 'signposts' along these lines are appropriate, then the law may need to provide for them. Indeed the law may take the form of requiring compliance with whatever signposts are displayed, coupled with rules about who is responsible for making decisions on the detailed requirements, and for displaying the relevant signposts.

Selecting an Appropriate Approach

The choice of approach in a particular context will depend on who the audiences are for the law, and on the viability and cost of the various potential institutional arrangements for implementing that law. It will also depend on the acceptability of differences in outcomes in similar cases, and on whether certain types of error are more problematic than others.

Predictability is always in principle desirable – it enhances the accessibility of law, consistent with rule of law objectives, and increases the prospect of the law changing behaviour in the desired way (ie, not being a damp squib). Predictability is also closely linked to consistency of outcomes, which is also in principle desirable – the law should not be a lottery that depends on which decision-maker you happen to encounter on the day. But sometimes a high level of predictability is not achievable, and sometimes the difficulty and cost of providing precise rules in advance is not justified. The appropriate level of precision – the extent to which rules should be preferred to standards – primarily turns on how frequently the issue arises, and on the nature of the audiences for the legislation.[5]

So for example laws regulating the use of hazardous chemicals or setting minimum standards for rental accommodation have a very broad audience which includes many small businesses and individuals, and will probably also depend on many enforcement officers and courts or tribunals in different centres. It would be very costly for all of the people affected by laws of this kind to have to acquire information about how a broad standard would apply to their activities. And they are often not well placed to do so: they do not have the relevant expertise, or the resources to pay for advice from people with that expertise. It will be much more efficient – and the risk of error at every point will be much reduced – if a (competent, and adequately resourced) government agency does the detailed work. So for example a hazardous substances regulator can identify the substances that are subject to regulation, and issue detailed requirements for how each category of substance must be dealt with. That information can be made available online very simply and inexpensively. The task of enforcement agencies and courts will also be greatly simplified if there are more detailed rules – which is important for frequently occurring issues.

Conversely, prohibitions on the misuse of monopoly power are primarily relevant to a small audience of well-resourced businesses and sophisticated regulatory agencies. Issues of this kind arise relatively infrequently. And they arise in many different contexts. So publishing detailed guidance in advance on what firms with monopoly power may not do in all those different contexts is almost certainly unworkable in practice. A prohibition in the form of a broad standard seems inevitable in this field.

Most of the discussion in this chapter has focused on legislation that seeks to regulate behaviour. Similar points can be made in relation to other forms of legislation – for example, legislation setting out entitlements or benefits for certain groups, or legislation setting default rules that apply to certain forms of consensual dealings (such as contracts for the sale of goods). The more frequently the issue arises, the greater the net benefit from providing detailed rules in advance. The less frequently an issue arises, and the more disparate the contexts in which it may arise, the stronger the case for a broad standard rather than a rule. And as with regulatory statutes, this is not a binary choice: there are many hybrid approaches along the spectrum from broad standards to detailed rules.

The starting point should be to strive for the greatest level of accessibility and predictability for users that is reasonably achievable. At the risk of repeating myself, that significantly enhances the prospect of achieving the outcomes that the law seeks to bring about. Where a high level of accessibility and predictability cannot be achieved in the primary legislation itself, because the level of detail required cannot efficiently be dealt with at that level or because the legislation needs to adapt to changing circumstances (ie, needs to be adaptive legislation), consideration should be given to providing for more detailed rules to be issued by the executive or an executive agency, or for signposts of some kind that tell users what they need to do, when they need to do it.

Lawmakers should be cautious about resorting to broad standards (or broad discretions) on their own, without any mechanism that provides end users and other relevant audiences with more detailed rules or guidance in at least some cases. They should do so only where they are satisfied that there is no other workable approach, or that the cost and difficulty of providing further guidance outweighs the likely benefits.

---

[1] Thomas Erskine Holland, 'The Reform of the Statute Book' (1866) 6 *The Fortnightly Review* 334, citing Gilbert Burnet, *Bishop Burnet's History of the Reformation of the Church of England* (London, Richard Chiswell, 1679).

[2] Cass R Sunstein, *Simpler: The Future of Government* (New York, Simon & Schuster, 2013) 1.

[3] On the noise associated with standards, see Daniel Kahneman, Olivier Sibony and Cass R Sunstein, *Noise* (New York, Little, Brown Spark, 2021) ch 28.

[4] See House of Commons Justice Committee, *Criminal Cases Review Commission* (HC 2014–15, 850) para 31.

[5] See Kahneman, Sibony and Sunstein (n 3) ch 28, and the discussion of rules and standards in the context of adaptive legislation in ch 11 above. See also Anthony I Ogus, *Regulation: Legal Form and Economic Theory* (Oxford, Hart Publishing, 1994, reissued 2004) chs 6 and 8; Louis Kaplow, 'Rules Versus Standards: An Economic Analysis' (1992) 42 *Duke Law Journal* 557, and the works cited at fn 1 of that article.

PART III

The Checklists

16

Checklists for Law Makers?

The Structure of the Checklists

In part III of this book I suggest a set of checklists for use by lawmakers – the people involved in designing our laws. That includes the ultimate decision-makers on the content of the law – legislators; their advisers, including government officials and consultants; law drafters; and the many people who seek to influence the shape of the law. The primary checklist is framed around 10 important questions that need to be considered whenever you set out to frame a new law, or amend an existing law. It is accompanied by three secondary checklists that feed into the primary checklist. Each secondary checklist focuses on specific aspects of the overall analysis: the people who are intended to benefit from the law; the people who are required to comply with the law; and the institutions responsible for administering the law. For any given project some checklists, and some items in the checklists, will be more relevant than others. If you work through the checklists systematically, you should be in a position to identify the key factors that could result in the proposed law failing to meet its goals.

The checklists are not READ-DO checklists, or DO-CONFIRM checklists. They do not satisfy Atul Gawande's 'checklist for checklists' in the appendix to *The Checklist Manifesto*. I would have loved to produce such a checklist (or set of checklists) – that would have been a significant breakthrough! But law-making is too wide-ranging and complex an exercise to be reduced to a single checklist, or even a set of checklists. The most common causes of failed laws stem from failure to gather relevant information, failure to ask relevant questions, and failure to recognise and provide for uncertainty, rather than failure to take specific and well-defined actions. Failures of analysis, rather than failures to act.

So the structure of the checklists in this book is designed to help lawmakers who are considering whether legislation is an appropriate tool to advance a policy goal, and what any such legislation might look like, to identify the key questions they need to address along the way. It breaks down those broad questions – can legislation help to advance this policy goal? what should the legislation look like? – into more focused and more manageable issues. It suggests some ways of tackling those issues. The resulting checklists – especially the primary checklist – are longer, more comprehensive and more open-textured than the checklists Gawande describes. But significant abbreviation or simplification would mean leaving out key steps that have a significant impact on the risk of failure. In the context of law reform processes whose length is usually measured in months, sometimes years, brevity – while still desirable – is at less of a premium than in the high-pressure environment of an aeroplane cockpit or a surgical theatre.

The checklists are designed to provide what the authors of *Noise* call 'decision hygiene', in a form tailored to the legal design process. They draw on the 'Mediating Assessments Protocol' described in that book – the process of breaking down the ultimate complex decision that needs to be made into multiple independent assessments, ensuring (so far as possible) that each one is evaluated independently of the others, and resisting premature intuitions about the final decision.[1] The opportunity for independent assessment of each issue is limited, in the law-making context, by the iterative nature of the process. It is usually necessary to revisit issues as the law passes through various stages of development, and additional information relevant to each issue becomes progressively available (in particular, through consultation with affected groups). But returning to the checklists at each stage (and practising actively open-minded thinking) should help to ensure that new information is factored into each separate question to which it is relevant, and that question reassessed, rather than simply putting the new information into a large unstructured 'bucket' where it risks being crowded out by confirmation bias and the halo effect.

For ease of reference the checklists are summarised in Appendix 1.

The suggestion that legal designers should use checklists is not a new one. Several other forms of checklist are in common use in the legal design context.[2] The most widely used are Regulatory Impact Assessments (RIAs), also called Regulatory Impact Statements (RIS). This policy analysis tool is now standard throughout the OECD and in many other countries.[3] Other widely used checklists in this context are the legislative drafting manuals (sometimes in-house, sometimes publicly available) developed by governmental drafting agencies.[4] These manuals typically provide guidance on technical aspects of legislation (including structure), drafting style and issues that arise frequently when drafting legislation. They are much narrower in scope than the checklists set out below. And in some countries there is guidance on the design and content of legislation which incorporates a checklist of issues to be addressed: for example, New Zealand's *Legislation Guidelines*.[5] But these guidelines are more detailed, and more focused on legal substance, than my checklists.

There is a substantial overlap – unsurprisingly – between the questions addressed in an RIA and the topics covered by the checklists set out below.[6] But my experience, and the research on human decision-making and its flaws summarised in earlier chapters, suggest that there is real value in having a more structured checklist targeted specifically at the design of legislation. A checklist that breaks the broad policy questions posed in an RIA down into more detailed questions inspired by the ways in which legislation fails to achieve its goals, and the factors that contribute to those failures. My hope is that the checklists set out below will provide another, more specific, tool for legal designers that can be used in conjunction with preparing an RIA. Use of the checklists in a law reform project should also enhance the quality of an RIA for that project.

How should the Checklists be Used?

The checklists in this book are designed to be used as a starting point for your own project-specific checklists. You can take the checklist summary in Appendix 1, and adapt it to your own project. The checklists can then be used by the team working on the project to ensure that key issues are identified and addressed in a structured and timely way, and that the risk of failure is minimised. They can also be used by senior advisers – or politicians – as a mechanism for confirming that the necessary work has been done, and that areas of significant risk have not been overlooked.

Within a project team working on proposed legislation, each checklist should have an 'owner' responsible for ensuring it is used, and used effectively. Often it will make sense for the team leader to be the owner of the primary checklist. The other checklist owners have more focused roles, which I describe in the relevant chapters below. The benefits checklist owner, for example, would have primary responsibility for ensuring that information has been gathered about the circumstances, interests and views of the people who are intended to benefit from the legislation. And for advocating, within the team, for design choices that would make access to those benefits as simple and easy as possible.

Ideally, the checklists should be used from the inception of a project, at the point where a team begins work on a policy issue and is looking at whether legislation is an appropriate instrument to advance the project's policy goals. Although I refer throughout to 'proposed legislation', the checklists do not assume that a particular legislative proposal is already on the table. Rather, they are meant to help you work out whether it makes sense to legislate to pursue a particular social or economic policy objective, and what any relevant legislation might look like.

'Blank slate' policy work, where a policy concern is identified and there is no existing legislation directly addressing that topic, is relatively unusual. It is much more common for concerns to arise about how existing legislation is operating, either generally or in a particular context.

Where a genuinely novel concern does emerge, the checklists are intended to provide a structure for thinking about the potential for legislation to contribute to the overall policy response to that concern, and for thinking about what any legislation might look like.

More often, existing legislation provides a starting point for a project. An agency decides to review the way in which that legislation is operating, or is tasked with carrying out a review. In this scenario the checklists provide a structure for assessing how the existing legislation is working, where it is failing to achieve its policy goals, and how that legislation could be amended, or institutional arrangements changed, in order to advance those goals.

In all of these scenarios, the checklists provide a framework for analysis, not a straitjacket. I have tried to set the items out in a logical order. Some items in the primary checklist do need to be tackled before moving on to subsequent items. But work on other items can be done in parallel.

It is also likely that work on the checklists will be iterative, in the sense that work on later items may require you to loop back to address earlier items again in the light of what you have learned. If for example a review of experience elsewhere (or a trial in your own society) raises concerns about the adequacy of the existing institutional arrangements for implementing proposed legislation, you may need to loop back to item 4 in the primary checklist (what institutions will the legislation depend on?) and consider alternative options. Unfortunately, these are not the sort of checklists where an item can be checked off once, and stay checked off for the rest of the life of the project. Law reform just isn't that tidy a process.

The need to keep earlier items under review means that there should be periodic reviews of where the project is up to by reference to the checklists as a whole. The timing of these reviews will depend on the scale of the project and the time available to complete it. Careful thought needs to be given to the best way to ensure that these reviews factor in information from all participants in the project about the state of play in relation to each item. There should be a simple, open, efficient way to capture any new information and any concerns about the adequacy of the work done to date under each item, as the project goes along. It is not possible, in this book, to discuss how those information flows should be managed. For helpful ideas, which you will need to customise for your project, I suggest reading the discussion in Atul Gawande's *Checklist Manifesto* about how complex building projects are run, and Cass Sunstein and Reid Hastie's *Wiser: Getting Beyond Groupthink to Make Groups Smarter.*[7]

Agencies that have a continuing responsibility for the operation of particular laws should aim to monitor the operation of those laws even in the absence of specific proposals for change.[8] They should be gathering information on a continuous basis about item 1 (what is the current position?), item 2 (the law's policy goals) and item 4 (the capacity and operational effectiveness of relevant institutions). They should periodically review those items. This groundwork will enable the agency to initiate reforms where concerns are identified. It will also provide a springboard for work on proposals for reform that originate outside the agency – for example, from politicians or stakeholders.

Many law reform projects are long-term exercises, and it should be possible to work through the checklists systematically. But sometimes – in most countries, more often than one might wish – time frames are tight and options are limited by political commitments or other constraints. Sometimes the pressure to review and reform the law is acute but amorphous – a minister wants to respond swiftly to public expectations that they will do something about a crisis, or about an issue that has become politically salient, but does not have firm views about what the response should be. In this context, advisers will have the opportunity to identify options for responding to the policy concern, which may or may not include legislation, and to give advice on the form that any legislation might take. The checklists are at least as important in this context as they are in less time-constrained projects. They provide a structure for assessing what you do already know about the issue, what you do not know, and the risks that are involved in legislating on the basis of limited knowledge. They emphasise the importance of thinking about adaptability – an importance that is heightened in circumstances where important information is unavailable when the legislation is first developed (at speed!) but will emerge further down the track. Some stages of the analysis will inevitably be curtailed – in particular, there will be little time for extensive research and information-gathering under item 1. But in my experience the pay-off from a small amount of well-targeted proactive information-gathering is substantial. One-to-one engagement with a carefully chosen list of well-informed stakeholders can provide a great deal of information relatively quickly.

The most challenging scenario from an adviser's perspective is where there is already a commitment to the form that legislation will take at the time the project gets under way. For example, where a new government has campaigned on a commitment to change the law in a particular way, or where a senior politician forms a firm view about a reform before seeking policy advice from officials, or becomes impatient with the pace of officials' work and reaches a view on the basis of their own engagement with stakeholders and political advisers. Margaret Thatcher is reputed to have said to officials, shortly after being elected as Prime Minister of the United Kingdom, 'Don't tell me what – I know what. Tell me how'. She is not the only political leader with clear views about what they plan to do. The 'what' may be locked down before your advice is sought.

In this scenario also the checklists remain useful, though time pressure is likely to limit how much work can be done on each item. The checklists can help with the 'how', even if the 'what' has already been decided. And, critically, the checklists will help to identify risks of failure, and the ways in which those risks might be managed. All but the most single-minded politicians will want to understand where those risks lie, and what can be done to manage them.

The advice that is hardest to give, and that risks not being well received, is advice that legislation to which there is already some level of commitment is likely to fail: it is likely to be a damp squib, or to produce undesired consequences. Before giving advice along those lines, a prudent adviser will want to be sure of the concerns that they are raising. The checklists will help to assess these risks in a structured way, and can provide a framework for giving advice about those risks. Responsible politicians should welcome frank advice, as long as it is well founded. But it is only human to be reluctant to hear that a project to which you have publicly committed is flawed. Especially if there is a risk that the media will get hold of the advice, or that your political opponents will use it against you. In many countries, the pressure on advisers not to give unwelcome advice is strong, and my impression is that this pressure has increased in recent decades. There is no easy solution here. But an institutional commitment to using checklists along the lines set out in this book can make it easier for advisers to raise concerns of this kind, by providing a structure within which such issues are identified and addressed as a matter of course. Advisers are simply working through a standard risk-assessment process, not singling out particular proposals for special criticism. Politicians and their advisers have a shared responsibility to maintain a culture in which frank advice can be given and received, however unwelcome. Checklists along these lines, used properly, can support that culture.

---

[1] See Daniel Kahneman, Olivier Sibony and Cass R Sunstein, *Noise* (New York, Little, Brown Spark, 2021) ch 25, and the 'Review and Conclusion' 361–75.

[2] And others have been proposed – for example the concise and thoughtful checklist for legislative instructions suggested by Helen Xanthaki, *Drafting Legislation: Art and Technology of Rules for Regulation* (Oxford, Hart Publishing, 2014) 36–37.

[3] See OECD, *OECD Best Practice Principles for Regulatory Policy* (Paris, OECD Publishing, 2020); Stephan Naundorf and Claudio M Radaelli, 'Regulatory Evaluation Ex Ante and Ex Post: Best Practice, Guidance and Methods' in Ulrich Karpen and Helen Xanthaki (eds), *Legislation in Europe: A Country by Country Guide* (Oxford, Hart Publishing, 2020).

[4] See, eg, the Australian Office of Parliamentary Counsel's drafting manuals, available at: www.opc. gov.au/drafting-resources/drafting-manuals; and the United Kingdom Office of Parliamentary Counsel 'Drafting Guidance' (June 2020), available at: www.assets.publishing.service.gov.uk/government/ uploads/system/uploads/attachment_data/file/892409/OPC_drafting_guidance_June_2020-1.pdf.

[5] Legislation Design and Advisory Committee, *Legislation Guidelines: 2021 Edition* ch 10, available at: www.ldac.org.nz/assets/documents/LDAC-Legislation-Guidelines-2021-edition.pdf. See also the United Kingdom Office of the Parliamentary Counsel's *Common Legislative Solutions: A Guide to Tackling Recurring Policy Issues in Legislation* (Cabinet Office, March 2021), available at: www.gov.uk/government/ publications/common-legislative-solutions-a-guide-to-tackling-recurring-policy-issues-in-legislation.

[6] The core questions that are addressed in an RIA are:

- What, in general terms, is the problem to be addressed?
- What is the specific policy objective to be achieved?
- What are the different ways of achieving that policy objective (including regulatory and non-regulatory options)? The 'no-action' or baseline scenario should always be one of the options considered. Where the policy options that are being considered include legislation, the enactment of that legislation will be another option (or there may be more than one option involving legislation, if different legislative approaches are under consideration).
- What are the costs and benefits associated with each of the options under consideration? Where a regulatory proposal would have significant impacts, assessment of costs, benefits and risks should be quantitative where possible. Impacts that are difficult or impossible to quantify should be described qualitatively.

[7] Atul Gawande, *The Checklist Manifesto: How to Get Things Right*, 1st edn (New York, Metropolitan Books, 2009) ch 3; Cass R Sunstein and Reid Hastie, *Wiser: Getting Beyond Groupthink to Make Groups Smarter* (Boston, MA, Harvard Business Review Press, 2015).

[8] This is one aspect of regulatory stewardship – see ch 11, nn 9 and 15 above.

17

The Primary Checklist

The first checklist I describe is an overarching 'primary' checklist. It breaks down broad questions about a proposal to make legislation into 10 more focused questions. It dovetails with three more specific checklists: a 'benefits checklist' that focuses on the people who are intended to benefit from the legislation; a 'compliance checklist' that focuses on the people who are required to comply with obligations imposed by the legislation; and an 'institutions checklist' that focuses on the institutions responsible for implementation of the legislation.

The primary checklist contains 10 items:

1. What is the current position?
2. What is the legislation aiming to change?
3. Who are the audiences for the legislation?
4. What institutions will the legislation depend on? Do they have the capacity to play their role?
5. Has this been tried elsewhere? How did that go? How relevant is their experience?
6. Is a trial/pilot an option?
7. How will the legislation contribute to changes in behaviour?
8. Can the legislation adapt to take account of new information and/or changed circumstances?
9. Does the legislation take cross-border issues into account?
10. Telling the story: the narrative explaining the reasons for the reform.

Item 1: What is the Current Position?

As I explained in chapter six, the essential starting-point, before any legislative design process can get properly under way, is to capture as rich as possible a description of where we are now. In the law-making context, that has two main dimensions:

a. What is the current law (in the field being reviewed, together with background laws where relevant)?
b. How does the law operate in practice?

It is important that your description of the current position covers all the people who encounter the issue that the law addresses, not just those who come to the attention of officials, or who are involved in court proceedings. So for example if the issue is division of relationship property, the current position needs to be described in relation to all couples who separate, not just the tiny percentage who go to court to resolve property issues.

As explained in chapter six, the information-gathering process should include, but should not be confined to, identifying and obtaining relevant data held by government agencies and reviewing decisions from courts and other decision-makers. Consultation with the people directly affected by the relevant issue, and with others who have hands-on experience of how the current system operates (or fails to operate), is essential in order to build a rich and accurate picture of how people currently behave – and why they do what they do. Passively soliciting submissions from stakeholders is not enough.

I suggest you develop a decision map along the lines described in chapter six, which identifies who the relevant decision-makers are (citizens, businesses, government agencies, courts etc), and the time frames, costs and outcomes of those decisions.

It is important to expressly record what you do *not* know about the current position, as well as what you do know. The gaps in your knowledge are important pieces in the puzzle when it comes to considering the form that the legislation should take.

Item 2: What is the Legislation Aiming to Change?

Once we have described the current position, we come to the next key question: what is it that we are aiming to change? And how do we want to change it? These questions are explored in more detail in chapter seven above.

The key issues to address under this item are:

a.   What is the problem? More specifically, what aspects of the current behaviours described under item 1 are problematic?

b.   What is the desired outcome? How will the behaviour of relevant actors need to change in order to achieve this outcome?

The desired outcome should be expressed in terms that identify whose behaviour will change, and how it will change. Is the goal to change the behaviour of every person in a relevant group? Almost all of them? A majority? Some smaller proportion? Clarity about the scope of the desired change, as well as about its nature, is essential when it comes to designing the proposed legislation and thinking about how it will be implemented in practice.

Item 3: Who are the Audiences for the Legislation?

The process of identifying the change in outcomes that we want the proposed legislation to deliver, and the people whose behaviour would need to change in order for us to see those outcomes, leads logically into the next question: to whom will the legislation be addressed? Who needs to be aware of and act on the proposed law if we are to achieve the desired outcome? How will each audience be informed about what the law requires them to do, or enables them to do?

These issues are discussed in more detail in chapter eight above.

Item 4: What Institutions will the Legislation Depend on? Do they have the Capacity to Play their Role?

This item in the primary checklist focuses on identifying the relevant institutions, and assessing their capacity and will to perform their role. The fundamental importance of those institutions to the success or failure of a legislative project is discussed in chapter nine above.

Under this heading you should:

a. Identify all institutions (officials, agencies, courts etc) that have a role to play in implementing the legislation.
b. Consider whether each of those institutions has the capacity and the will to perform their role.
c. Consider what steps can be taken to address any concerns about institutional capacity.

These issues are addressed in more detail in the institutions checklist in chapter twenty below, which feeds into this item in the primary checklist.

Item 5: Has this been Tried Elsewhere? How did that Go? How Relevant is their Experience?

In chapter ten we examined the many ways in which the experience of similar societies can inform our own legal design projects. We also identified some critical questions that need to be asked when drawing on models from other societies.

The key questions to ask under this item are:

a. Is there a well-established and successful international model that should be used as a starting point for the proposed legislation?
b. What precedents are there in comparable societies for the proposed approach adopted in the legislation?

c. Was the approach a success in those other societies? How do we know?
d. Will success elsewhere translate into your society's social, economic and institutional setting?

Item 6: Is a Trial/Pilot an Option?

In chapter ten we also looked at how trials and pilots can be used to shed light on the likelihood that the desired change will in fact result from proposed legislation. The key questions to address under this item are:

a. Is a trial/pilot an option? Are there any practical or ethical reasons not to conduct a trial or pilot, to support more informed decision-making?
b. Should the legislation be amended to enable a trial/pilot to be conducted, with a subsequent roll-out if it is successful?

Item 7: How will the Legislation Contribute to Changes in Behaviour?

Chapter eleven addresses the most difficult of all the issues in this checklist: how likely is it that the proposed legislation will produce the desired changes? This complex issue can be broken down into a number of more manageable – though still challenging – questions:

a. How is the proposed legislation likely to operate in practice? What will change as compared with the status quo? Why – what is your theory of change? What will stay the same? Why? (It can be helpful to set this out in an amended version of the item 1 decision map, which identifies the changes that the proposed legislation is intended to make.)
b. What aspects of the post-legislation scenario are difficult to predict with reasonable confidence?

I strongly encourage you to conduct a pre-mortem for the legislation. Assume that a few years out it has failed, and ask what sort of failure is most likely:

a. Is the legislation a damp squib? Did it overshoot? Did it produce nasty surprises, or backfire?
b. What factors may have caused or contributed to that failure?
c. Can the risk of failure be reduced by adjusting default settings?
d. Can the risk of failure be reduced by reducing the complexity of the legislation as it is experienced in practice by end users or other relevant audiences?

The benefits checklist in chapter eighteen and the compliance checklist in chapter nineteen feed into this item of the primary checklist.

Item 8: Can the Legislation Adapt to take Account of New Information and/or Changed Circumstances?

It is likely – perhaps inevitable – that any legislative scheme will require adjustments from time to time in order to achieve its existing goals. These issues were explored in chapters eleven and twelve above. The key points to address under this item are as follows:

a.   What are the areas of greatest uncertainty? (The current position? Future social and economic change? The nature and extent of the changes in behaviour that will result from the legislation?)

b.   What mechanisms will there be for gathering relevant information in key areas of uncertainty? In particular, what mechanisms will there be for gathering information about how the legislation is operating in practice, and assessing that information against the legislation's goals?

c.   How can the law be structured to enable it to adapt to reflect new information about how it is working in practice, and changes in circumstances? How can the law be designed to be adaptive legislation? Is it appropriate to use techniques such as:

   i.   delegated rule-making?
   ii. legislating principles/standards coupled with (adaptable) default rules, safe harbours, provision of guidance by agencies?

d.   Is the legislation framed in a way that enables it to adapt to changing technologies? (see chapter twelve).

e.   Should there be express provision for reviews?

Item 9: Does the Legislation take Cross-Border Issues into Account?

The practical significance of cross-border issues for design of legislation is explained briefly in chapter thirteen. These issues are overlooked all too often. Under this item you should identify the cross-border issues that are relevant to the proposed legislation, and consider how the legislation should take those issues into account:

a.   What cross-border issues are likely to arise in the context of the proposed legislation?

   i.   Are relevant actors outside the jurisdiction?
   ii.   Is relevant property outside the jurisdiction?
   iii. Is relevant information outside the jurisdiction?
   iv.   Is there a risk that the laws of more than one country will apply to some activities, giving rise to conflicting obligations or complexity or unnecessary duplication?

    v.   Conversely, is there a risk of a regulatory gap (ie, no country's law both applies and is practically effective in relation to certain actors or activities)?

    vi.   Is there scope for unilateral or mutual recognition of outcomes in other countries?

    vii.   Will enforcement need to take place abroad?

    viii.   Is there a need for cross-border regulatory cooperation in order for the law to be effective? With which other countries?

b.   What are the appropriate connecting factors for the legislation to apply?

c.   How will the legislation be enforced in practice, where relevant actors (or their assets) are outside the jurisdiction?

Item 10: Telling the Story – The Narrative Explaining the Reasons for the Reform

Throughout this book I have warned against designing laws on the basis of plausible narratives constructed on the basis of limited information. I have emphasised the need to break issues down into their component parts; gather relevant information; and avoid the risk of over-confidence in the stories we tell ourselves about the status quo, and about how the proposed legislation will bring about change.

But when it comes to explaining a proposed reform, it would be difficult to overstate the importance of being able to tell a simple, cogent story about the reasons for that reform and about the way it is being implemented. The proposed reform will need to be explained in the political arena: the legislator responsible for the reform may need to bring their colleagues on board; support may be needed from other political groupings; the reform may need to be summarised for legislators. The merits of the proposed reform will need to be explained in a range of public forums, and in the media. The process of designing the legislation, and implementing it, will usually involve a number of officials and agencies all of whom need to understand the rationale for the reform. Things will go better if there is a carefully developed narrative that is simple, clear, accurate – and consistent across all these different contexts.

If you have worked your way through the earlier items in this checklist, you will be well placed to help develop a narrative that explains what the proposed legislation is intended to achieve, and how it will do this. The narrative needs to be as simple as possible. The key elements of this narrative are likely to be:

- The problem: what is happening now (item 1), and why is it undesirable (item 2)?
- The desired outcome: what is the legislation intended to change (item 2)?
- The solution: how will the proposed legislation help to bring about the desired outcome (item 7)?

Sometimes it is helpful to point to other places where similar laws have been successful (item 5).

This narrative will be an important explanatory tool. It will also be a helpful litmus test for the clarity and coherence of your own thinking, and for the consistency of the draft legislation with the original policy goal.

18

Benefits Checklist

At the risk of stating the painfully obvious, the purpose of most legislation is to provide benefits of some kind to one or more groups of people. Sometimes the intended benefit is diffuse – constitutional laws, and many criminal laws, are intended to benefit all members of a society. More often, the legislation is intended to benefit a particular group – tenants, or people whose relationship has ended, or consumers, or business owners.

But surprisingly often, legislation operates in a way that makes it unnecessarily difficult for the end users who are intended to benefit from the legislation (its 'beneficiaries', as I will call them in this chapter) to find out about the benefits it provides, or to access those benefits. The result is a damp squib – the legislation fails to achieve its policy goals.

The purpose of the benefits checklist is to identify risks of failure of this kind, and to prompt consideration of ways to manage those risks.

The most effective way for a team working on a legislative project to make use of this checklist is to appoint an owner of the checklist, who will take the lead in ensuring that the checklist is used effectively. Their role includes gathering information about the circumstances of the beneficiaries, their interests and their views. And advocating, within the team, for design choices that would make access to the benefits those beneficiaries are intended to receive as simple and easy as possible. Allocating this role to a specific team member should help to ensure that this information is obtained and shared with other team members, reducing the risk of the 'groupthink' that can contribute to these important issues being overlooked or discounted.

The benefits checklist contains five items:

B1 Who is the legislation intended to benefit? What benefits are those beneficiaries intended to obtain?

B2 What criteria do the beneficiaries need to meet to qualify for those benefits?

B3 How will the beneficiaries become aware of the availability of those benefits, and how to obtain them?

B4 Can receipt of those benefits be made a default setting that does not require any specific action from beneficiaries?

B5 If beneficiaries are required to make an active decision, or take active steps, what can be done to make this as simple and easy as possible?

Each of these items is discussed briefly below.

B1: Who is the Legislation Intended to Benefit? What Benefits are those Beneficiaries Intended to Obtain?

You will have given some thought to this question already, in the course of tackling item 2 of the primary checklist. If the legislation works as intended, who will be better off? The answer to this question is obvious if the legislation provides for certain people to have enforceable rights or claims against others. A law that provides consumers with guarantees in relation to goods and services, and gives them rights against the providers of those goods and services, is intended to benefit consumers. A law that provides for incorporation of businesses is intended to provide direct benefits to owners of businesses (as well as indirect benefits to the economy as a whole). The answer is less obvious, but no less important, where the law protects the interests of a group in less direct ways – for example, laws in relation to building construction that are intended to ensure the safety of people using those buildings, and people in the vicinity of those buildings.

Often there will be more than one group of beneficiaries. We can think of bail laws, for example, as intended to benefit two distinct groups:

a. The public: the law aims to support the efficient and effective administration of justice in the public interest by ensuring that people accused of an offence attend court hearings, and to protect public safety while dangerous offenders await trial.
b. People accused of committing offences: the law aims to protect the liberty of individuals charged with an offence unless and until they have been found guilty of an offence by a court and sentenced to a term of imprisonment.

As this example illustrates, identifying the benefits that the legislation is intended to provide to each relevant group is inextricably linked to the process of identifying those groups.

It is difficult to design legislation to be effective if you are not clear about who is intended to benefit from that legislation, and about the benefits that the legislation is intended to provide to the relevant group or groups.

As the bail law example illustrates, the goals of the legislation may be in tension with each other. The legislation will have to strike a balance between those goals. The benefit the law seeks to provide to one group needs to be weighed against the benefit the law seeks to provide to other groups. A clear focus on the interests of all relevant groups, and the trade-offs involved in leaning one way or another, will improve the quality of both policy analysis and legislative design.

Once each relevant beneficiary group has been identified, an 'owner' of this checklist should be appointed with responsibility for working through the checklist and reviewing it from the perspective of that group. If there is more than one beneficiary group, and their interests are potentially inconsistent – as in the bail law example above – you may want to appoint more than one owner, each of whom will focus on a particular class of beneficiaries. But if time or resource constraints preclude having multiple owners of this list, it is better to have one than none.

B2: What Criteria do the Beneficiaries Need to Meet to Qualify for those Benefits?

The second item in this checklist is closely related to the first. It seeks to spell out in more detail the boundaries of each beneficiary group, and how people will be identified as members of that group. Suppose for example that the legislation will provide for financial assistance to tertiary students who would otherwise struggle to afford further education and training. In the course of addressing item 1, you may have identified the beneficiary group as 'tertiary students in need', or 'prospective students who cannot afford the cost of tertiary study'. Under this item, you will spell out in more detail the criteria for qualifying for financial support under the legislation.

This item is important because it links the purpose of the legislation – its policy goals – with the implementation issues that are raised by items B3–B5. The more targeted the provision of benefits under the legislation, and the more closely the criteria are tied to its policy goals, the more complex the legislation is likely to be to administer. If for example stringent criteria are adopted for financial need, more information will be needed about the student and their family circumstances in order to apply those criteria. A student seeking to obtain financial support will need to invest more time and effort in the process. The process will also be more time-consuming and resource-intensive for the agency responsible for applying the criteria. This increases the social cost of administering the programme, and can significantly increase the risk that people who are intended to benefit from it will fail to navigate the system and obtain those benefits. Adopting criteria framed in terms of broad standards or a discretionary test that depend on the exercise of judgement by an agency will have similar consequences: increased complexity and increased time and cost for applicants and for the agency.[1] And the broader the standard or discretion, the less predictable the outcomes for applicants, and the greater the risk of outcomes inconsistent with the policy goals of the legislation: false negatives, false positives, or both.

If the criteria are less stringent, on the other hand, then implementation is likely to be simpler and there will be fewer barriers to access to the scheme by the intended beneficiaries. But other people who are not the intended beneficiaries are more likely to be able to access the scheme: it will be more costly to fund, and will benefit people who do not need the support it provides. Money will be spent on this scheme that could be used to fund other pressing social goals.

Similar issues arise in other contexts. The policy goal of planning legislation is to set appropriate limits on how landowners use their land, in the interests of the people affected by those uses: it addresses costs imposed on others (externalities) that result from decisions by landowners. If the legislation provides for affected people to have rights of objection in relation to development proposals, what criteria will apply? Can anyone object, even if they do not live nearby? If they live in a different city? Can business competitors object – a right that is likely to be used for strategic purposes to hinder competition?

As these examples illustrate, choices about the criteria that will be set out in legislation in order to qualify for the benefits it provides will have important consequences for the complexity of the legislation, for the predictability of its operation, for ease of access to those benefits for the intended beneficiaries, and for implementation costs for the society as a whole. Decisions about these criteria are likely to be iterative: in light of the answers to items B3–B5, it may be necessary to revisit the criteria identified under this item.

B3: How will the Beneficiaries Become Aware of the Availability of those Benefits, and How to Obtain them?

Item 3 of the primary checklist asks who the audiences are for the proposed legislation, and how each audience will become aware of the implications of the legislation for them. Item B3 of the benefits checklist feeds into this exercise by asking how a key group – the intended beneficiaries – will become aware of the potential benefits the legislation provides and what they need to do in order to obtain those benefits.

Returning to the planning law example, people who are not aware of a land development proposal, or who do not know about an ability they have to object to the proposal if it has certain adverse effects, will not be able to exercise that right of objection. The law needs to ensure that this beneficiary group is adequately informed about proposals, and about their rights in connection with those proposals. This may require different levels of notification – personal notice to immediate neighbours, for example, coupled with an appropriate form of public notice.

The famous *Miranda* warning that United States case law requires people to be given when arrested, advising them of their rights (including the right to remain silent), is a good example of a process for ensuring that a person is made aware of their entitlements under the law at the time that those entitlements are of particular relevance. In many other countries, legislation provides for similar warnings. These important rights are essentially useless in practice if you do not know you have them at the time when you need them most. Or if you do not understand them.

Even in contexts where receipt of benefits under legislation is automatic, requiring no positive action on the part of the beneficiary, it will often be necessary to ensure that beneficiaries are made aware of those benefits to ensure that they are taken up. Suppose for example that a law is passed entitling children aged five and under to free dental care, and the law is implemented by providing for dentists to recover payment for these treatments direct from a funding agency. The beneficiary does not need to make a payment upfront and then apply for reimbursement, or engage with the funder, or provide any information apart from the basic personal information they provide to their dentist. Even so, if a child's parents do not know that they can take their child to the dentist without having to pay, they may not do so because they are concerned about their ability to meet the cost.

This is a critical item on the checklist. A lack of awareness on the part of intended beneficiaries about the benefits available under a legal framework is likely to lead to 'damp squib' failures.

B4: Can Receipt of those Benefits be made a Default Setting that does not require any Specific Action from Beneficiaries?

The simpler and easier it is for the intended beneficiaries to receive a benefit under the legislation, the more likely it is that they will receive those benefits in practice, and the more likely it is that the law will achieve its policy goals. The most effective way to remove barriers to access to benefits by the intended beneficiaries is to make receipt of the benefits a default setting: the benefit is provided without the need for any positive decision or other action on the part of a beneficiary. The importance of default settings is discussed in more detail in chapter fourteen above.

In practice, making receipt of benefits a default setting usually involves one of the following three approaches:

- Universal provision of the benefit – so there is no need to apply any criteria to determine eligibility. In New York City, for example, school lunches are provided free to all children attending elementary school. This avoids the need for a means-testing mechanism, reducing administration costs for the relevant agencies and reducing the barriers to access for beneficiaries that were previously created by the need to fill in forms and establish eligibility. Universal provision also removes the stigma associated with taking advantage of means-tested school lunches; a stigma which can hinder uptake of this kind of benefit.

- Use of information that is otherwise available to determine eligibility. The information may have been provided at an earlier time, or in another context. Or there may be an acceptable proxy for the eligibility criteria that can be used to identify a subset of the beneficiary group (perhaps coupled with a mechanism to identify those who are missed by the proxy), or to identify a somewhat broader group to whom the benefits can be extended. New Zealand's 'Kiwisaver' retirement savings scheme, described in more detail in chapter ten above, provides for every person who begins a new job to be enrolled in the scheme by default, unless they opt out. This mechanism does not capture the full class of intended beneficiaries of the scheme – essentially, all working-age people. Supplementary arrangements are needed for existing employees and for the self-employed. But over time it creates a default setting for a very large proportion of the target group.

- Proactive identification (usually by a public agency) of people who qualify as beneficiaries. In practice this often overlaps with the second approach: information obtained in another context is used to identify potential beneficiaries, and their eligibility is then proactively assessed by an agency.

Each of these approaches raises a set of challenges that will need to be weighed against ease of access. Universal provision of a benefit is usually (though not invariably) more costly than targeted provision of the same benefit. The second and third options may raise privacy concerns, if information provided for one purpose is used for another purpose. The third option risks failure to identify beneficiaries, and under-provision of benefits. In practice, these challenges often lead to some sort of requirement for beneficiaries to take active steps to seek a benefit, and establish that they qualify for it. That leads into item B5.

B5: If Beneficiaries are Required to make an Active Decision, or take Active Steps, What can be Done to make this as Simple and Easy as Possible?

If it is not possible to make receipt of the benefit a default setting, then beneficiaries will be required to make an active decision, or take active steps, in order to receive the benefit. The purpose of this item in the checklist is to ensure careful identification and scrutiny of the steps they are required to take, to assess the impact of those requirements on the ability of the legislation to achieve its policy goals.

The first step in this analysis is to identify in detail each step that a person will be required to take to qualify for the benefit – each form that will have to be filled in, each item of information that they will need to gather in order to fill in and submit the form, each queue that they will have to join, each phone call they will need to make, and anything else they will need to do in order to reach the end point of the process.

Each and every one of those steps should be carefully scrutinised to test whether it is actually necessary. The overall process – the time and cost and hassle involved in getting from start to finish – should also be considered. Is it realistic? The practicalities of each step, and of the overall process, should be tested with people from the relevant group: they will have the best understanding of the practical hurdles involved.

Options that might be considered to improve ease of access to benefits under the legislation include:

- Dispensing with criteria for access to the benefit that are costly and time-consuming to apply, with the result that beneficiaries face significant barriers to accessing the intended benefit.
- Dispensing with, or simplifying, steps in the process of applying for and receiving the benefit. Does a form really need to be filled in at, or delivered to, the agency's office? Can the information be provided online in advance? Can the need to visit an office in person be dispensed with completely? Can two steps, each requiring a visit or the provision of information, be combined into one? Can payments be made electronically, rather than in cash or by cheque?

- Enhancing transparency and accountability in relation to the time taken to make decisions, the process for making the decisions, and the outcomes of those decisions. The caseload and backlog for different offices can be tracked, and causes of delays investigated. The figures can be made public. In environments where corruption is a concern, providing for random allocation of cases and for public decision-making in real time can remove opportunities to seek bribes or other benefits;

- Simplifying the process for departing from the default 'no benefit' setting. Can the initial process of accessing the benefit be made simpler and faster, with any problem cases identified and resolved after the event? One example discussed in chapter fourteen above is the child support scheme in New Zealand, which provides for an initial 'formula assessment' using a relatively simple algorithm. The outcome of the formula assessment can be reviewed by an official (or, on appeal, a judge), applying a more sophisticated test. But in the interim the amount assessed using the formula is paid to the custodial parent to be spent for the benefit of the child who has an immediate need for support, and the liable parent must make payments – there is a preliminary binding determination of the amount payable. The time and cost involved in accessing a benefit can be significantly reduced if an initial decision is made using an algorithm that is reasonably accurate, though imperfect, with any problems addressed at a subsequent stage. An algorithm may also be used to triage cases into easy cases that can be dealt with automatically, harder cases requiring additional information before they are dealt with automatically, and the most complex cases which a human decision-maker will need to consider. If 80 per cent of cases are relatively simple and can be automated, they should be; only the genuinely difficult cases should go through a more sophisticated and time-consuming process.

- Ensuring that the information sought from beneficiaries is no more extensive than is necessary for the relevant purpose.

- Ensuring that information already provided to the same agency by a beneficiary on a previous occasion need not be provided again – for example, by pre-filling hard copy or online forms.

- Providing beneficiaries with the option of authorising access to information provided to other agencies (or to a shared public sector data repository, if there is one), or held by third parties (for example, their bank), to avoid the need to provide that information in the current context.

- Empowering a public agency to enforce rights on behalf of individuals or groups. Transferring responsibility for enforcement of a law to an appropriately skilled and resourced institution can be an effective way to address the risk of that law becoming a damp squib because of the difficulty, delay and cost that invoking the law would present for the people who are intended to benefit from it. So for example public agencies may be given a role in enforcing rights of employees or tenants. A consumer protection agency may have the ability to bring proceedings on behalf of consumers. A privacy regulator may be empowered to seek remedies for privacy breaches on behalf of the affected individuals. An ombudsman may have the ability to investigate grievances about various kinds of government decision. But resource constraints can limit the practical value of provisions of this kind. It is one thing to provide for this approach in legislation; it is another for this approach to deliver widespread effective results. If the agency's resources are modest, this approach may make only a small difference to the effectiveness of the law.

- Providing direct assistance to participants in a claims process, or providing funding for them to obtain such assistance. In many countries the availability of legal aid for participation in civil proceedings has been curtailed over the last decade or so, as public expenditure has come under increasing pressure. It seems unlikely that legal designers will be able to rely on this approach in many countries in the foreseeable future, as it runs against that trend, so it may be necessary to find more creative solutions to access issues.

- Reducing barriers to access to court-based processes through class action regimes, which may be coupled with litigation funding mechanisms. The extent to which generic regimes of this kind are available and effective should be taken into account when assessing access issues. Where there is no generally applicable class action regime, one option for making some laws more effective in practice may be to provide tailored class action regimes for the purposes of that law – for example, enabling one borrower to bring proceedings challenging oppressive provisions in a lender's standard form credit contract on behalf of all similarly situated borrowers dealing with that lender.

- Providing access to dispute resolution mechanisms (generic or tailored to the particular context) that are simpler, faster and less costly than full-blown court proceedings – at least as a first step.[2] These may be administered by human decision-makers, but with reduced formality and easier access. One option is to provide for claims to be made and information provided online: many current online dispute resolution initiatives take this form.[3] In some contexts, the dispute resolution process may be automated, with or without provision for review by a human decision-maker. The design of automated dispute resolution mechanisms is a vast topic, beyond the scope of this book. But automation, and in particular AI, is of growing importance as a tool for delivering meaningful access to some form of neutral and binding dispute resolution. Critics are quick to point out the limits of automation of dispute resolution mechanisms. Those limits are certainly significant. But the critics need to explain what better, practically workable alternatives they can put forward: measuring automated dispute resolution tools against an unattainable (because unaffordable) ideal adds little to the debate.

The issue of access to the benefits that a proposed law is intended to provide is a pressing one. It needs to be squarely faced, and serious attempts made to address it. There are more tools in the toolbox than most legal designers appreciate. Those tools can improve the position even where they cannot resolve the issue completely.

In cases where, despite the use of those tools, the law will still not be accessible in practice to many of its intended beneficiaries, that should be acknowledged and factored into decisions about the viability and value of the proposed legislation.

---

[1] Some methods of reducing complexity are discussed in ch 10 above.

[2] Many countries provide a relatively swift and inexpensive dispute resolution process for low value civil claims: eg, New Zealand's Disputes Tribunal, which hears some types of civil claim up to a ceiling of NZ$30,000, and the English Small Claims Court which hears some civil claims up to a ceiling of £10,000. But such tribunals often do not have jurisdiction to hear common types of claim, for example family law disputes, and the ceiling on the value of claims they can hear limits their relevance. Usually legal representation is not required, and in some of these processes (eg, in New Zealand) it is actually prohibited. This keeps direct costs down, but a prohibition on legal representation can be problematic for parties who need support to advance their claim effectively. Expanding the scope of processes of this kind is one option to enhance access to the protection of the law – either by bringing additional categories of claim within their scope, or by lifting the monetary value ceiling. Tailored processes that perform a similar function, but with particular subject-matter expertise, are another option.

[3] See Online Dispute Resolution Advisory Group, *Online Dispute Resolution for Low Value Civil Claims* (Civil Justice Council, February 2015), available at: www.judiciary.uk/reviews/online-dispute-resolution/odr-report-february-2015/.

19

Compliance Checklist

As we saw in chapter two, one common cause of damp squibs is widespread failure to comply with requirements imposed by the law. A great deal of non-compliance with legal requirements results from people not being aware of the requirement, or forgetting about it, or postponing the action required by the law because it is time-consuming and tedious. If we design laws and institutions that take account of common human failings and make allowances for those failings, our laws will work much better.

Where the law requires a person to take some active steps in order to comply with the law, legal designers should focus on making it as easy as possible for people to take those steps. The easier it is, the more likely it is that people will do it. This seems pretty obvious – but I have encountered a great deal of legislation that requires the people to whom it is addressed to jump through unnecessary hoops, and even more legislation that misses opportunities to simplify life for well-intentioned people who want to comply with the law provided they know what it requires, and doing so isn't unreasonably difficult.

The compliance checklist is intended to test the need for requirements imposed by the law, and to focus attention on how compliance with genuinely necessary requirements can be made as simple as possible, and as attractive as possible. It contains five items:

C1   Who is required to take steps to comply with the legislation? What is each relevant compliance group required to do?
C2   Can some compliance obligations be reduced or eliminated?
C3   How will each compliance group be made aware of their obligations?
C4   What can be done to make compliance as simple and easy as possible?
C5   What can be done to encourage compliance?

Each of these items is discussed briefly below.

As with the benefits checklist, I suggest appointing an owner of the compliance checklist who takes the lead in ensuring that the checklist is used effectively. Their role includes gathering information about the circumstances, interests and views of the people required to comply with the proposed legislation. And advocating within the team for design choices that would make compliance as easy and attractive as practicable for these people.

C1: Who is Required to take Steps to Comply with the Legislation? What is each Relevant Compliance Group Required to Do?

If the proposed legislation works as intended, who will need to change their behaviour to comply with requirements imposed by that legislation? What will each of these 'compliance groups' be required to do, and in what circumstances? You will have given these questions some thought already in the context of item 2 of the primary checklist. For the purposes of this item, those questions need to be answered in more detail. The decision map you prepare in the context of the primary checklist should help with this exercise – and this exercise will in turn feed into the decision map.

Once each relevant compliance group has been identified, an 'owner' of this checklist needs to be appointed to work through the checklist and review it from the perspective of that group. If there is more than one compliance group, and their interests are potentially inconsistent, you may want to appoint more than one owner, each of whom will focus on a particular group. But as in the benefits context, resource and time constraints may preclude this.

C2: Can Some Compliance Obligations be Reduced or Eliminated?

The next question to ask is whether it really is necessary for the relevant group to take a particular action in order to achieve the legislation's policy goals. Can some compliance obligations be eliminated, without compromising the effectiveness of the law? In many countries, for example, tax laws significantly simplify compliance by taxpayers with their tax obligations by:

- Providing for automatic deductions of tax from salaries, and from investment returns. Individual taxpayers do not need to do anything in order to pay the amount of tax estimated to be payable in respect of these forms of income.

- Not requiring some categories of taxpayer to file a tax return. If the only income a taxpayer receives is in the form of salary and investment returns that are subject to deductions of tax at source, then the government has all relevant information and does not require a return to ensure sufficient tax is paid. (A taxpayer may want to file a return to claim a refund, but this is optional. And in some tax systems, even this is unnecessary, as assessment and payment of refunds is automated for some categories of taxpayer.)

Another closely related option is to reduce the frequency with which people are required to take positive steps to comply with the law. Can obligations that are currently performed monthly be reduced in frequency so that they need only be addressed every two or three months? It can make a big difference to a business, in particular a small business, if it is only required to provide information or make payments to an agency quarterly rather than monthly. The vehicle licensing legislation in New Zealand was recently amended to provide that car owners only need to have their cars inspected by an authorised safety inspector every three years, rather than every year. Improvements in the quality and safety of vehicles on the road meant that the frequency and overall cost of these inspections could be reduced by two-thirds without materially compromising safety goals.

There are also many ways in which the scope of legal requirements – what the legislation requires a person to do – can be reduced. In particular, many laws require people and businesses to provide information for various purposes. Often the default setting is that on every occasion a prescribed form must be completed, or a standardised set of information provided, whether this is being done for the first time or the hundredth time, and whether or not the relevant agency already holds some or all of that information. The effectiveness of the legislation can be increased, and the burden on affected people and businesses reduced, by modifying this default so that only information that is not already held by the agency actually needs to be provided. Where a government agency requires information to be updated or confirmed for a particular purpose, for example, and that agency already holds some or all of the relevant information, it can provide a partly or fully completed form and ask the recipient to correct or update anything that is inaccurate, and confirm its correctness. This can often be done online, simplifying the process further still. This approach has been adopted in some countries where companies are required to file annual returns setting out current information about matters such as the location of the head office of the company, and about its directors and shareholders. The registry sends out by post or email, or provides an online link to, a form that already contains the most recent information about these matters held by the registry. If the information is still current, a simple confirmation suffices. If not, then updated information can be filled in and the form can then be submitted – ideally by clicking a 'submit' button online, rather than by posting a hard copy form or delivering that form to the registry. Where a process of this kind is moved online, it is also a simple matter to send reminders by email or text message to ensure that deadlines are not overlooked.

Some governments are taking this approach further by ensuring that individuals and businesses are not required to provide the same information to multiple government agencies on different occasions. This is a common complaint from small businesses in particular: in many countries they spend a significant amount of time filling in the same information on slightly different forms issued by different agencies for different purposes, and sending it to all of those agencies. If relevant information has been provided by a business to agency A, and agency B needs to receive some or all of the same information, you should consider whether it is possible for that information to be made available by agency A direct to agency B. Agency B can then confine its requirements to any genuinely new information that it requires. Or the government can create a centralised data repository, in which individuals and businesses can choose to keep relevant information, and those individuals and businesses can then authorise an agency to access that information in order to reduce the need to provide the information on multiple occasions. This approach requires investment in data technology, and safeguards to ensure appropriate levels of data integrity and privacy. But it has the potential to significantly reduce or simplify compliance obligations.

There are many other ways in which legislation can be designed to make compliance easier and simpler. Some of these are discussed below. But the starting point should always be to ask if imposing a compliance obligation can be avoided, or the frequency or scope of the obligation reduced. Once the truly necessary requirements have been identified, attention can turn to making it as easy and attractive as possible to comply with those requirements.

C3: How will each Compliance Group be made Aware of their Obligations?

How will each relevant compliance group become aware of what they are required to do in practice? This topic was touched on under item 3 of the primary checklist. You should consider how each relevant group will become aware that they have obligations under the legislation, and how they will obtain the necessary information to know what practical steps they must take in order to comply.

In some contexts, a compliance group will obtain this information direct from the legislation. But this is unusual: few people or businesses have the capacity to read and understand legislation and translate it into the specific actions they are required to take in order to comply with their obligations. In some contexts the members of a compliance group will seek legal advice, or advice from other professionals, about their compliance obligations. But in most circumstances this also is unrealistic, for reasons of time and cost.

Careful thought needs to be given to how information about the law's requirements will be obtained by each compliance group. Should the law provide for 'signposts' – contextually relevant information about compliance obligations such as speed limits, road markings, or warning signs? For information about compliance obligations to be provided by an agency? Should that information be made available passively on a website or in brochures, or should it be provided as and when it is relevant – for example, warnings about customs and biosecurity obligations addressed to arriving travellers at an airport? What status will the detailed guidance provided by an agency have? Must it be complied with (for example, will the legislation provide for the issue of rules by the agency, and for penalties for non-compliance with those rules)? Will compliance with the requirements prescribed by the agency be treated as compliance with the legislation (a form of safe harbour)? Or is the information provided for assistance only? Are decisions (or some form of binding ruling) available in particular cases in advance? What other forms of assistance are available, whether proactively or on request, to enable a person to understand what they need to do in order to comply?

If a compliance group cannot readily obtain information at a practically useful level of detail about their obligations, they are much less likely to comply with those obligations. The law risks being a damp squib. This is a critical issue to test, both at a level of theory and by engaging with members of the relevant group to explore how proposed approaches will work in practice.

C4: What can be Done to Make Compliance as Simple and Easy as Possible?

Under item C2, you will have considered whether it is necessary to require a compliance group to take particular steps. Under item C3, you will have considered how the compliance group will become aware of the steps that they are required to take. The focus of this item is on how compliance can be made as simple and easy as possible. Ease of compliance is another critical issue that needs to be addressed both at a level of principle and through engagement with members of the relevant group.

The first component of this exercise overlaps with item C3. The more complex a legal obligation, the harder it is for a compliance group to understand what they are required to do in practice to comply with that obligation. They may be well aware of a legal obligation which is framed as a standard – for example, to take all practicable steps to reduce health and safety risks for employees in the workplace. But complex issues arise about what a standard of this kind requires in practice in particular settings. Complexity can also arise where laws are lengthy and detailed, for example where multiple provisions of the law are relevant to the same scenario. Many tax laws suffer from this form of complexity. Complexity can also arise from overlapping (and different) requirements imposed by different laws. The issue of complexity is an important one, discussed in more detail in chapter fifteen above. Reducing complexity hinges on the interplay between the substantive law and the institutional arrangements for implementing that law.

The second component of this exercise focuses on the practical steps required by the law. Can these be made less burdensome? Less time-consuming or costly? Can compliance be facilitated, for example by making it a default position? Can 'architecture' – the physical or online environment in which the relevant conduct occurs – facilitate compliance?[1] Can reminders be provided electronically – for example, using email or text messages to provide reminders that documents must be filed at a companies registry, reminders that tax payments are due, or reminders of court appearances or probation appointments? This is an especially important issue to explore with the relevant compliance group, and with advisers to that group.

C5: What can be Done to Encourage Compliance?

Even if it is clear what the law requires a person to do, and even if unnecessary barriers to compliance have been removed, many people will remain reluctant to comply with laws that impose a significant burden on them. Few people pay taxes with enthusiasm, to take just one example. That brings us to the next topic: making it more attractive to comply with the law – or, put another way, making it less attractive to fail to do so.

Compliance is problematic where it is costly. In particular, compliance is likely to be poor where the gains from non-compliance significantly exceed the expected cost of non-compliance. This trade-off will vary significantly depending on context – a decision map backed by interviews with stakeholders should help to identify where this is likely to be an issue.

Compliance is also problematic where the law runs counter to established social beliefs or practices. The options for addressing this issue depend very much on context. If the law seeks to encourage people to wear seatbelts, for example, in a country where this is uncommon, then a law requiring the wearing of seatbelts needs to be accompanied by effective education about the risks of not wearing seatbelts, and effective enforcement of the requirement. Compliance can be made easier by requiring new cars to be fitted with seatbelts when sold, and existing cars retrofitted with seatbelts within a specified time frame. It is much easier to wear a seatbelt (and to get into the habit of putting it on) if every car you get into has seatbelts! (A retrofitting requirement may be able to be enforced through vehicle licensing requirements, especially if these already include periodic inspections.) Consideration can be given to options for making compliance more attractive through technology – for example, requiring vehicles to be fitted with alarms that sound if a seatbelt is not fastened, or disabling technology that prevents the car from moving until seatbelts are fastened.

Suppose, to take another example, that legislation seeks to prevent discrimination by employers on the basis of race or gender or sexual orientation. Education and enforcement will be important. Other mechanisms for encouraging compliance with such laws include reporting obligations in relation to hiring decisions and relative remuneration levels. The obligation could be to make a report to a public agency, or to address the issue in published reports of a kind that large businesses in many countries are already required to produce.

The key point for present purposes is that simply passing a law that requires people to change behaviour that is deeply ingrained will achieve very little, without more. That 'more' may have important implications for the content and structure of the law. It needs to be thought through at the time the law is being designed, not left for a later stage.

The traditional focus of legal designers seeking to encourage compliance with the law is to prescribe sanctions for non-compliance, often in the form of fines imposed through a penal process administered by a public agency, or through the courts. This is a simple and familiar technique. But it begs many questions:

- What, if anything, can be done to make compliance easier? In many contexts, simplifying the process of compliance will be more effective than increasing penalties for non-compliance or investing more resources in enforcement. This is yet another illustration of the important interplay between substantive law (including penalty rules) and institutions.

- What, if anything, can be done to reward compliance? If a tax payment or fee is due, for example, should the legislation provide for discounts for timely payment?

- What forms of sanction/deterrent are likely to be both effective and proportionate? Is it really appropriate to invoke the criminal process, with the cost and delay and stigma that involves? Or should there be a system of civil penalties? Administrative penalties? Administrative directions and/or court orders to carry out remedial work, ultimately backed by sanctions and/or cost recovery for that remedial work in the event of non-compliance? Step-in powers to enable an agency to take immediate action to achieve compliance, then recover the costs from the breacher? Rules providing for disgorgement of gains? Rules providing for compensation to be paid to people harmed by the conduct, or to an agency that will assist those who have been harmed? Rules providing for breachers to be barred from the relevant activity on an interim basis, or permanently? Regimes to facilitate and incentivise whistle-blowing? Taxes imposed on behaviour that the law seeks to discourage, so the behaviour is not prohibited but the cost of engaging in it increases? All relevant options need to be considered, and their likely effectiveness assessed, paying attention both to the theoretical effectiveness of such a remedy and to how it is likely to operate in practice in the relevant social and economic setting.

Where a law does use the familiar technique of imposing penalties for non-compliance, thought needs to be given to how those penalties are set by the law. If they are fixed sums, or fixed maximum sums, then inflation is likely to mean they become meaningless over time. Section 13 of the Taranaki Botanic Garden Act 1876, still in force in New Zealand, prohibits certain conduct in the garden such as lighting fires and breaking or cutting trees or plants – and provides for penalties for breach 'not exceeding ten dollars'. That's about the cost of two cups of coffee. It's not going to alter anyone's behaviour, even assuming that would-be fire-lighters know about the penalty in the first place.[2] The Impounding Act 1955, which deals with the impounding of stray stock, imposes fines for a wide range of offences – up to a maximum of $500. If this was an appropriate maximum in 1955, then the corresponding figure today allowing for inflation would be more than $13,000. The prescribed penalties are essentially meaningless today. Many countries use simple mechanisms to maintain the real value of financial penalties: failure to do so is quite simply poor legal design.

Another design issue in the context of financial penalties is that the impact of a given penalty on an individual or business, and the strength of the incentive it creates, will vary significantly depending on the wealth of that individual or business. A penalty that is significant, perhaps unaffordable, for many people will be trivial to others. A number of countries have adopted mechanisms to adjust penalties to take this into account – for example, 'day fines' calculated by reference to an individual's daily income. This may not be appropriate in all contexts. But thought should be given to whether, if an approach like this is not adopted, the incentives created by prescribed penalties will be immaterial for many of the people whose behaviour is intended to be influenced by those penalties. If the answer is that this doesn't matter much because the incentives created by penalties are not an important factor in securing compliance, then the appropriateness of providing for financial penalties needs to be revisited.

At least as important as the level of prescribed penalties is the likelihood of enforcement action: if the prospect of enforcement is remote then even the most hefty penalties are likely to be ineffective. The fundamental question for any legal designer is, as I have emphasised above, how the law will change behaviour. It is not possible to make meaningful judgements about the likely extent of compliance with a proposed law without taking into account the practical realities for compliance groups in relation to enforcement of that law. Changing the law to provide for more severe sanctions will not make any difference at all, if the main reason the existing law does not work is that it is not effectively enforced. I have often seen reforms focus on the law on paper – because that is relatively easy and inexpensive to change – when the real issue was institutional capacity to enforce the law.

---

[1] For a discussion of the ways in which architecture shapes behaviour, and code as architecture in the online context, see Lawrence Lessig, *Code and Other Laws of Cyberspace* (New York, Basic Books, 1999).

[2] The prohibited conduct would almost certainly constitute an offence under other general laws, and be subject to more serious penalties under those laws – but that raises very starkly the question of what purpose the 1876 penalty provision continues to serve. Retaining outdated provisions of this kind is at best pointless, and risks undermining respect for the law as an institution.

20

Institutions Checklist

As I have emphasised on a number of occasions, whether legislation succeeds in achieving its policy goals depends on the institutions responsible for its implementation. If the relevant institutions do not have the capacity and the will to implement the legislation effectively, failure is certain. The only question is the likely nature of that failure. 'Damp squib' failure is pretty much guaranteed. There is also often a real risk of nasty surprises, and perhaps backfires.

The institutions checklist focuses on this critical element of effective implementation of proposed legislation. It contains three items:

I1   What institutions will play a role in implementing the legislation? What decisions and actions will they be required to take?
I2   Will each of those institutions have the capacity and will to perform its role?
I3   How can any concerns about institutional capacity be addressed?

As with the other specific checklists, it is desirable to appoint an 'owner' of this checklist whose role is to develop a detailed understanding of the relevant institutions, their strengths and weaknesses, and the options for addressing any capacity concerns. Their role includes identifying risks associated with implementation of the legislation by the relevant institutions, and advocating changes to the legislation or to the institutional framework, or both, to ensure that those risks are addressed. These issues are complex and messy. As a result, there are often pressures within a project to postpone these issues until later, or simply ignore them and treat the relevant institutions as a 'black box' whose workings need not be examined. Those pressures make appointing an owner of this checklist, whose job it is to raise these issues, all the more important.

I1: What Institutions will Play a Role in Implementing the Legislation? What Decisions and Actions will they be Required to Take?

The first item in this checklist overlaps with item 4 of the primary checklist, and feeds into it. Identifying the institutions that will play a role in implementing proposed legislation is a fundamentally important task in any legal design project. Every relevant institution needs to be identified – including agencies with specific responsibility in relation to the legislation, and any general institutions such as the courts which are expected to play a role in implementation of the legislation.

It is also important to focus in some detail on the role that each institution will be expected to play, by identifying each distinct function that the institution will need to perform in connection with the legislation. What decisions and actions will each relevant institution be required to take? How often will they need to act? Is this a low-volume, high-complexity role? Or a high-volume, low-complexity role? Or – most challenging of all – a high-volume, high-complexity role? Will a single person or body make all of the decisions, or will there be multiple decision-makers?

A detailed decision map should be prepared showing all relevant institutions, all relevant functions of each institution, and the expected volume of each type of decision. The intended time frames for making each of these decisions should also be identified: often these will be critical to the effective operation of the legislation.

I2: Will each of those Institutions have the Capacity and Will to Perform its Role?

This item also overlaps with item 4 in the primary checklist, and feeds into it. It involves a detailed inquiry into the capacity and will of the institution to perform each of the specific functions identified under item I1 above. The volume, complexity and intended time frames for each decision are the key benchmarks against which capacity should be assessed. You will also need to consider the practical consequences of a lack of capacity in the context of each relevant function. What are the likely consequences of errors in making decisions? Are some types of error more likely than others? Are some types of error more problematic than others? What mechanisms exist to identify and correct errors? Is there a risk of inconsistency in outcomes, and if so, how much of a concern is that? What are the likely consequences of delay in making decisions beyond the intended time frames? These questions should be considered in relation to specific cases, and in relation to the overall regime. For example, it is usually the case that occasional errors or occasional delays are undesirable, but unavoidable and tolerable. However frequent errors, or pervasive and significant delays, can undermine the whole regime and cause it to fail in multiple ways.

Where a relevant institution already exists, the starting point for these enquiries should be a review of its current capacity and performance. If it is already performing the relevant function, it should be possible to gather data about volumes and time frames and outcomes. Assessing the quality of its performance is often more difficult. There may be relevant data – for example, frequency of appeals or reviews of its decisions, and the outcomes of those processes. But consultation with stakeholders is also essential, to provide a more complete picture of the institution's perceived strengths and weaknesses. Any concerns that are identified can then be followed up to ascertain whether, and to what extent, they are well-founded.

If the institution already exists, but is being given a new function, information about its existing capacity and the performance of its existing functions will help you form a view about its likely capacity to perform the new role. You will also need to consider what additional resources and systems the institution would need to perform the new role.

It is especially challenging to reach an informed view about institutional capacity issues where the proposal is to establish a new institution to implement the legislation. The ability of the institution to perform its intended role cannot be assessed based on known resources and an existing track record. But the difficulty of this task is not a good reason to ignore it. Pilots and dry runs are valuable options for assessing the necessary resources and systems, and any capacity issues that are likely to be encountered. It will often be essential to set up an establishment unit to identify the resources and systems that the institution will need in order to operate effectively, and to work towards the establishment of the institution. That establishment unit should be closely involved in the legal design process to ensure that the legal framework and the implementation framework dovetail neatly together.

I3: How can any Concerns about Institutional Capacity be Addressed?

Where there are concerns about the capacity of an institution – existing or proposed – to perform the functions that proposed legislation would confer on it, there are three basic options:

- Find ways to reduce the dependence of the proposed reform on that institution.
- Take action to address those institutional capacity issues.
- Reconsider the viability of the proposed reform.

These options are discussed in more detail in chapter nine above. If it is not possible to reduce the dependence of the proposed legislation on a weak institution, and there is no assurance that the institution will be able to develop the capacity and the will to perform its function within a reasonable time frame, then serious thought needs to be given to the overall viability of the proposed law. In the absence of concrete plans for implementation of proposed legislation by the relevant institutions, based on a realistic assessment of their existing or future capacity, the risk of failure is high.

21

Improving the Checklists

The astute reader may by this time be wondering whether, in preparing these checklists, I am making the same assumptions and falling victim to the same over-confidence that I warned against back in chapter three. What, you may be wondering, is my basis for thinking the checklists will work? Has there been a trial, or a pilot of some kind? Or have I just come up with a good story about how the world can be improved by the use of these checklists, without any grounding in the facts?

These are fair questions. The answer has four parts.

First, the value of a more structured approach to making complex decisions is well established. My experience of law reform in many countries over many years, and my work as a judge, confirm that the legal design process is vulnerable to the flaws that such a process is designed to mitigate. There is abundant room for us to do better. And there is good reason to think that an approach along these lines should help.

Second, there is no magic in the detail of the checklists. Their core function is to ensure that key questions about the proposed legislation – questions that on any view are relevant to its future effectiveness – are asked in a timely way. They are intended to ensure that legal design work avoids the pitfalls that are apparent when we look at how and why laws have failed in the past. And to reduce the risk that we will succumb, in our legal design work, to well-documented frailties in our human decision-making processes. They are not intended as a detailed prescription for each and every legal design project.

Third, the checklists are an attempt to distil, and set out in a systematic way, the approach that I have developed over time in my own policy advice work. That approach has enabled me to ask some practically important questions, and test proposals for legislation, in a way that has provided useful insights into the likely effectiveness of proposed legislation. They are the product of my personal experience. But they have not been tested in any broader or more systematic way.

Fourth – you are the pilots! And the checklists are adaptive tools that can be customised to respond to new information about how they work in practice. I look forward to hearing from readers who have used the checklists, who can tell me what works in their environment and what can be improved to be more useful for them and for others. I am sure there are important issues I have overlooked, and useful design options I have not mentioned.

I have established a website for this book at www.makinglawsthatwork.net. On it you will find a version of the checklists that you can download and customise for your own projects, and a feedback form so you can tell me about your experience of working with the checklists. With the benefit of your experience, I will be able to refine and improve the checklists – and the book as a whole. I hope that you will take the time to provide some feedback, to ensure that the second edition of this book is better than the first.

Appendices

Appendix 1: Legislation Checklists

The Primary Checklist

1. What is the current position?

   (a) What is the current law (in the field being reviewed, together with background laws where relevant)?

   (b) How does the law operate (or fail to operate) in practice?

   > i. Describe the current position in relation to *all* the people who encounter the issue that the law addresses, not just those who come to the attention of officials or appear before a court. It is important to identify what you do *not* know about the current position, as well as what you do know.

   > ii. Prepare a decision map showing what decisions are made by each relevant actor (citizens, businesses, government agencies, courts etc), with as much detail as possible about each stage in the process (numbers, time frames, costs etc).

2. What is the legislation aiming to change?

   (a) What is the problem? More specifically, what aspects of the current behaviours described under item 1 are problematic?

   (b) What is the desired outcome? How will the behaviour of relevant actors need to change in order to achieve this outcome?

3. Who are the audiences for the legislation?

   (a) To whom is the proposed legislation addressed? Who (citizens, businesses, officials, agencies, courts etc) needs to understand and act on the legislation in order to achieve the desired outcome?

   (b) How will each of these audiences become aware of what the law requires them to do, or enables them to do?

4. What institutions will the legislation depend on?

   (a) Identify all institutions (officials, agencies, courts etc) that have a role to play in implementing the legislation (this should be apparent from the decision map).

   (b) Will each of those institutions have the capacity and the will to perform their role?

   (c) What steps can be taken to address any concerns about institutional capacity?

   (d) Cross-refer to the **institutions checklist**.

5. Has this been tried elsewhere?

   (a) Is there a well-established and successful international model that should be used as a starting point for the proposed legislation?

   (b) What precedents are there in comparable societies for the proposed approach adopted in the legislation?

   (c) Was the approach a success in those other societies? How do we know?

   (d) Will success elsewhere translate into your society's social, economic and institutional setting?

6. Is a trial/pilot an option?

   (a) Are there any practical or ethical reasons not to conduct a trial or pilot, to support more informed decision-making?

   (b) Should the legislation be amended to enable a trial/pilot to be conducted, with a subsequent roll-out if it is successful?

7. How will the legislation contribute to changes in behaviour?

   (a) How is the proposed legislation likely to operate in practice?

      i. Prepare an amended version of the item 1 decision map to show how the proposed legislation is intended to operate in practice.

      ii. What do you expect will change as a result of the legislation, and why? What do you expect will stay the same, and why?

      iii. What aspects of the post-legislation scenario are difficult to predict with reasonable confidence?

   (b) Conduct a pre-mortem for the legislation: assume that a few years out it has failed, and ask:

      i. What sort of failure is most likely? Is the legislation a damp squib? Did it overshoot? Did it produce nasty surprises, or backfire?

      ii. What factors may have caused or contributed to that failure?

      iii. Can the risk of failure be reduced by adjusting default settings?

      iv. Can the risk of failure be reduced by reducing the complexity of the legislation from the perspective of end-users and other relevant audiences?

   (c) Cross-refer to the **benefits checklist**.

   (d) Cross-refer to the **compliance checklist**.

8. Can the legislation adapt to take account of new information and/or changed circumstances?

   (a) What are the areas of greatest uncertainty? (The current position? Future social and economic change? The nature and extent of the changes in behaviour that will result from the legislation?)

   (b) What mechanisms will there be for gathering relevant information in key areas of uncertainty? In particular, what mechanisms will there be for gathering information about how the legislation is operating in practice, and assessing that information against the legislation's goals?

(c) How can the law be structured to enable it to adapt to reflect new information about how it is working in practice, and changes in circumstances? ie, how can we make this adaptive legislation? Is it appropriate to use any of the following techniques:

   i. Delegated rule-making?

   ii. Legislating principles/standards coupled with (adaptable) default rules?

   iii. Safe harbours?

   iv. Provision of guidance by agencies?

   v. Advance ruling regimes?

(d) Is the legislation framed in a way that enables it to adapt to changing technologies?

(e) Should there be express provision for reviews?

9. Does the legislation take cross-border issues into account?

(a) What cross-border issues are likely to arise in this context?

   i. Are relevant actors outside the jurisdiction?

   ii. Is relevant property outside the jurisdiction?

   iii. Is relevant information outside the jurisdiction?

   iv. Is there a risk that the laws of more than one country will apply to some activities, giving rise to conflicting obligations or complexity or unnecessary duplication? Conversely, is there a risk of a regulatory gap (ie, no country's law applies and is practically effective in relation to certain actors or activities)?

   v. Is there scope for unilateral or mutual recognition of outcomes in other countries?

   vi. Will enforcement need to take place abroad?

   vii. Is there a need for cross-border regulatory cooperation in order for the law to be effective? With which other countries?

(b) What are the appropriate connecting factors for the legislation to apply?

(c) How will the legislation be enforced in practice, where relevant actors (or their assets) are outside the jurisdiction?

10. Telling the story: The narrative explaining the reasons for the reform.

Develop a narrative that explains what the proposed legislation is intended to achieve, and how it will do this. Key elements in the narrative include:

   i. The problem: what is happening now (item 1), and why is it undesirable (item 2)?

   ii. The desired outcome: what is the legislation intended to change (item 2)?

   iii. The solution: how will the proposed legislation help to bring about the desired outcome (item 7)?

Benefits Checklist

B1   Who is the legislation intended to benefit? What benefits are those beneficiaries intended to obtain?

   (a) Identify the groups that the legislation is intended to benefit.
   (b) Identify the benefits that each of those groups is intended to obtain.
   (c) What trade-offs are there between these different groups/benefits?

B2   What criteria do the beneficiaries need to meet to qualify for those benefits?

   (a) Identify the criteria that a person must meet to qualify for the benefits provided under the legislation.
   (b) What are the implications of those criteria for the complexity of the legislation, for the predictability of its operation, for ease of access to those benefits for the intended beneficiaries, and for the cost of implementing the regime?

B3   How will those beneficiaries become aware of the availability of those benefits, and how to obtain them?

   (a) How will beneficiaries become aware of the availability of those benefits?
   (b) How will beneficiaries become aware of what they need to do to obtain those benefits?
   (c) When will beneficiaries need this information? What steps can be taken to ensure it is available and understood at this time? Should the law provide for 'signposts', or other methods of providing information as and when it is relevant?

B4   Can receipt of those benefits be made a default setting that does not require any specific action from beneficiaries?

   (a) Is it appropriate for the benefit to be universal?
   (b) Can existing information be used to identify qualifying beneficiaries?
   (c) Can an agency be given a proactive role in identifying beneficiaries?

B5   If beneficiaries are required to make an active decision, or take active steps, what can be done to make this as simple and easy as possible?

   (a) Identify in detail each step that a person will be required to take to qualify for the benefit.
   (b) Review whether each of these steps is necessary.
   (c) Review the overall process – is it workable and realistic for beneficiaries?
   (d) Consider what can be done to make access to benefits for intended beneficiaries simpler and easier, for example by reducing the number of steps required, not requiring information to be provided if an agency already holds it, allowing beneficiaries to authorise the use of information held by other agencies so they do not have to provide it again, providing support/assistance for applicants

Compliance Checklist

C1 Who is required to take steps to comply with the legislation? What is each relevant compliance group required to do?

    (a) Who will need to change their behaviour to comply with requirements imposed by that legislation?

    (b) What will each compliance group be required to do, and in what circumstances?

C2 Can some compliance obligations be reduced or eliminated?

    (a) Can some compliance obligations be eliminated, without compromising the effectiveness of the law?

    (b) Is it possible to reduce the frequency with which people are required to take positive steps to comply with the law?

    (c) Is it possible to reduce the scope of any of the compliance obligations (for example, by not requiring information to be provided which is already held by the agency, or by another agency)?

C3 How will each compliance group be made aware of their obligations?

    (a) How will each compliance group become aware that they have obligations under the legislation?

    (b) How will the members of each group obtain the necessary information to know what practical steps they must take in order to comply?

    (c) Should the law provide for 'signposts' or other methods of providing information as and when it is relevant?

    (d) What status will any detailed information provided by an agency have?

    (e) What other forms of assistance are available, whether proactively or on request, to enable a person to understand what they need to do in order to comply?

C4 What can be done to make compliance as simple and easy as possible?

    (a) Can compliance be made the default outcome, to remove the need for active steps to be taken?

    (b) Can complexity be reduced to facilitate compliance?

    (c) Can the practical steps required to comply with the law be made less burdensome – less costly or less time-consuming?

C5 What can be done to encourage compliance?

    (a) What are the costs of compliance?

    (b) What other barriers are there to compliance (for example, established social practices/attitudes)?

    (c) What can be done to remind people of their obligations as and when those obligations are relevant?

    (d) What are the practical consequences of non-compliance? Is non-compliance attractive as a result of low/ineffective enforcement, inadequate sanctions etc?

(e) Can the legislation provide for more effective and proportionate sanctions/deterrents?

(f) Can the legislation or institutional arrangements be modified to address concerns about effective enforcement?

Institutions Checklist

I1   What institutions will play a role in implementing the legislation? What decisions and actions will they be required to take?

    (a) What institutions will play a role in implementing the legislation?

    (b) What decisions/actions will each relevant institution be required to take?

    (c) How often will they need to act?

    (d) Within what time frames?

    (e) How complex are those decisions?

    (f) Will a single person or body make all of the decisions, or will there be multiple decision-makers?

I2   Will each of those institutions have the capacity and will to perform its role?

    (a) Describe in detail the capacity of each relevant institution, and (if it is an existing institution) its performance to date.

    (b) Is the capacity of each institution likely to be adequate to perform its identified functions?

    (c) What are the likely consequences of errors in making decisions?

    (d) Are some types of error more likely than others?

    (e) Are some types of error more problematic than others?

    (f) What mechanisms exist to identify and correct errors?

    (g) Is there a risk of inconsistency in outcomes, and if so, how much of a concern is that?

    (h) What are the likely consequences of delay in making decisions beyond the intended time frames?

I3   How can any concerns about institutional capacity be addressed?

    (a) Can default rules be modified to reduce dependence on the institution?

    (b) Can the complexity of decisions that the institution is required to make be reduced?

    (c) Can responsibility for a function be transferred to another institution (existing or new) that is more likely to have the capacity and will to perform that function?

    (d) Can the institution be strengthened/established in a way that ensures it will have the necessary capacity within a reasonable time frame?

    (e) If none of these is workable, reconsider the proposed legislation in light of the high risk of failure due to institutional factors.

Appendix 2: Background Reading for Legal Designers

Highly Recommended Reading

Atul Gawande, *The Checklist Manifesto: How to Get Things Right*, 1st edn (New York, Metropolitan Books, 2009)

Daniel Kahneman, *Thinking, Fast and Slow* (New York, Farrar, Straus and Giroux, 2011)

Daniel Kahneman, Olivier Sibony and Cass R Sunstein, *Noise* (New York, Little, Brown Spark, 2021)

Anthony King and Ivor Crewe, *The Blunders of our Governments* (London, Oneworld Publications, 2013)

Cass R Sunstein, *Simpler: The Future of Government* (New York, Simon & Schuster, 2013)

Cass R Sunstein, *The Cost–Benefit Revolution* (Cambridge, MA, MIT Press, 2018)

Cass R Sunstein and Reid Hastie, *Wiser: Getting Beyond Groupthink to Make Groups Smarter* (Boston, MA, Harvard Business Review Press, 2015)

Suggested Reading

Robert Baldwin, Martin Cave and Martin Lodge, *Understanding Regulation: Theory, Strategy and Practice*, 2nd edn (Oxford, Oxford University Press, 2013)

Tom Bingham, *The Rule of Law* (London, Penguin Books, 2011)

Andrew Burrows, *Thinking About Statutes: Interpretation, Interaction, Improvement* (Cambridge, Cambridge University Press, 2018)

Lawrence M Friedman, *Impact: How Law Affects Behavior* (Cambridge, MA, Harvard University Press, 2016)

David Halpern, *Inside the Nudge Unit: How Small Changes Can Make a Big Difference* (London, WH Allen, 2015)

Michael Howlett, *Designing Public Policies: Principles and Instruments*, 2nd edn (Abingdon, Routledge, 2019)

Robert Cooter and Thomas Ulen, *Law and Economics*, 6th edn (Boston, MA, Addison-Wesley, 2016), available at: www.econ.jku.at/t3/staff/winterebmer/teaching/law_economics/ss19/6th_edition.pdf

Maria Mousmouti, *Designing Effective Legislation* (Cheltenham, Edward Elgar Publishing, 2019)

Sendhil Mullainathan and Eldar Shafir, *Scarcity: Why Having Too Little Means So Much* (London, Allen Lane, 2013)

Anthony I Ogus, *Regulation: Legal Form and Economic Theory* (Oxford, Hart Publishing, 1994, reissued 2004)

Nate Silver, *The Signal and the Noise: The Art and Science of Prediction* (London, Penguin Books, 2013)

Seth Stephens-Davidowitz, *Everybody Lies: Big Data, New Data and What the Internet Can Tell Us About Who We Really Are* (New York, HarperCollins, 2017)

Philip E Tetlock and Dan Gardner, *Superforecasting: The Art and Science of Prediction* (New York, Broadway Books, 2015)

Richard H Thaler and Cass R Sunstein, *Nudge: Improving Decisions about Health, Wealth and Happiness* (New Haven, CT, Yale University Press, 2008)

Jeremy Waldron, *Law and Disagreement* (Oxford, Oxford University Press, 1999)

Duncan J Watts, *Everything is Obvious* *Once You Know the Answer* (New York, Crown Business, 2011)

Helen Xanthaki, *Drafting Legislation: Art and Technology of Rules for Regulation* (Oxford, Hart Publishing, 2014)

Edward E Zajac, *Political Economy of Fairness* (Cambridge, MA, MIT Press, 1996)

INDEX